THE EXCLUSIONARY RULE OF EVIDENCE

This is an intriguing book. By exploring the complex "rules" in English and American law which exclude the use of evidence obtained by illegal or unfair methods, Dr Hsieh seeks to establish comparable rules for China, in order to "extract the firewood from under the cauldron". Dr Hsieh recognises that an exclusionary rule is only one small but important tool in the regulation of police practice. His focus on removing barriers to the protection of defendants' rights is refreshing.

Nicola Padfield, University of Cambridge, UK

AF833586

INTERNATIONAL AND COMPARATIVE CRIMINAL JUSTICE

Series Editors:

Mark Findlay, *Institute of Criminology, University of Sydney, Australia*
Ralph Henham, *Nottingham Law School, Nottingham Trent University, UK*

This series explores the new and rapidly developing field of international and comparative criminal justice and engages with its most important emerging themes and debates. It focuses on three interrelated aspects of scholarship which go to the root of understanding the nature and significance of international criminal justice in the broader context of globalization and global governance. These include: the theoretical and methodological problems posed by the development of international and comparative criminal justice; comparative contextual analysis; the reciprocal relationship between comparative and international criminal justice and contributions which endeavor to build understandings of global justice on foundations of comparative contextual analysis.

Other titles in the series:

Developing Restorative Justice Jurisprudence
Rethinking Responses to Criminal Wrongdoing
Tony Foley
ISBN 978 1 4094 6533 1

International Criminal Law
Using or Abusing Legality?
Edwin Bikundo
ISBN 978 1 4094 3867 0

The Dual State
Edited by Eric Wilson
ISBN 978 1 4094 31077

Policing in Hong Kong
Kam C. Wong
ISBN 978 1 4094 1060 7

Criminal Law Reform and Transitional Justice
Human Rights Perspectives for Sudan
Edited by Lutz Oette
ISBN 978 1 4094 3100 8

The Exclusionary Rule of Evidence

Comparative Analysis and Proposals for Reform

KUO-HSING HSIEH
National Chung Cheng University, Taiwan

Routledge
Taylor & Francis Group
LONDON AND NEW YORK

First published 2014 by Ashgate Publishing

2 Park Square, Milton Park, Abingdon, Oxfordshire OX14 4RN
52 Vanderbilt Avenue, New York, NY 10017

Routledge is an imprint of the Taylor & Francis Group, an informa business

First issued in paperback 2020

Copyright © 2014 Kuo-hsing Hsieh

Kuo-hsing Hsieh has asserted his right under the Copyright, Designs and Patents Act, 1988, to be identified as the author of this work.

All rights reserved. No part of this book may be reprinted or reproduced or utilised in any form or by any electronic, mechanical, or other means, now known or hereafter invented, including photocopying and recording, or in any information storage or retrieval system, without permission in writing from the publishers.

Notice:
Product or corporate names may be trademarks or registered trademarks, and are used only for identification and explanation without intent to infringe.

British Library Cataloguing in Publication Data
A catalogue record for this book is available from the British Library

The Library of Congress has cataloged the printed edition as follows:
Hsieh, Kuo-hsing, author.
The exclusionary rule of evidence : comparative analysis and proposals for reform / by Kuo-Hsing Hsieh.
pages cm. -- (International and comparative criminal justice)
Includes bibliographical references and index.
ISBN 978-1-4724-1067-2 (hardback)
1. Exclusionary rule (Evidence)--China 2. Admissible evidence--China.
3. Police questioning--China. 4. Torture--China--Prevention. 5. Law reform--China.
6. Exclusionary rule (Evidence)--Great Britain. 7. Exclusionary rule (Evidence)--United States. I. Title.
KNQ4679.X54 2014
347'.062--dc23

2014015619

ISBN 978-1-4724-1067-2 (hbk)
ISBN 978-0-367-60005-1 (pbk)

To my parents,
謝仲方先生與潘清女士,
for love and support beyond measure

Contents

Preface

If there is any fixed star in our constitutional and criminal procedure constellation, it is that torture is illegal and torture-introduced evidence is inadmissible. The purposes of this book are to (1) assess the exclusionary rule in the United Kingdom and United States; (2) explore the theoretical constitutional foundation of the rule; and (3) establish the Chinese exclusionary rule in criminal practice. The current Chinese legal structure for combating police torture is not adequately armed. The fight against police torture has been plagued by many legal loopholes and practical hurdles. Currently, there is no exclusionary rule in practice. If the wrongful conviction of the innocent is a pressing issue in China today, police torture is the flashpoint. Police torture in China is the prevalent evil, not the isolated anecdote. This book combines diagnosis and prescription—the problem of police torture in China and the solution of the exclusionary rule. The ultimate goal of the research is to find a suitable exclusionary rule for China to solve the serious problem of police torture and wrongdoing.

At the level of theory, my exclusionary rule framework is grounded in the separation of powers. Previous research about the separation of powers doctrine has focused almost entirely on constitutional law and political theory. It has completely ignored the special role that the doctrine plays in the criminal justice system, a role consisting of the exercise of a reviewing function to ensure executive compliance with the criminal law. Separation of powers is a core component of the constitution's system of checks and balances, a system in which each branch of the government is endowed with a constitutional control over the others.

Without any judicial supervision or due process, the potential for arbitrary enforcement is high. The alternatives to the exclusionary rule are mainly illusory and of no practical avail. History also demonstrates that the very idea of protecting the defendant's right is completely empty unless it is linked to an efficient mechanism. China grants the police too much power and has too little judicial supervision over police investigations. It creates imbalance in the existing Chinese criminal justice system. It is such an imbalance, and the lack of separation of powers in the criminal justice system, that poses a significant and growing threat for the protection of defendants' rights.

Kuo-hsing Hsieh
National Chung Cheng University
May 2014

Acknowledgements

The research was funded through scholarships and research grants from the University of Edinburgh, the W.A. Wilson Education Fund, and the National Chung Cheng University. For their generous support, I would like first to express my appreciation to these bodies.

I appreciate the help and encouragement that I have received in working on this book. I got support from Professor Zenon Bankowski who supplied me with professional and supportive advice throughout my research. I am also deeply thankful for help in understanding evidence law for the scientific perspective from Professor Burkhard Schafer, who discussed problems with me to clear my mind. I am grateful to Professor Gerry Maher QC for his infinite wisdom and insight into the criminal justice system. Professor James Chalmers guided my understanding of evidence law from the very beginning. Many thanks to him for invaluable guidance and commentary. They gave me all the support that I needed. I benefited from helpful discussions at all meetings with them. Without their invaluable commentary the book would not have been possible.

In addition, I was very fortunate to have two extremely patient and inspiring examiners: Professor Peter Duff and Dr. Sharon Cowan. I am deeply indebted to them for all the unforgettable generous support, gentleness, and their insightful suggestions during the Ph.D. viva. Special thanks go to Dr. Cowan for her tireless enthusiasm, assistance, extremely invaluable advice, pointing out minor slips, encouraging and supporting me in various ways.

Above all, I express my gratitude to my parents, for their assistance, encouragement and lifelong belief in the value of education. My thanks also go to my wife, Dr. Wei Ouyang, who has been enormously supportive throughout the period in which this book was written, to Yen-Chen Hsieh, whose birth on October 4, 2012 provided motivation for completing the book.

Chapter 1
Introduction

1.1 We Are So Very Much Alike

The power of a police officer in conducting a search is immense. He or she is entitled forcibly to enter the citizen's home, even at midnight, to wake a person from sleep, rummage in his or her drawers, papers, letters and most private possessions, or upset the entire building. Although the particularity clause of the warrant defines the scope of a search, it is said that the police allegedly abuse their search authority.[1]

The conduct of some police officers can only be described as outrageous and totally inconsistent with their responsibilities. In 1992, for example, London police arrived at Mr. Hsu's residence because a previous lodger complained to the police that Hsu was preventing her from collecting her belongings from his home. The officers demanded entrance but Hsu refused to admit them without a search warrant. The door was forcibly opened. They had no search warrant. He was arrested forcefully. He was punched in the face and kicked in the back (he later passed blood in his urine). He was also racially abused and placed in a cell for over one hour. He went home only to find that his house had been entered and some of his own property was missing. He had a predisposition to depression and was socially and culturally isolated and he was still suffering symptoms of a post traumatic distress disorder three years after the incident.[2]

Some people have even lost their lives during police searches in the United States. For example, in 2006, a police SWAT (Special Weapons and Tactics) team in Atlanta stormed a house and shot a 92-year-old woman, Kathryn Johnston, who lived alone in the roughest neighborhood in Georgia. The police claimed that they had bought drugs at the home from a man known only as Sam and were returning to search the residence.[3]

The historical background of the exclusionary rule was rooted in English and American experiences. In 1604, the sheriff broke into Semayne's home and seized

---

1 *R v. Reading JJ ex p. South West Meats Ltd* (1992) 4 Admin LR 401. This case illustrates ways in which the police can abuse their powers of search and seizure, even with a warrant. Large quantities of documents were removed from the premises which obviously did not fall within the terms of the warrant, contrary to Section 8(2) of the Police and Criminal Evidence Act (PACE) 1984.

2 *Thompson & Hsu v. The Commissioner of Police for the Metropolis,* [1998] QB 498, 505–7.

3 "92-year-old Killed in Roughest Neighborhood in Georgia". Available at: http://www.cnn.com/2006/US/11/22/woman.shot.ap/index.html accessed Oct. 10, 2013.

his property in the United Kingdom. Sir Edward Coke declared that "[t]he house of everyone to him is his castle and fortress."[4]

In 1761, there was widespread objection against the writs of assistance in all American colonies. These writs were general search warrants that permitted the authorities, especially customs officials, to search whoever and wherever they pleased for any reason—or for no reason, without any necessity for a showing of probable cause. The officials did not need to have specific suspicions about any person in any place. Section 5(2) of the Act of Frauds of 1662 provided:

> And it shall be lawful to or for any Person or Persons, authorized by Writ of Assistance under the Seal of his Majesty's Court of Exchequer, to take a Constable … or other publick Officer inhabiting near unto the Place, and in the Day-time to enter … Any House … Or other Place, and in Case of Resistance to break open Doors, Chests, Trunks and other Package, there to seize, and from thence to bring, any Kind of Goods or Merchandize whatsoever, prohibited, and to put and secure the same in his Majesty's Store-house.[5]

A group of Boston merchants retained Attorney James Otis, Jr. to challenge the legality of the writs of assistance for the first time. Otis attacked the writs:

> It appears to me the worst instrument of arbitrary power, the most destructive of English liberty, and to the fundamental principles of law that was ever found in an English law book. It is the power that places the liberty of every man in the hands of every petty officer … One of the most essential branches of English liberty is the freedom of one's house. *A man's house is his castle*; and whilst he is quiet, he is well guarded as a prince in his castle. This writ, if it should be declared legal, would totally annihilate this privilege. Custom house officers may enter our houses when they please—we are commanded to permit their entry—their menial servants may entry—may break locks, bars and everything in their way—and whether they break through malice or revenge, no man, no court can inquire—bare suspicion without oath is sufficient.[6]

Although the Superior Court upheld the legality of the writs, John Adams, one of the fathers of American independence, had recalled Otis's memorable speech as the prologue to the American Revolution.[7]

---

4 Semayne's Case, [1558–1774] ALL E.R. 62, 63 (K.B. 1604).

5 J.W. Hall, Jr., *Search and Seizure* (2nd edn, Michie, Charlottesville 1991) 7.

6 M.H. Smith, *The Writs of Assistance Case* (University of California Press, Berkeley 1978) 344 (emphasis added).

7 *Boyd v. United States*, 116 U.S. 616, 625 (1886); J.W. Landynski, *Search and Seizure and the Supreme Court: A Study in Constitutional Interpretation* (Baltimore, Johns Hopkins University Press, 1966) 37.

There were two most famous related English cases decided by Lord Charles Pratt Camden.[8] The first is *Wilkes v. Wood*.[9] The case was famous on both sides of the Atlantic. Broad search and seizure power for the first time was introduced in England by the Tudors.[10] General warrants were frequently used to close down libelous printers during the era of the infamous Star Chamber.[11] In 1763, John Wilkes, a Member of the House of Commons, published a pamphlet series vehemently attacking the British government. Lord Halifax, the Secretary of State, issued a general warrant and ordered four messengers to search for, arrest and seize the authors, printers, and publisher, as well as their papers. Wilkes' bureau was thoroughly ransacked, and all his books and private papers were seized and taken away. Forty-nine persons were arrested and five houses were searched in three days on the strength of that single warrant. Wilkes filed suits for trespass and challenged the legality of the general warrant in civil damage suits. Chief Justice Charles Pratt held the general warrants were null and void and that Wilkes could recover damages of £5,000 for the illegal search and seizure:

> To enter a man's house by virtue of a nameless warrant, in order to procure evidence, is worse than the Spanish Inquisition; a law under which no Englishman would wish to live an hour … If such a power is truly invested in a secretary of state, and he can delegate this power, it certainly may affect the person and property of every man in this kingdom, and is totally subversive of the liberty of the subject.[12]

The second is *Entick v. Carrington*.[13] In 1762, according to the executive warrant issued by the Earl of Halifax, the Secretary of State, the defendants Nathan Carrington and others, with force and arms broke and entered John Entick's dwelling-house, broke open the doors, chests, drawers, searched and examined all the rooms in his dwelling, house and all the boxes, and took away hundreds of printed charts, pamphlets and papers. Entick was suspected of publishing seditious libels. He sued the defendants for trespass. The jury found that the defendants did trespass and awarded Entick £300. This judgment exercised great influence on the subsequent case law on search in England as well as in the United States. Lord Camden dismissed Star Chamber precedent and condemned the invasion of homes and found the warrant was wholly illegal and void:

---

8 Chief Justice Charles Pratt elevated to the peerage as Lord Camden after *Wilkes*.

9 98 Eng. Rep. 489 (CD 1763).

10 J.W. Landynski, *Search and Seizure and the Supreme Court: A Study in Constitutional Interpretation* (Baltimore, Johns Hopkins University Press, 1966) 20.

11 Potter Stewart, "The Road to *Mapp v. Ohio* and Beyond: The Origins, Development and Future of the Exclusionary Rule in Search-and-Seizure Cases" (1983) 83 *Columbia Law Review* 1365, 1369.

12 19 Howell's State Trials, 1153 (C.P. 1763).

13 19 Howell's State Trials, 1029 (C.P. 1765).

> If this point should be determined in favor of the jurisdiction, the secret cabinets and bureaus of every subject in this kingdom will be thrown open to the search and inspection of a messenger, whenever the Secretary of State shall think fit to charge, or even to suspect, a person to be the author, printer, or publisher of a seditious libel … If this is the law it would be found in our books, but no such law ever existed in this country. Our law holds the property of every man so sacred that no man can set his foot upon his neighbour's close without his leave. If he does, he is a trespasser, though he does no damage at all; if he will tread upon his neighbour's ground, he must justify it by law … We can safely say there is no law in this country to justify the defendants in what they have done; if there was, it would destroy all the comforts of society, for papers are often the dearest property a man can have.[14]

As news spread about the ruling, Lord Camden was hailed both in England and America for his bold and clear-eyed expression of the common law and the rights of Englishmen.[15] The United States Supreme Court described *Entick* as "one of the landmarks of English liberty" and "one of the permanent monuments of English liberty."[16]

During the last half of the eighteenth century, English and Americans were both suffering a recurrence of highhanded search and seizure measures, which violated the maxim that "a man's house is his castle." That is why both James Otis, Jr. and Lord Camden decried the evil of uneven, unchecked and progressively oppressive executive power of the officers. The roots of the exclusionary rule can be found in the common law distaste for intrusions by state officials.

The United Kingdom (except Scotland) and United States share the same common law roots from England.[17] In the past, English judges have often prided themselves as protectors of citizens' rights.[18] At first sight, the similarities of two respective criminal justice systems are particularly striking in many ways, for example the emphasis on the adversary system, the presumption of innocence, and the sense of fundamental fairness required for a just procedure. Equally striking, however, is the lack of similarity between the two systems in significant areas, for instance the process employed to correct wrongful convictions[19] and the admissibility of illegally or unfairly obtained physical evidence in criminal trials.

14 19 Howell's State Trials, 1029 (C.P. 1765).

15 A.R. Amar, "The Fourth Amendment, Boston, and the Writs of Assistance" (1996) 30 *Suffolk University Law Review* 53, 65.

16 *Boyd v. United States*, 116 U.S. 616, 626 (1886).

17 M.R. Damaška, *The Faces of Justice and State Authority: A Comparative Approach to the Legal Process* (Yale University Press, New Haven 1986) 8–15.

18 David Dixon, *Law in Policing: Legal Regulation and Police Practices* (Clarendon Press, Oxford 1997) 70.

19 Lissa Griffin, "The Correction of Wrongful Convictions: A Comparative Perspective" (2001) 16 *American University International Law Review* 1241, 1241–2.

1.2 But Oh the Difference

Perhaps the most striking thing about the exclusionary rule of evidence is that nobody seems to have very clear idea what it is. Although the exclusionary rule is widely considered a hallmark of Anglo-American criminal evidence, courts and scholars have not formulated a universal definition of the rule. My definition is "a rule that excludes evidence obtained by illegal or unfair methods," for example, by illegal search or torture. This research argues that the whole point of the rule is to regulate the intrusions and thus constrain every species of arbitrary or oppressive government. Historically,[20] there are at least three differences of the exclusionary rule between the two criminal justice systems.

First, the English judges seemed reluctant to exclude illegal evidence from 1978.

From the 1960s, English courts have increasingly extended police powers, especially in search and seizure and pre-charge detention for investigation.[21] Since 1978, courts were almost unwilling to exercise their discretion to exclude illegally or unfairly obtained evidence. I find this a dispiriting development. For instance, in *R v. Houghton and Franciosy*,[22] the Court ruled that a judge was right not to exclude a confession even though the defendant had been unlawfully arrested, unlawfully detained incommunicado for five days, and questioned without caution. In general, judges in post-war England and Wales became increasingly accommodating to police demands for additional powers: they retreated from control of police, while senior judges in America (in the 1960s) and Australia (in the 1980s) attempted to advance it.[23] In the leading case of *R v. Sang*,[24] Lord Diplock noted: "[The trial judge] has no discretion to refuse to admit relevant admissible evidence on the ground that it was obtained by improper or unfair means. The court is not concerned with how it was obtained."[25]

In the United States, under the exclusionary rule, evidence which is obtained by an unlawful search and seizure is excluded from admissibility in accordance with the Fourth Amendment to the United States Constitution. This provision provides that:

> The right of the people to be secure in their persons, houses, papers, and effects, against unreasonable searches and seizures, shall not be violated, and no warrants shall issue, but upon probable cause, supported by oath or affirmation,

---

20 For further analysis see 2.1.

21 Ibid., ch. 4.

22 (1978) 68 Cr App Rep 197.

23 David Dixon, *Law in Policing: Legal Regulation and Police Practices* (Clarendon Press, Oxford 1997) 142.

24 [1980] AC 402.

25 Ibid., 437.

> and particularly describing the place to be searched, and the persons or things to be seized.[26]

In 1914, in *Weeks v. United States* the Court first held that "in a federal prosecution the Fourth Amendment barred the use of evidence secured through an illegal search and seizure."[27] Justice Day noted: "The effect of the Fourth Amendment is to put the courts of the United States ... against all unreasonable searches and seizures under the guise of law. This protection reaches all alike, whether accused of crime or not."[28]

Second, the rationales for the exclusionary rule are very different.

The English courts have repudiated the idea of using exclusion of illegally obtained evidence as a deterrent against police misconduct. It was believed that it was not the judges' role to discipline police officers in courts.

In contrast, the United States Supreme Court in *Weeks* first recognized that the only effective way to deter police misconduct is to exclude illegal evidence.[29] Since 1961, the Court has systematically ignored all but the deterrence rationale for the exclusionary rule. The essence of the rationale is that it allows the courts to control the activities of the law enforcement agencies and dissuade them from encroaching unjustifiably on the civil liberties of citizens. For example, in *United States v. Calandra*, Justice Powell observed that the exclusionary rule is "A judicially created remedy designed to safeguard Fourth Amendment rights generally through its *deterrent* effect."[30]

Third, there is a significant difference, it should be observed, about the admissibility of derivative evidence from illegally obtained real evidence and inadmissible confessions.

It is important to distinguish the *exclusionary rule* and the *fruit of poisonous tree doctrine*. The two are often mixed up. The former deals with the evidence

---

26 Articles 8 and 24 of the Canadian Charter of Rights and Freedoms are relevant in this context: Article 8 declares that "everyone has the right to be secure against unreasonable search or seizure," while Article 24 reinforces the rule that "(1) anyone whose rights or freedoms, as guaranteed by this Charter, have been infringed or denied may apply to a court of competent jurisdiction to obtain such remedy as the court considers appropriate and just in the circumstances. (2) where, in proceedings under subsection (1), a court concludes that evidence was obtained in manner that infringed or denied any rights or freedoms guaranteed by this Charter, the evidence shall be excluded if it is established that, having regard to all the circumstances, the admission of it in the proceedings would bring the administration of justice into disrepute." In addition, the New Zealand Charter has a similar provision. Articles 21 of the New Zealand Bill of Rights Act 1990 provides that "everyone has the right to be secure against unreasonable search or seizure, whether of the person, property, or correspondence or otherwise."

27 232 U.S. 383, 398 (1914).

28 232 U.S. 383, 391–2 (1914).

29 232 U.S. 383, 391 (1914).

30 414 U.S. 338, 348 (1974) (emphasis added).

which is directly derived from an illegal search or interrogation. The latter, however, concerns evidence discovered as a consequence of an illegal search. For example, an illegal search may find out a key to a railway station locker where the money of a robbery is being kept. Or a confession obtained by torture may reveal the whereabouts of the murder knife.

Under English law, evidence derived from an illegal confession is admissible. In *R v. Warickshall*,[31] Warickshall was charged with being an accessory after the fact to theft and with receiving the stolen property. The issue was the admissibility of stolen goods which had been found in her bed, to which her confession had led the authorities. The confession was made after the defendant was promised that she would not be prosecuted if she confessed. After she made a full confession, however, a prosecution took place.

Counsel argued that "as the fact of finding the stolen property in her custody had been obtained through the means of an inadmissible confession, the proof of the fact that ought to also be rejected; for otherwise the faith which the prosecutor had pledged would be violated, and the prisoner made the deluded instrument of her own conviction."[32] Her confession was excluded as evidence, but the real evidence was included.[33] The position in this case became broadly accepted.

In addition, the Criminal Law Revision Committee of 1972 (CLRC) endorsed this practice. The Criminal Law Revision Committee recommended that the fact that evidence of a confession is inadmissible under the clause shall not affect the admissibility in evidence of any facts discovered as a result of the confession.[34] Although the confession is inadmissible, evidence of the fact discovered is admissible. Clause (5) of the Draft Criminal Evidence Bill provides:

> The fact that a confession is wholly or partly excluded in pursuance of section (2) or (3) shall not affect the admissibility in evidence—(a) of any facts discovered as a result of the confession; or (b) as regards any fact so discovered as a result of a statement made by the accused; or (c) where the confession is relevant as showing that the accused speaks, writes or expresses himself in a particular way, of so much of the confession as is necessary to show this about him.[35]

The Criminal Law Revision Committee mentioned the criticism that it is illogical not to apply fully one or other of the reliability and disciplinary principle—either, first, to apply the reliability principle and admit the whole evidence, or, to apply the disciplinary principle and exclude the derivative

31 1 Leach 263, 168 Eng. Rep. 234 (O.B. 1783).

32 Ibid.

33 Ibid.

34 The Criminal Law Revision Committee, "Eleventh Report, Evidence (General)" (Cm 4991, 1972) [56], [68].

35 The Criminal Law Revision Committee, "Eleventh Report, Evidence (General)" (Cm 4991, 1972) draft bill cl2 (5).

evidence. Responding to above criticism, it merely said "there are sufficient practical reasons for accepting the mixture of the two principles as the basis of the law."[36] The Committee, however, neither provides any practical reason nor explains why they include the derivative evidence. Maybe the central practical reason is that it is too dangerous to exclude derivative evidence.

This recommendation was implemented in Section 76(4) of the Police and Criminal Evidence Act (PACE) 1984 which explicitly rejects the admissibility of derivative evidence and provides:

> The fact that a confession is wholly or partly excluded in pursuance of this section shall not affect the admissibility in evidence—(a) of any facts discovered as a result of the confession; or (b) where the confession is relevant as showing that the accused speaks, writes or expresses himself in a particular way, of so much of the confession as is necessary to show that he does so.[37]

In contrast to the English approach, in the United States the derivative evidence should be excluded if there is close connection between the initial illegality and subsequently discovered evidence. In addition, Justice Frankfurter first coined the phrase "fruit of poisonous tree" in *Nardone v. United States*[38] in 1939 and stated: "[T]o forbid the direct use of methods [but] to put no curb on their full indirect use would only invite the very methods deemed inconsistent with ethical standards and destructive of personal liberty."[39]

1.3 Criminal Justice Models

The construction of models serves multiple purposes and functions. First, models provide a useful way to cope with the complexity of the criminal process. They simplify the details of the process, highlight common themes and trends, evaluate criminal procedure values, and then assist in understanding the structure and content of the criminal justice system. They recognize "the value choices that underlie the details of the criminal process."[40] In Beloof's word, the models remain "useful constellations above the sea of the criminal process."[41] Second, they provide positive descriptions of the actual operation of the criminal justice

36 The Criminal Law Revision Committee, "Eleventh Report, Evidence (General)" (Cm 4991, 1972) [56].

37 Section 76 (4) of PACE.

38 308 U.S. 338 (1939).

39 308 U.S. 338, 340 (1939).

40 Herbert Packer, *The Limits of the Criminal Sanction* (Stanford University Press, Stanford 1968) 153.

41 Douglas Beloof, "The Third Model of Criminal Process: The Victim Participation Model" (1999) 1999 *Utah Law Review* 289, 289.

system and a guide to judge the operational practices of the criminal operation in the criminal process. Third, the models assist in revealing the relationship of criminal process to substantive criminal law[42] and evidence law. The models help us understand the criminal process as dynamic, rather than static. In the context of the exclusionary rule, models may proffer a normative guide to what values ought to influence the law of evidence.

The criminal process refers to the wide range of actors and operational practices which respond to crime. The most successful attempt to construct models of the criminal process was achieved by Herbert Packer (1925–72); these models have had remarkable durability. In his pioneering work, Packer first neatly synthesized the themes and identified two conceptual models of the criminal process: the crime control model and the due process model.[43] He attempts to abstract two value systems that compete for priority in the operation of the criminal process. The models were extremes of a spectrum.

This section explores different aspects of Packer's two models, including the perspective of the exclusionary rule, as the rule is central to the relationship between Packer's models of criminal justice. At the heart of the contention which surrounds the subject of the exclusionary rule lie two broad and conflicting concerns. The first is the concern for crime control, and the desire to include *every* single piece of evidence (including illegally obtained evidence), as long as the evidence can prove that the defendant is factually guilty. The second is the concern with due process, and the desire to exclude illegally obtained evidence. The debates and case law of the exclusionary rule can be analyzed in terms of whether a decision favors one or the other model. The model may provide guidance in deciding whether to exclude illegally obtained evidence. Packer's models contain a basis and framework for evaluating the functioning of the criminal justice system. These best-known models can be used as ideal-types to analyze and expound trends in the criminal process.

The section begins with Packer's two dichotomized models of the criminal justice system. I will illuminate the differences between the two models. The essence of the two models can be captured by evocative metaphors: "assembly line"[44] and "obstacle course."[45] The difference between the crime control model and due process model is that they disagree on four fundamental questions. The

42 Herbert Packer, *The Limits of the Criminal Sanction* (Stanford University Press, Stanford 1968) 152.

43 Herbert Packer, "Two Models of the Criminal Process" (1964) 113 *University of Pennsylvania Law Review* 1, 2.

44 Herbert Packer, "Two Models of the Criminal Process' in George Cole (ed.), *Criminal Justice: Law and Politics* (5th edn, Pacific Grove Brooks/Cole, California 1988) 15, 20; Herbert Packer, *The Limits of the Criminal Sanction* (Stanford University Press, Stanford 1969) 159.

45 Herbert Packer, *The Limits of the Criminal Sanction* (Stanford University Press, Stanford 1968) 163.

first question asks what the primary purpose of a criminal process is. The second question asks whether we should impose specific restraints on broad investigative powers of the police in order to protect the rights of the accused. The third question asks whether we should condone intrusive uses of state power in pursuit of the suppression of crime and tolerate wrongful conviction of the innocent defendants. Lastly, the fourth question asks whether we should exclude credible evidence for the sole reason that the methods used to obtain it were illegal or unfair.

The suppression of crime is the exclusive predominant function for structuring the criminal process. In the words of Packer, "repression of criminal conduct is the most important function to be performed by the criminal process."[46] The crime control model's emphasis on repressing crime leads it to reject safeguards which restrict the apprehension and conviction of offenders. The model was based on societal interests in law and order. According to Packer, "[t]he failure of law enforcement to bring criminal conduct under tight control is viewed as leading to the breakdown of public order and thence to the disappearance of an important condition of human freedom."[47]

Given its utilitarian nature, the combination of high crime and reality of limited law enforcement resources, the crime control model, therefore, stresses efficiency, which is defined in terms of speed and finality.[48] To achieve such speed and finality[49] and fulfill its purpose, first, the model aims to produce "efficiency" by disposing of criminal cases swiftly and dealing with the maximum number of cases in a criminal justice system with limited resources. The key to achieving that end is "the efficiency with which the criminal process operates to screen suspects, determine guilt, and secure appropriate dispositions of persons convicted of crime."[50] Second, this prompts calls for the police to be equipped with broad investigative powers, for example, search, seizure, and arrest people for interrogating, to apprehend criminals efficiently. These broad powers are often the quickest methods to establish whether the defendant is factually guilty.[51] The limitation on the police interrogation is that designed to ensure the reliability of the defendant's statements.

The model operated under an assumption that "preliminary screening processes operated by the police and the prosecuting officials contain adequate guarantees of reliable fact finding."[52] Packer describes this model as a high speed

46 Ibid., 153.

47 Ibid.

48 Ibid., 159.

49 In other words, low rates of appeal.

50 Ibid., 158.

51 Ibid., 177.

52 Herbert Packer, "Two Models of the Criminal Process" (1964) 113 *University of Pennsylvania Law Review* 1, 13.

"assembly line conveyor belt"[53] operated by the police and prosecutors. It can be described in terms of a criminal justice system for conveying suspects through from interrogation to conviction. The criminal process is merely an "assembly line" that processes criminal cases as quick as possible. The "assembly line" is primarily concerned with efficiency. It focuses on efficiency in apprehending, trying, and convicting offenders.

Key to the formulation of the model is the concept of "factual guilt," in which the accused committed the criminal act. This model is premised on a preference for fact-finding centered in police investigations and the belief that executive officials[54] identify those persons who are "factually guilty." Once identified, to obtain a conviction and impose punishment as quickly as possible. The model depends on quick resolution of questions of factual guilt through informal investigation processes and interrogations with minimal oversight. In order to efficiently achieve the conviction and punishment of the factually guilty, it should be avoided to expend unnecessary resources. The function of the trial is *not* important in the model because its center of gravity lies in "the early, administrative fact-finding stages."[55] Court based processes are truncated or rejected as there is no reason to waste time on elaborate courtroom procedures.

The model regards the state as an ally. Its "benevolent" view of state power means that it is willing to entrust the state with wider powers in order to give it great leeway in its efforts to tackle crime. The model emphasizes the suppression of crime, and so is willing to condone more intrusive uses of state power in pursuit of this aim. The wrongful conviction of the innocent is not seen as a problem. Mistakes are acceptable as long as they do not interfere with the repression of crime. Where there is sufficient reliable evidence of guilt, even the most serious misconduct by the police should not result in the conviction being quashed.

Credible evidence is not excluded simply because the methods to obtain it were illegal. The crime control model *cannot* tolerate that credible evidence is excluded for the sole reason that the methods used to obtain it were illegal or improper. To let factually guilty go free on such a "technicality" undermines crime control. The exclusionary rule, therefore, is viewed by the police as an unnecessary complication of the task of detecting and apprehending criminals, and suppressing crime.[56]

---

53 Herbert Packer, "Two Models of the Criminal Process' in George Cole (ed.), *Criminal Justice: Law and Politics* (5th edn, Pacific Grove Brooks/Cole, California 1988) 15, 20; Herbert Packer, *The Limits of the Criminal Sanction* (Stanford University Press, Stanford 1968) 159.

54 For example, the police and prosecutors.

55 Herbert Packer, *The Limits of the Criminal Sanction* (Stanford University Press, Stanford 1968) 162.

56 Jerome Skolnick, *Justice without Trial: Law Enforcement in Democratic Society* (2nd edn, John Wiley and Sons, New York 1975) 227.

In addition, the police should also have wide powers to conduct searches as only the factually guilty have something to hide.[57] The model also opposes the search and seizure exclusionary rule. According to the model, illegally obtained physical evidence should be admissible at trial. Illegally obtained guns, drugs and stolen property should not be excluded as they reveal the truth. It does not matter how the police obtained them.[58] If the evidence is reliable, as Justice Crompton has claimed in 1861 in England: "[i]t matters not how you get it; if you steal it even, it would be admissible."[59]

By contrast, Packer's due process model represents a human rights approach to the criminal process. The model has its predominant goal the regulation of governmental intrusions in individual rights and the protection of the rights of the accused, which, it is assumed, will protect the rights of the individual. The model was based on the primacy of the rights of the individual in relation of the state, and emphasized protection of defendants, from official oppression. The model is concerned with ensuring sufficient protection for the individual against state power. Thus, the model is mindful of the potential for abuse and so insists on strict safeguards and based on the value of prevention of abuse of state power.

The model is concerned with state power, the possibilities of abuse inherent in official power,[60] "the primacy of the individual,"[61] the protection of individual rights, the rights of the defendant, fairness to the defendant, and "quality control."[62] The model stresses quality and thoroughness. The basic motivation underlying the model, according to Packer, is a desire to minimize mistakes in ascertaining guilt.[63] Conviction of those who are innocent is totally unacceptable and must be avoided.

The model is skeptical of the administrative investigative process and its capacity to accurately assess guilt without judicial oversight. Thus, the model may impose procedural restrictions on application of criminal law even if these restrictions will limit the efficiency of the application.[64] Packer describes this model as an "obstacle course"[65] in which lawyers argue before judges that the prosecution may be rejected because the defendant's rights have been violated. Quality control takes priority over quantitative outputs under this model. This

57 Herbert Packer, *The Limits of the Criminal Sanction* (Stanford University Press, Stanford 1968) 196.

58 Ibid., 199.

59 *R v. Leatham* (1861) 8 Cox CC 498, 501.

60 Herbert Packer, *The Limits of the Criminal Sanction* (Stanford University Press, Stanford 1968) 165–6.

61 Ibid., 165.

62 Ibid.

63 Ibid.

64 Abraham Goldstein, "Reflections on Two Models: Inquisitorial Themes in American Criminal Procedure" (1974) 26 *Stanford Law Review* 1009, 1009–11.

65 Herbert Packer, *The Limits of the Criminal Sanction* (Stanford University Press, Stanford 1968) 163.

model operates according to the preoccupation of limiting state power over the individual.

The model is skeptical of the motivations and fact-finding skills of law enforcement officers and animated by a fundamental distrust of the fact-finding process. The model insists instead on adherence to "formal, adjudicative, adversary fact-finding processes in which the factual case against the accused is publicly heard by an impartial tribunal."[66] To prevent such abuse the model subjects the exercise of investigative power to certain checks and balances. In addition, the model emphasizes the distinction between legal and factual guilt. There is a key concept of the model: "legal guilt," in the sense that a defendant is deemed to be guilty only after the state establishes the fact by meeting the procedural demands of the system.[67]

The model sees the criminal process as "conforming to the rule of law ... emphasizing legal guilt over factual guilt."[68] The model uses the criminal process to police itself by its commitment to the concept of "legal guilt."[69] The model will not sacrifice the rights of the individual on the altar of "efficiency." The model "stresses the possibilities of error."[70] Mistakes should be eliminated to the fullest extent possible. Thus, the model places great weight on avoiding mistakes. Wrongful conviction of the innocent defendants is intolerable. All possible steps should be taken to prevent abuses of state power. As Blackstone has stated, "[i]t is better that ten guilty persons escape, than that one innocent suffer."[71]

The exclusionary rule is symbolic of the due process model as courts will be more concerned with constitutional violation than discovering the truth about factual guilt. According to the model, strong "prophylactic and deterrent"[72] exclusionary rules are necessary because much police abuse can never be remedied. Instead of focusing on factual guilt, the prosecutor and judge should put their efforts into establishing legal guilt beyond a reasonable doubt on the basis of legally obtained evidence. Illegally obtained confessions should be excluded because they infringe the rights of the accused and were obtained through police misconduct.

---

66 Ibid., 163–4.

67 Peter Arenella, "Rethinking the Functions of Criminal Procedure: The Warren and Burger Courts' Competing Ideologies" (1983) 72 *Georgia Law Journal* 185, 211.

68 Jerome Skolnick, *Justice without Trial: Law Enforcement in Democratic Society* (2nd edn, John Wiley and Sons, New York 1975) 182.

69 Herbert Packer, *The Limits of the Criminal Sanction* (Stanford University Press, Stanford 1968) 166.

70 Ibid., 163.

71 William Blackstone, *Commentaries on the Laws of England* (Clarendon Press, Oxford 1769) 352.

72 Herbert Packer, *The Limits of the Criminal Sanction* (Stanford University Press, Stanford 1968) 168.

1.4 Problematic Trends

The exclusionary rule is one of the most difficult,[73] controversial[74] and complex[75] doctrines in criminal procedure and evidence law. The difficulties are both in theory and practice. In theory, it is difficult to provide a compelling rationale for the rule; in practice, the extent of the rule is unclear. This rule is multifaceted and ever-changing. Dennis has also noticed that "the law in this area is complex and still developing."[76]

There are several types of evidence to be considered for exclusion. In this book these types fall into two main categories: (1) confessions: confessions obtained by torture or oppression; (2) non-confessional evidence: evidence secured by illegal

---

73 Ross and Chalmers noted that "when it has been established that a piece of evidence has been obtained illegally or irregularly, the question as to whether in a particular case it is admissible or inadmissible is frequently one of difficulty." Margaret Ross and James Chalmers, *Walker and Walker: The Law of Evidence in Scotland* (Tottel, Edinburgh 2006) 6; Ashworth and Redmayne noted that "[w]here the police have evidence against a suspect by unfair or illegally means, the courts face a difficult question: whether or not to admit the evidence ... The issues involved here are complex ... The exclusion of improperly obtained evidence is a difficult topic." Andrew Ashworth and Mike Redmayne, *The Criminal Process* (3rd edn, Oxford University Press, Oxford 2005) 314, 332.

74 Shanks noted that "few court-made rules have endured so much criticism or provoked so many attacks." B.F. Shanks, "Comparative Analysis of the Exclusionary Rule and Its Alternatives" (1983) 57 *Tulane Law Review* 648, 651; Orfield noted that "[t]he exclusionary rule is one of the most controversial and divisive issues in American constitutional law." Myron Orfield, Jr., "The Exclusionary Rule and Deterrence: An Empirical Study of Chicago Narcotics Officers" (1987) 54 *University of Chicago Law Review* 1016, 1016; Fennelly noted that "no other doctrine in American criminal jurisprudence has generated more controversy or possessed such determined critics and supporters." J.E. Fennelly, "Inevitable Discovery, the Exclusionary Rule and Military Due Process" (1991) 131 *Military Law Review* 109, 129; Damaška noted that "[d]espite intense scholarly efforts to provide clarity in this area, the precise scope of rules whose violation may lead to exclusion remains uncertain everywhere and highly controversial." M.R. Damaška, *Evidence Law Adrift* (Yale University Press, New Haven 1997) 23; Dripps noted that "[f]ew debates in American law are as sustained, or as bitter, as the debate over the exclusionary rule." Donald Dripps, "The Case for Contingent Exclusionary Rule" (2001) 38 *American Criminal Law Review* 1, 1; Ashworth noted that "the right to be tried on evidence not obtained by violation of fundamental rights ... is a controversial right. It is not contained in the Convention as such; there are signs of its recognition in some decisions and not in others. It is accepted in English law to some degree, but not as a general proposition." Andrew Ashworth, *Human Rights, Serious Crime and Criminal Procedure* (Sweet & Maxwell, London 2002) 35.

75 The Royal Commission on Criminal Procedure of 1981 described this is a "complex and controversial" field. The Royal Commission on Criminal Procedure, "Report" (Cm 8092, 1981) [4.126].

76 I.H. Dennis, *The Law of Evidence* (3rd edn, Sweet & Maxwell, London 2008) 295.

search and seizure. A detailed consideration of all types of illegally or unfairly obtained evidence is beyond the scope of this research; there are far too many breaches of police powers. I am now mainly concerned with evidence obtained by torture and illegal searches.

Some of the previous studies are insufficient and incomplete in terms of their scope and depth. They over-simplified this complicated issue. My intention here is to take matters further by providing a more principled discussion of the rule. First, Tapper notes that "in England, illegally obtained evidence is admissible as a matter of law, provided that it involves neither a reference to an inadmissible confession of guilt, nor the commission of an act of contempt of court."[77] Zander argues that "[b]roadly, confessions were liable to be excluded, whilst other evidence was normally admitted in evidence."[78]

As a matter of fact, in the past two decades, there has been a trend in Europe to increasingly expand the use of the exclusionary rule, including the United Kingdom. In 1984, the English criminal justice system began a process of reconstruction. There are four grounds of exclusion under of the PACE. Section 76(2) requires exclusion of confession (a) obtained by oppression or (b) likely to have been rendered unreliable by anything said or done by anyone.[79] What matters is how the confession was obtained, not whether it may have been true or not. If the confession was obtained by oppression, the judge is bound to exclude the admissions. His decision is mandatory rather than discretionary. Section 78(1) provides that: "the court may refuse to allow evidence … if it appears … that … the admission of the evidence would have such an adverse effect on the fairness of the proceedings that the court ought not to admit it."[80] In addition, Section 82(3) saves "pre-existing common law powers … to exclude evidence whose prejudicial effect outweighed its probative value."[81]

For the first time in the history of British criminal justice, the judiciary were given statutory power to exclude improperly obtained non-confessional evidence.[82] Judges do not need to consider whether they have discretion to exclude relevant evidence.

In the United States, since 1970s, the Supreme Court has gradually moved in a conservative direction, limited the scope and application of the rule

77 Colin Tapper, *Cross and Tapper on Evidence* (11th edn, Oxford University Press, Oxford 2007) 547.

78 Michael Zander, *Cases and Materials on the English Legal System* (10th edn, Cambridge University Press, Cambridge 2007) 470.

79 PACE, ch. 60, Section 76 (2) (Eng.).

80 Ibid., Section 78 (1).

81 David Feldman, "Regulating Treatment of Suspects in Police Stations: Judicial Interpretation of Detention Provisions in the Police and Criminal Evidence Act 1984" (1990) *Criminal Law Review* 452, 453.

82 Sybil Sharpe, "Covert Policing: A Comparative View" (1996) 25 *Anglo-American Law Review* 163, 165.

and has repeatedly created exceptions. Presently, there exist the following exceptions: independent source,[83] good faith,[84] inevitable discovery,[85] purged taint,[86] impeachment,[87] harmless error exception[88] and rule of attenuation.[89] The Court backed away from a very strict application of the search and seizure exclusionary rule.

The exclusionary rule is very controversial. Some judges, including the Chief Justice Burger, opposed the rule. For example, in *Bivens v. Six Unknown Named Agents of Federal Bureau of Narcotics*,[90] F.B.I. agents raided a suspect's home, handcuffed him in front of his family, and searched for drugs. Finding none, they took him to the station house where he was strip searched, interrogated, and eventually released. The suspect, Bivens, then brought a civil action against the federal government.

Although the Court held that the plaintiff was entitled to recover money damages for any injuries he had suffered as a result of the agents' violation of the Fourth Amendment, in Chief Justice Burger's dissent, he characterized the exclusionary rule as "an unworkable and irrational concept of law," totally rejected the rule and attacked the rule for inadequately protecting the rights of suspects and wrongfully punishing prosecutors, who are powerless to correct police misconduct.[91]

In 1995, the Senate was considering completely eliminating the exclusionary rule in the proposed Violent Crime Control and Law Enforcement Improvement Act of 1995, although it didn't succeed, which stated that:

> Evidence which is obtained as a result of a search or seizure shall not be excluded in a proceeding in a court of the United States, on the ground that the search or seizure was in violation of the Fourth Amendment to the constitution of the United States, if the search or seizure was carried out in circumstances justifying an objectively reasonable belief that it was in conformity with the Fourth Amendment.[92]

Additionally, there are still many profound, crucial and difficult questions unanswered. Many of these important issues have been simply ignored. These questions are full of conflicts and dilemmas. For example, (1) Does and should the

83 *Segura v. United States*, 371 U.S. 471 (1963).

84 *United States v. Leon*, 468 U.S. 897 (1984).

85 *Nix v. Williams*, 467 U.S. 431 (1984).

86 *Won Sun v. United States*, 371 U.S. 471 (1963).

87 *Walder v. United States*, 347 U.S. 62 (1954).

88 *Chapman v. California*, 386 U.S. 18 (1967).

89 *Nardone v. United States*, 308 U.S. 338 (1939).

90 403 U.S. 388 (1971) (Burger, C.J., dissenting).

91 Ibid.

92 Exclusionary Rule Reform Act of 1995 Report Together with Dissenting Views (1995), Report 104–17, 104th Cong., 1st Sess.

exclusionary rule not only just apply to ordinary criminals, but also to terrorists,[93] murderers and rapists? Should we carve out categories of people for whom the full force of the rule does not apply? I will argue strongly that the rule must apply to everyone.

(2) How to bridge the gap between confessional and non-confessional evidence? There is a huge gap between them. As a matter of law, the general rule about non-confessional evidence is that "the test to be applied in considering whether evidence is admissible is whether it is relevant to the matters in issue. If it is, it is admissible, and the court is not concerned with how the evidence was obtained."[94] If reliable evidence exists, it would be regrettable not to use it, and to risk the acquittal of a guilty person; why cannot we apply this approach to confessional evidence to obtain more evidence and apprehend more criminals? If an involuntary confession is corroborated and there is no doubt about its trustworthiness, can the criminal justice system make use of it? In general, if a confession had been obtained by police methods that rendered it involuntary or coerced—and thus violated due process law—it had to be excluded, however verifiable. It was so clear and simple. But why is it not that simple when non-confessional evidence is obtained in violation of due process, when the police have violated a constitutional protection that is basic to a free society?[95] Lord Devlin has aptly observed that:

> [i]f the court is prepared to exclude admissions given in answer to improper questioning, however potent evidence they may be of the commission of a crime, and if it does so because the benefit to the law of fair interrogation outweighs the justice of the individual case, ought it not to follow the same principle where documents are unlawfully seized?[96]

(3) Why do some of the police prefer using illegal or unfair methods to procure evidence? Should the police be permitted to use deception to extract confessions from suspects? If it is not a judge's function to discipline the police, who should

93 Although much has recently been written on the issue of the prohibition of torture in the context of terrorism, the discussion has expended very little attention on the question of whether evidence obtained by torture would be admissible. See Alan Dershowitz, *Why Terrorism Works: Understanding the Threat Responding to the Challenge* (Yale University Press, New Haven 2002); Oren Gross, "Are Torture Warrants Warranted? Pragmatic Absolutism and Official Disobedience" (2003) 88 *Minnesota Law Review* 1481 (discussing the issue of the prohibition of torture).

94 *Kuruma Son of Kaniu v. Reginam*, [1955] 1 All ER 236. Professors Robert and Zuckerman also criticized that "this pat rationalization is far too quick, and proves much too much." Paul Roberts and Adrian Zuckerman, *Criminal Evidence* (Oxford University Press, Oxford 2004) 150.

95 Yale Kamisar, "The Writings of John Barker Waite and Thomas Davies on the Search and Seizure Exclusionary Rule" (2002) 100 *Michigan Law Review* 1821, 1828.

96 Patrick Devlin, *The Criminal Prosecution in England* (Yale University Press, New Haven 1958) 53.

take responsibility for regulating police misconduct? According to my research and over 10 years' prosecutor and criminal judge experience, I firmly argue that the police system will not seriously discipline their "brothers" who go beyond permissible limits in their eagerness to secure valuable evidence against the "bad guys."[97] Some high-ranking police officers who ordered that pain be inflicted on the suspect even considered themselves crime fighters.[98] It is rather a naïve view of depending on the police to safeguard civil rights.

(4) The exclusionary rule reveals the fundamental tension between the social need for order and individuals' desire for privacy and liberty. Can both ideologies be pursued simultaneously without compromise? In the leading case of *Lawrie v. Muir* in Scotland, Lord Justice-General Cooper highlighted that:

> The law must strive to reconcile two highly important interests which are liable to come into conflict—(*a*) the interest of the citizen to be protected from illegal or irregular invasions of his liberties by the authorities, and (*b*) the interest of the State to secure that evidence bearing upon the commission of crime and necessary to enable justice to be done shall not be withheld from Courts of law on any merely formal or technical ground.[99]

---

97 Hsieh Kuo-hsing (2004), "美國證據排除法則之思辨" [Rethinking the Exclusionary Rule of Evidence in the United States] 49 *Criminal Law Review* 62, 81.

98 In 2002, the Frankfurt police had arrested Magnus Gaefgen, who was accused of kidnapping an 11-year-old boy. Wolfgang Daschner, Frankfurt Police Vice-President, ordered his subordinates to try to extract the necessary information "by means of the infliction of pain, under medical supervision and subject to prior warning." Gaefgen testified that a police officer told him that a specialist was being flown by helicopter to Frankfurt who could "inflict on me pain of a sort I had never before experienced." Within 20 minutes after being so threatened, Gaefgen crumpled and admitted he had killed the child less than two hours after the boy was abducted. He then led police to the body. The actual infliction of pain, which in fact had been arranged by fetching a specially trained police officer, was not necessary. In 2003, Gaefgen was sentenced to life imprisonment. The information provided by him under the impression of the unlawful threat was not admitted as evidence. Daschner pleaded "either I violated the rights of the suspect, or I put at risk the life of the victim. In weighing up the options it was clear to me what I had to do, and *I would do the same again.*" In 2004, Daschner was fined €10,800 and the subordinate police officer was fined €3,600 by the Regional Court at Frankfurt. See John Hooper, "Kidnap Case Presents Germans with Ugly Dilemma over Torture" *The Guardian*, Feb. 27, 2003, at 18; Hannah Cleaver, "Kidnapper Gets Life for Murder of Banker's Son in £700,000 Plot" *Daily Telegraph*, July 29, 2003, at 11; Roger Boyes, "Police Chief Sanctioned "Torture to Save a Life"" *The Times*, Nov. 19, 2004, at 38 (emphasis added); Florian Jessberger, "Bad Torture—Good Torture? What International Criminal Lawyers May Learn from the Recent Trial of Police Officers in Germany" (2005) 3 *Journal of International Criminal Justice* 1059, 1066.

99 1950 J.C. 19, 27.

The crucial question is, "How to balance the two conflicting interests?" The dilemma is the gravity of serious crimes always will by definition exceed the gravity of almost any illegal or irregular invasions of citizens' liberties.

(5) What is the admissibility of evidence obtained in breach of Article 8 of the European Convention for the Protection of Human Rights and Fundamental Rights (ECHR)?

The British Parliament incorporated the ECHR in its domestic law by the Human Rights Act 1998, which became effective in 2000. The Act requires British courts to act in accordance with rights protected by the Convention. For example, Article 3, which guarantees freedom from torture and inhuman and degrading treatment, is relevant to the possible exclusion of a confession. Article 6, the most litigated provision of the ECHR in the ECtHR,[100] offers sophisticated protections for the right to a fair trial.

Many of the covert and intrusive methods used by police violated the suspect's right to respect for a private life, in breach of Article 8. In *Khan v. United Kingdom*,[101] Khan visited a friend in Sheffield in 1993 who was under investigation for dealing in heroin. The police placed an aural surveillance device on his friend's house. Khan was arrested subsequently because the police obtained recordings of a conversation in the course of which Khan admitted that he had been involved in another importation of drugs case. The issue is whether the evidence was admissible. The House of Lords held that the trial judge had been justified in not excluding the evidence.[102]

Khan pursued his case to the European Court of Human Rights (ECtHR) and alleged that his right of privacy under Article 8 had been violated. In addition, as the only evidence in the case had been obtained in breach of the Convention, it should follow that his right to a fair trial under Article 6 had also been violated. The ECtHR held that the admission of evidence obtained by means of a listening device in breach of Article 8 did not automatically render the proceedings unfair.

The question, however, raises two separate issues: first, does it make a fair trial where evidence is relied on which was obtained in breach of the human rights guaranteed by the Convention; secondly, is such evidence admissible? I argue that the security of one's privacy against intrusion by the government is inextricable from the conception of fair trial.

Some decisions of the ECtHR have generated a power controversy; since Articles 3, 6 and 8 cover some of the most crucial areas of criminal procedure the issues bring into sharp focus the classic dilemma of order versus liberty in the civil societies.

---

100 Paul Roberts, "Does Article 6 of the European Convention on Human Rights Require Reasoned Verdicts in Criminal Trials?" (2011) *Human Rights Law Review* 213, 214.

101 *Khan v. United Kingdom* (App no 35394/97) (2001) 31 EHRR 45.

102 *R v. Khan (Sultan)*, [1997] AC 558, 582.

By comparing the criminal procedure of other countries, we might find good reasons to maintain or change the Anglo-American approach towards the exclusionary rule. In order to predict more accurately in which direction we may go, it is important for us to be aware of other countries' situation.

(6) Does China desire to solve the problem of police torture? Why is this problem still so serious? Why cannot current mechanisms play their roles? What are the attitudes of Chinese criminal judges towards illegally obtained evidence? Which is the appropriate application of the exclusionary rule for China?

All of these questions have not been thought through, while some important issues have been simply ignored. Finding answers to these questions is very critical. It will help China to prevent police torture and police malfeasance leading to imprisonment or even execution of innocent persons.

Referring to the original contribution in this book , I will address two points. The first point, quite simply, is that this research is the first systematic investigation of the exclusionary rule of evidence in the United Kingdom,[103] United States[104] and China.[105] It will explore the interesting similarities and differences about the exclusionary rule issues in the United Kingdom and the United States. Although the judicial attitudes on indictment in the United Kingdom, United States and China provide the basis for much of the discussion in the book , the position in a variety of other jurisdictions is analyzed where it is felt that such analyses throw light on the particular issue under discussion. The exclusionary rule remains an unexplored issue before Chinese courts[106] and, hence, is not a subject of much contention. In the past, the Chinese legal community who cared about their personal safety

---

103 It mainly refers to English law. In addition, there has been little analysis of the exclusionary rule and its related issues in Scotland. The Scottish decisions perceive themselves to be steering somewhat of a middle course between the automatic exclusion and the unquestioned admissibility. It seems that the Scottish judges have taken a more robust protection of the exclusionary rule than their English counterparts. It is a topic that requires further examination. See Peter Duff, "Admissibility of Improperly Obtained Physical Evidence in the Scottish Criminal Trial: The Search for Principle" (2004) 8 *Edinburgh Law Review* 152, 152–3 (analyzing the exclusionary rule in Scotland).

104 It mainly refers to the federal/constitutional law.

105 To date, there is absolutely no analysis of court cases about the exclusionary rule in China. This research will explore the judicial attitudes towards illegally obtained evidence. In addition, from the Qin dynasty (221–207 B.C.), torture was part of the ordinary criminal procedure. Not only the suspects but also the informant and witness maybe suffered from torture. This research will explore the relationship between the traditional legal culture and Chinese criminal procedure law in practice.

106 In this book, I have selected these Chinese cases among a great many cases with great effort and care, and I have selected them largely because they are of interest to me. Many of them have also received a great deal of attention in China. In addition, it is extremely difficult to collect complete criminal judgments in China, especially if the cases involve police torture or police misconduct.

avoided publishing on human rights and torture issues. The political climate produced a chilling effect upon the quality of scholarship.

Although the corpus of writing on the Chinese criminal justice system has slightly expanded in recent years, significant gaps in our knowledge of the origin, development, and potential impact of the exclusionary rule remain. It is easy to criticize the Chinese criminal justice system. However, unlike commentators who contentedly note the broad short-comings of Chinese criminal process but stop there, I propose reforms, using the experiences in the United Kingdom and the United States as a model. Comparative criminal procedure law is particularly germane in exclusionary rule cases because it can help us to develop a sounder approach to some structural issues.

This book will combine diagnosis and prescription—the problem of police torture and the solution of the exclusionary rule. I challenge the widespread idea that the Chinese government has no desire to solve the problem of police torture and establish the exclusionary rule. The crucial question is which type of exclusionary rule is suitable for China. The research explores the importance of the rule in the quest for abolishing police torture. This research will begin a conversation between the Chinese criminal justice system and the Anglo-American criminal justice system. I will provide the most suitable approach for the exclusionary rule in China.

The second point is this research will make a timely contribution.

The timing is perfect. In 2011, I predicted China would adopt the exclusionary rule within a few years and it happened. Over 10 cities and provinces[107] have already adopted the confession exclusionary rule according to judicial interpretations. Some scholars started to notice the importance of the rule, although they have focused on the confession exclusionary rule. Now is the perfect time to introduce the rule to China for a solution to police torture. It is becoming increasingly clear that a series of chilling torture cases might provide China with the incentive to establish the exclusionary rule in practice.

1.5 Structure

Three underlying themes in the book are, first, the rationales on which the exclusionary rule in criminal trials is premised; secondly, the theoretical constitutional foundation of the rule, and, thirdly, reform of the rule. Attention will have been drawn to the following interrelated issues:

1. What are the rationales of the exclusionary rule?
2. We will elevate the exclusionary rule to a new level of constitutional status. This is not merely a matter of evidence law. But what on earth is the theoretical constitutional foundation of the rule?

107 See 7.3.

3. Should police torture be subject to a blanket prohibition? Should the exclusionary rule not apply to suspects who committed some serious cases, for example, murderers, career armed robbers and rapists?
4. Are there alternatives to the exclusionary rule in practice?
5. Why is the problem of police torture still so serious in China? Should China adopt the exclusionary rule in practice? If the answer is yes, which approach is suitable for China?

The arrangement of this study is as follows: this chapter is the introduction to the study, which concerns the problematic trends of the research, and the key issues in this area. The opportunity is taken here for extended discussion and comparison of a variety of work which is much cited, but rarely analyzed in depth. In this chapter, I have also elaborated on the way in which this project will be carried out.

The first part of this research (Chapters 2, 3 and 4) discusses lessons from the past—the Anglo-American exclusionary rule. Chapter 2 addresses the evolution of the exclusionary rule (both the confession exclusionary rule, and the search and seizure exclusionary rule) in the United Kingdom and the United States. It will mainly examine the leading cases concerning the rule addressed by the courts in the House of Lords and United States Supreme Court and refer to decisions of lower courts in the same jurisdiction as well. This book will evaluate different approaches found in the case law of these courts. Further, the rationales for the exclusionary rule are still unclear. In England there are two completely different perspectives regarding the rule. To utilitarians, to exclude evidence is to exclude the root of justice; the rule is the obstacle to truth-finding. To libertarians, the rule is to prevent abuse of power and to protect the liberty of the individual. In the United States, by contrast, no other doctrine in criminal procedure and evidence jurisprudence has possessed such loyal supporters and opponents. This chapter then examines rationales for the rule in criminal trials.

Chapter 3 continues by exploring various issues of the acrimonious debates for the exclusionary rule. The chapter is a contribution to the debates on the exclusionary rule. This chapter will examine the supporting and opposing opinions on the rule. It delves into the question: whether there exists an alternative plan to the exclusionary rule. Next, it analyzes the cost-benefit balancing of the exclusionary rule. This chapter also examines the myths of the exclusionary rule.

Chapter 4 canvasses the theoretical constitutional foundation of the exclusionary rule. The separation of powers doctrine is a major principle of the United States Constitution. This chapter will explore the relationship between the separation of powers doctrine and the rule. This chapter next turns to the analysis of the interactions of the court, exclusionary rule and police. To date, no substantial literature addresses the relationship between the three.

The second part (Chapters 5, 6 and 7) of this study concentrates on the exclusionary rule in China. Part II is the heart of this book. Chapter 5 argues that the current Chinese legal structure for combating police torture is not adequately armed with the possibility, and that the fight against police torture has been plagued by many legal loopholes. The first section of this chapter describes the nature and magnitude of the problem of police torture in China. It considers the reasons why the police make use of torture to obtain evidence. This chapter next turns to the wide powers of Chinese police. This chapter then challenges the proposal that the ban on police torture should be lifted. I argue that prohibition on police torture is absolute and the confessions obtained by torture cannot be justified under any circumstances.

Chapter 6 explores the operation of the exclusionary rule in China. First of all, the major purpose of this section is to canvass the attitude of Chinese criminal judges towards illegally obtained evidence. This chapter then deals with whether, where torture is alleged, the burden of proof should fall on the suspect or prosecution. Finally, it turns to an analysis of evidence obtained by searches and seizures.

The seventh chapter turns to the most pressing concern for exploring the appropriate approach of the exclusionary rule for China. It begins with the threshold question: what is the appropriate approach for China to shape the exclusionary rule in criminal practice? In the first place, I will examine why we need to establish the exclusionary rule in China in practice. In the second place, it then turns to address the admissibility of illegally obtained physical evidence. Lastly, it depicts several regional rules of criminal evidence and analyzes the possible effects of each regional rule that can occur when the court dealing with the admissibility of illegally obtained evidence. I show how some exceptions are dangerous because they will replace the exclusionary rule per se.

Chapter 8, the concluding chapter, as well as drawing together and synthesizing a number of themes which have been explored in, and which have underlain, the preceding chapters, presents some proposals for reform of the existing law and judicial interpretations.

PART I
Lessons from the Past: The Anglo-American Exclusionary Rule

Introduction

The book will first consider the approaches to illegally obtained evidence employed by England and the United States. The first part of the book reflects upon the development of the Anglo-American exclusionary rule, with separate chapters covering (1) evolution and rationales, (2) the exclusionary rule debates and (3) theoretical constitutional foundation.

I focus on the origins of the exclusionary rule in England and the United States, including its evolution since the beginning of the eighteenth century. I begin my work by examining evolution of the exclusionary rule going all the way back to 1740s in England.[1] Since 1886, the United States Supreme Court has required that evidence in violation of the Fourth Amendment be excluded.[2] I will trace the history of the exclusionary rule to show that the rule is about controlling executive power. Then I will examine the varying justifications for the exclusionary rule. As regards rationales, although the United States Supreme Court recognizes the deterrence rationale as the exclusionary rule's primary purpose, this book asserts that the effect of the exclusionary rule is much greater than mere deterrence.

Further, the exclusionary rule has attracted much controversy and debate. After exploring the history of the exclusionary rule,[3] the work then moves to the ongoing debates of the exclusionary rule.[4] No single principle of criminal procedure and evidence has generated more debate than the exclusionary rule. Opponents of the exclusionary rule claim that the rule causes criminals to go free, without textual basis, the rule is not an effective deterrent, and the rule is limited to the United States and common law countries;[5] therefore, it is invariably argued, the exclusionary rule should be abolished. Unfortunately, however, these claims cannot

---

1 J.H. Langbein, *The Origins of Adversary Criminal Trial* (Oxford University Press, Oxford 2003) 218–33.

2 *Boyd v. United States*, 116 U.S. 618 (1886).

3 See 2.1.

4 See Chapter 3.

5 See 3.1.1–3.1.5.

be substantiated. In addition, commentators have also been engaged in a long and lively debate as to whether there exist alternatives to the exclusionary rule.[6] In theory, there are three types of alternative remedies: the criminal remedy, the civil remedy and the administrative remedy. However, upon closer consideration, no workable alternative to the exclusionary rule exists.

Next, according to the cost-benefit balancing approach in the context of the exclusionary rule, in the view of the United States Supreme Court, if the costs of excluding valuable illegally obtained evidence outweigh the deterrent benefits gained, the rule will not be permitted.[7] In addition, Richard Posner takes the position that all Fourth Amendment issues should be resolved through cost-benefit balancing.[8] I wish I could believe that this were the case, but after close attention to the Court's Fourth Amendment cases, I cannot bring myself to that conclusion. As we will see, the cost-benefit balancing approach was not used properly to decide whether or not to exclude evidence obtained through illegal methods.[9] Quite the contrary, the deterrence-oriented cost-benefit balancing approach leads to a distortion of substantive exclusionary rule protection.[10]

An overarching theme in Chapter 4 is to lay the thorough theoretical foundation for analyzing issues around the exclusionary rule, by identifying the theoretical constitutional foundation for the rule (i.e., the *separation of powers*), analyzing the interrelationship between the court, exclusionary rule and police, and showing the result of lacking checks and balances in the criminal process. This book challenges the traditional perception of the exclusionary rule by developing it in the constitutional law context. The key question, the focus of the present book, is what the theoretical constitutional foundation of the exclusionary rule is. Critical examination of this question goes to the very roots of the exclusionary rule.

6 See 3.2.

7 See 3.3.1.

8 Richard Posner, 'Rethinking the Fourth Amendment' (1981) *The Supreme Court Review* 49, 74.

9 See 3.3.2.

10 See 3.3.

Chapter 2
Evolution and Rationales

2.1 Evolution

The history of the exclusionary rule is about controlling executive power. Some of the lawyer's histories of the rule are incorrect because they only take a narrow perspective of history. It is important to identify the virtues and limitations of the rule from the history, which helps us to evaluate the subsequent development and solve some difficult problems in contemporary exclusionary rule theory. The exclusionary rule opinions of both the House of Lords and the United States Supreme Court frequently invoke history as a foundation for decision. In this book, I will use historical evidence to support my arguments.

Broadly speaking, the exclusionary rule was born as early as the eighteenth century (between the 1740s and the 1770s), grew up in the nineteenth century, and matured in the twentieth century.

2.1.1 English Law

2.1.1.1 Confession exclusionary rule The starting point is confession evidence. The confession exclusionary rule refers to the rule that excludes confessions obtained by illegal or unfair methods, for example, fear of prejudice, hope of advantage, or oppression of any sort. The fundamental condition of the admissibility of confession evidence is that it must be voluntary. If the confession was voluntarily offered, it is admissible.

Peter Mirfield claimed that "in *Warickshall* itself we find that the first judicial statement of what is, without doubt, an exclusionary rule."[1] The confession exclusionary rule, however, long predated *Warickshall* in 1783. Langbein's examination of the *Old Bailey Sessions Papers* describes the criminal trials conducted in the Old Bailey from the 1670s until the eve of World War I provides insights into the way in which the exclusionary rule solidified at the court.

The exclusionary rule goes back some 275 years. At the trial of Tobias and Rachel Isaacs in 1740, after the prosecutor promised Rachel to be her friend and that she would not hurt her, she confessed. The report noted that "[t]he prosecutor was not allowed to proceed; and another witness afterwards offering to give an account of what she had confessed to him, was likewise stopped; because a confession obtained on a prosecutor of friendship or by false insinuations ought

1 Peter Mirfield, *Confessions* (Sweet & Maxwell, London 1985) 47, citing *The King v. Warickshall*, 1 Leach 263 (1783).

not to be given in evidence against a prisoner." The confession exclusionary rule was thereby applied at the Old Bailey in 1740.[2] In 1741, involuntary confessions were regarded as inadmissible because of the exclusionary rule in the trial of Charles White.[3]

Up to 1775, however, the authorities often extracted confessions from suspects by threats or promises and most of such extorted confessions were admissible. In *R v. Margaret Caroline Rudd*,[4] on application for release, the accused had been induced by promises. Lord Mansfield referred to the fact that:

> The instance has frequently happened of persons having made confessions under threats or promises: the consequence as frequently has been that such examinations and confessions *have not been made use of against them* on their trials.[5]

The court barred involuntary confessions which were obtained by threats or promises and established important precedents on the confession exclusionary rule in 1775. However, the judge did not state why involuntary confessions are inadmissible.

Subsequently, *R v. Warickshall*[6] is an important case on the confession exclusionary rule. Warickshall was indicted for receiving stolen goods. After the police made promises of favor, she confessed and property was found in her bed. The court held that the confession should be excluded because the positive inducements rendered the confession involuntary.

The Court of King's Bench said that "a confession forced from the mind by the flattery of hope, or by the torture of fear, comes in so questionable a shape when it is to be considered as the evidence of guilt, that no credit ought to be given to it; and therefore it is rejected."[7]

Next, in *Ibrahim v. The King*,[8] Ibrahim, a private in the Indian Army, was charged with murdering his officer. After the officer in command asked why he had done such a senseless act, he confessed. Lord Sumner confirmed the general principle and noted:

> It has long been established as a positive rule of English criminal law, that no statement by an accused is admissible in evidence against him unless it is shown by the prosecution to have been a voluntary statement, in the sense that it has

---

2 J.H. Langbein, *The Origins of Adversary Criminal Trial* (Oxford University Press, Oxford 2003) 218–33.

3 17 Howell's State Trials 1079.

4 1 Leach 115, 168 Eng. Rep. 160 (K.B. 1775).

5 1 Leach 115, 168 Eng. Rep. 160 (K.B. 1775) (emphasis added).

6 1 Leach 263–4, 168 Eng. Rep.234 (K.B. 1783).

7 1 Leach 263–4, 168 Eng. Rep. 234, 235 (K.B. 1783).

8 [1914] AC 599.

> not been obtained from him either by fear of prejudice or hope of advantage exercised or held out by a person in authority.[9]

In 1963, Lord Parker asserted that confessions obtained "in an oppressive manner" were inadmissible in *Callis v. Gunn.*[10]

Between 1972 to 1993, the admissibility of confession evidence was considered by two commissions (or committees). The first was by the Criminal Law Revision Committee of 1972.

In 1959, the Conservative Home Secretary created the Criminal Law Revision Committee (CLRC) which later submitted its Eleventh Report in 1972. It was the first committee to suggest several recommendations for reform of the confession exclusionary rule. The Criminal Law Revision Committee provided some changes to the confession law.[11] The Criminal Law Revision Committee preferred the crime control model[12] and argued that "all available and relevant evidence should be before the court. We have throughout aimed at reducing the exceptions to admissibility under the present law."[13] It believed that "strict and formal" evidence rules for the protection of accused persons no longer served a useful purpose but become a hindrance to justice.[14] Its basic ground was that the traditional evidence rule unduly favored the guilty.

The second was the Royal Commission on Criminal Procedure of 1981. The Royal Commission on Criminal Procedure (the Philips Commission), under the chairmanship of Sir Cyril Philips, was triggered by the *Confait*[15] case in 1979 and issued its report (the Philips Report) in 1981.[16]

In 1972, Maxwell Confait was found dead in his blazing room in London. Leighton (aged 15), Lattimore (aged 18 and mentally retarded) and Salih (aged 14) were interviewed by police neither in the presence of a solicitor nor the boys' parents. All boys said they were assaulted by the police during their interviews and then confessed to serious crimes they did not commit.[17] Leighton was convicted of murder, Lattimore of manslaughter and all three were convicted of arson. It was later established that their confessions had been false. In 1975, the Court of Appeal ruled that the convictions were unsafe.[18]

---

9 [1914] AC 599.

10 [1964] 1 QB 495.

11 [1914] AC 599, 609.

12 See 1.3.

13 The Criminal Law Revision Committee, "Eleventh Report, Evidence (General)" (Cm 4991, 1972) [20].

14 Ibid., [21].

15 [1975] 62 Crim. App. 53.

16 The Royal Commission on Criminal Procedure, "Report" (Cm 8092, 1981).

17 J.J. Eddleston, *Blind Justice: Miscarriages of Justice in Twentieth-Century Britain?* (ABC-CLIO, Oxford 2000) 358.

18 *R. v. Lattimore*, 62 Crim. App. 53 (1975).

Ironically, the basic ground of the recommendations put forward by the Commission was that the present law improperly favored the guilty. The framework of the Commission's approach can be outlined as follows.

First, the primary purpose of the Code of Practice for interviewing suspects is to obtain reliable confessions. The reliability of confessions obtained in its breach must be open to question.[19]

Secondly, the Commission, referring to the United States, argued that the obvious defect of using an automatic exclusionary rule is that it can only apply to a small portion of cases and this caused doubt about its effectiveness as a deterrent of police conduct.[20] The Commission observed that the reason why the United States Supreme Court developed the exclusionary rule was to protect the citizen's constitutional rights. In addition, there is a bewildering complexity and amount of law enforcement agencies. Few are under any federal government supervision or control.[21]

Thirdly, the members of the Commission had different opinions in relation to the exclusion of confession evidence issues. One wished to maintain the existing law on the exclusion of involuntary statements and hoped judges would exercise a wider discretion to exclude more evidence obscured in breach of other aspects of the rules. Another preferred a wider application of automatic exclusion, so that any evidence in violation of the rules would be inadmissible. The rest considered that Parliament should take the responsibility for deciding what the rules should be. The existing voluntariness rule should be abolished. If there was non-compliance by the police, the consequences should be known to them. Those consequences should depend on the purpose of the rule that has been breached. Confessions should continue to be automatically excluded if obtained as a result of violence, threats of violence, torture or inhuman or degrading treatment and by methods which society would regard as abhorrent.[22]

Generally speaking, the Commission considered that the exclusion of evidence is not a satisfactory way of enforcing compliance with rules.[23] The effective methods to ensure that suspects are treated in a humane and civilized manner would be contemporaneous controls and good supervision.[24] Although the report was widely criticized by commentators,[25] it gave rise to the Police and Criminal Evidence Act 1984.

---

19 The Royal Commission on Criminal Procedure, "Report" (Cm 8092, 1981) [4.133].

20 Ibid. [4.125].

21 Ibid. [4.126].

22 Ibid. [4.131], [4.132].

23 Ibid. [4.132].

24 Ibid. [4.117], [4.118].

25 Marquita Inman, "The Admissibility of Confessions" (1981) *Criminal Law Review* 469, 469–82.

Taken overall, both the Criminal Law Revision Committee and Royal Commission on Criminal Procedure are all in fact consistent with the crime control model.[26] Finally, PACE stipulates that a confession obtained by oppression must be excluded by the judge.[27]

2.1.1.2 Search and seizure exclusionary rule I now turn to consider the search and seizure exclusionary rule which refers to the rule that excludes real evidence secured by illegal search and seizure in England. From the mid-nineteenth century to today, English courts regarded the method of obtaining evidence and its admissibility as two different things. The traditional English approach on illegally obtained physical evidence after 1861 could be summarized by the dictum of Crompton J. in *R v. Leatham*[28] as follows: "it matters not how you get it; if you steal it even, it would be admissible in evidence."[29]

In the important 1955 decision of the Privy Council in *Kuruma, Son of Kaniu v. R*, the accused was subjected to an illegal search in what was the British colony of Kenya. The Judicial Committee upheld the conviction of a Kenyan for unlawful possession of two rounds of ammunition even though the evidence had been obtained by two police officers of a lower rank than those permitted to conduct searches. He was sentenced to death. *Kuruma* established the test of admissibility of non-confessional evidence that once the evidence is deemed relevant to the matters in issue, it is admissible. The court argued that it was not concerned with how the evidence was obtained. Lord Goddard made the following finding: "[T] he test to be applied in considering whether evidence is admissible is whether it is relevant to the matters in issue. If it is, it is admissible and the court is not concerned with how the evidence was obtained."[30]

In 1978 in *Jeffrey v. Black*[31] Lord Widgery CJ admitted that the judge has a discretion to exclude evidence, reasoning as follows:

> [T]he magistrates … have a general discretion to decline to allow any evidence to be called by the prosecution if they think that it would be unfair or oppressive to allow that to be done … It is a discretion which *every* criminal judge has *all the time* in respect of all the evidence which is tendered by the prosecution.[32]

26 See 1.3.
27 PACE Section 76 (2) a.
28 (1861) 8 Cox CC 498.
29 (1861) 8 Cox CC 498, 501.
30 *Kuruma, Son of Kaniu v. R*, [1955] 1 All ER 236 (appeal taken from E. Afi.).
31 [1978] 1 All ER 555.
32 [1978] 1 All ER 555, 559 (emphasis added).

In the leading case of *R v. Sang*[33] decided in 1980, the House of Lords abolished the discretion and claimed that there is no discretion for a trial judge to exclude real evidence which had been obtained irregularly.[34]

Before PACE, England had no legislated rule of evidence concerning illegally obtained physical evidence. In sum, the judicially developed law was that such evidence was admissible if it was relevant, although the courts had very limited discretion to exclude evidence when "the strict rules of admissibility would operate unfairly against the accused."[35] The method by which evidence has been obtained is irrelevant.

2.1.2 United States Law

2.1.2.1 Confession exclusionary rule No confession is admissible unless made freely and voluntarily and not under the influence of promises or threats. In United States criminal trials, coerced and involuntary confessions are inadmissible. The confession exclusionary rule is an important part of the Fourth and Fifth Amendments, and the due process clause of the Fourteenth Amendment to the United States Constitution. The Fifth Amendment states that no person "shall be compelled in any criminal case to be a witness against himself."[36] The Supreme Court had long since adopted a confession exclusionary rule, which stands as a bar against the conviction of any accused in court by means of coerced confessions.[37]

The roots of police torture can be traced to lynching in the early 1890s in the United States.[38] There were at least 4,000 public torture lynchings between 1882 and 1940. David Garland defines public torture lynchings as "lynchings that were highly publicized, took place before a large crowd, were staged with a degree of ritual, and involved elements of torture, mutilation, or unusual cruelty."[39] Public torture lynchings led directly to police whippings of black suspects to obtain a confession.[40]

As early as 1935, in the United States Supreme Court case *Brown v. Mississippi*,[41] the defendants were suspected of murder based solely on their confessions. Over the course of several days, one defendant was brutally whipped

---

33 [1980] AC 402.

34 [1980] AC 402, 436.

35 *Kuruma Son of Kaniu v. R*, [1955] 1 All ER 236, 239.

36 The Fifth Amendment provides that "[n]o person … shall be compelled in any criminal case to be a witness against himself …"

37 *Brown v. Mississippi*, 297 U.S. 278, 287.

38 J.H. Skolnick, "American Interrogation: From Torture to Trickery" in Sanford Levinson (ed.), *Torture: A Collection* (Oxford University Press, Oxford 2004) 105, 106.

39 David Garland, "Penal Excess and Surplus Meaning: Public Torture Lynchings in Twentieth-Century American" (2005) 39 *Law and Society Review* 793, 795. (Garland reviews history of public lynchings in the United States.)

40 J.H. Skolnick, "American Interrogation: From Torture to Trickery," 105, 107–8.

41 297 U.S. 278 (1935).

until he confessed. All defendants were severely whipped. The police declared that they would continue the whipping until the suspect confessed. Defendants then agreed to confess to such statements as the deputy would dictate. The confessions had been obtained in the exact contents as desired by the police. The police also warned defendants that if they changed their story at any time in any respect from the confessions, the perpetrators would administer the same torture again. The Court held the confessions extorted by torture were inadmissible and violated the due process required by the Fourteenth Amendment.[42]

In *White v. State of Texas*,[43] the defendant, an illiterate farmhand in Texas, was arrested without warrants and put in custody without the filing of charges. During the seven days of his arrest, armed police on several successive nights took him handcuffed from the jail up in the woods, whipped him, asked him each time about a confession. He was repeatedly asked whether he was ready to confess; then began to cry and "confessed." Because of the alleged confession, the defendant was convicted of rape and sentenced to death. The Court excluded the confessions in 1940.[44]

2.1.2.2 Search and seizure exclusionary rule The origin of the search and seizure exclusionary rule can be traced in the 1886 civil case of *Boyd v. United States*. In 1884, the government initiated a forfeiture proceeding against two businessmen for importing plate glass in violation of revenue law, demanded and obtained the invoice of the goods. Justice Bradley linked the Fourth and Fifth Amendment and reasoned that the use of illegally obtained evidence did not differ from compelling a man to give evidence against himself.[45]

The 1914 decision of the Supreme Court in *Weeks v. United States*[46] is a landmark case which has had an important and great influence on the subsequent course of search and seizure law. *Weeks* imposed the exclusionary rule upon federal law enforcement. The Fourth Amendment forbids the admission of evidence secured through an illegal search and seizure in a federal criminal trial.

Local police searched defendant Weeks' home and seized personal items and papers without a warrant. Later in the same day, a United States marshal, also without a search warrant, searched the defendant's room and seized additional property. Weeks was arrested, charged and convicted of illegally using the mails and maintaining a lottery.

The Court, standing squarely on the Fourth Amendment grounds, unanimously held that "[i]f letters and private documents can thus be seized and held and used in evidence against a citizen accused of an offense, the protection of the Fourth

42 297 U.S. 278, 287 (1935).
43 310 U.S. 530 (1940).
44 310 U.S. 530, 532 (1940).
45 116 U.S. 618, 630–34 (1886).
46 232 U.S. 383, 398 (1914).

Amendment, declaring his right to be secure against such searches and seizures, is of no value."[47]

In the 1949 case in *Wolf v. Colorado*,[48] the police suspected Dr. Wolf was dispensing abortions, went to his office without a warrant, seized his appointment books and searched through it to learn the names of his patients. The police thus obtained leads to some patients who were questioned, with the result that the abortion business came to light. An information was filed against the doctor. The books also were introduced in evidence against Wolf.

The Court had a chance to abolish the "silver platter" doctrine, which allowed the use of evidence obtained by illegal search conducted by state officers in federal criminal trials as long as federal officers were not involved in the constitution violation, i.e., the local officers turn such evidence over to federal officials on a "silver platter" to assist in the federal prosecution of a suspect.

However, the Court held that evidence secured in violation of the Fourth Amendment, although inadmissible in federal courts, could be used in state courts. The Fourth Amendment was deemed applicable to the states through the Fourteenth Amendment but permitted the states to select their own method for enforcing it. The exclusionary rule was not extended to the state law enforcement.[49]

In 1961, in *Mapp v. Ohio*,[50] the Court overruled *Wolf* and extended the rule to state criminal justice systems. The Court ruled that state courts have to exclude illegally obtained evidence in criminal proceedings in the same way as federal courts. Cleveland police received information that a bomber was hiding in Miss Mapp's home and demanded entrance. Mapp refused to admit them without a search warrant after telephoning her attorney. The police twisted her hand, handcuffed her very forcefully and then ransacked her house without a warrant. Mapp was convicted of possession of obscene materials and sentenced to seven years' imprisonment. The issue in this case is whether the exclusionary rule applies to the states. The Court held that:

> Since the Fourth Amendment's right of privacy has been declared enforceable against the States through the Due Process Clause of the Fourteenth Amendment, it is enforceable against them by the same sanction of exclusion as is used against the Federal Government.[51]

United States v. Leon[52] created the significant good faith exception in 1984. The Court held that the exclusionary rule should be modified to allow the admission of evidence when the police obtained a search warrant from a magistrate and relied

47 232 U.S. 383, 393 (1914).
48 338 U.S. 25 (1949).
49 338 U.S. 25, 27–8 (1949).
50 367 U.S. 643 (1961).
51 367 U.S. 643, 655 (1961).
52 468 U.S. 897 (1984).

on it in good faith—even though it turned out that the search was illegal because the warrant was ultimately found to be lacking probable cause.

Justice White, writing for the majority, explained that "when an officer acting with objective good faith has obtained a search warrant from the judge or magistrate and acted within its scope … there is no police illegality and thus nothing to deter."[53] The Court concluded that the rule cannot be expected to deter objectively reasonable police activity. The purpose of the exclusionary rule is to deter unlawful police conduct and, when the official action was pursued in complete good faith, excluding that evidence does not prevent future police misconduct.[54]

2.2 Rationales

> [T]here are two distinct issues (i) one concerns rules about the probative value of evidence; (ii) the other concerns rules about the exclusion of evidence for reasons other than reasons of evidentiary value. The question in (i) is how to deal with evidence the probative value of which is in doubt … Evidence gained from an involuntary confession … and it is difficult to know in any event how much weight it should be given … These are issues internal to proof. In (ii) the issue is whether certain kinds of evidence … should be excluded, in order to advance other values or policies, such as … the protection of an accused against the police. These are issues external to proof … The exclusion of evidence in order to uphold those values may mean the loss of probative evidence and thus a lower level of accuracy.
>
> D.J. Galligan[55]

Identifying the source and basis of the exclusionary rule is of more than academic significance. The question of the rationales for the exclusionary rule determines whether the rule survives. At the outset, the fundamental question was stated to be: why should courts exclude illegally or unfairly obtained evidence? This section examines the rationales behind the exclusionary rule. The courts have been reluctant to provide insight and guidance into the constitutional underpinnings for the exclusionary rule when justifying their admissibility decisions.

Additionally, no decision by the court has ever fully explored and established consistently the justifications behind the exclusionary rule. The jurisprudence on the principles behind the rule is unconvincing and inconsistent. To date, the

---

53 468 U.S. 897, 921 (1984).

54 For further analysis of *Leon*, see 3.3.1.

55 D.J. Galligan, "More Scepticism about Scepticism" (1988) 8 *Oxford Journal of Legal Studies* 249, 255.

rationales of the rule are still unclear. Some rationales failed to adapt to changing social and technological developments.[56]

Traditionally, in common law the exclusionary rule has only been concerned by reference to the internal rationale. The internal consideration is to ensure the reliability of evidence. However, lacking the trustworthiness of evidence is not the only basis for excluding them.

This section will have two primary considerations: the *internal rationale*, i.e., the reliability rationale which is more relevant to the confession exclusionary rule; the *external rationale*, the dominant consideration, which is relevant to both the confession exclusionary rule, and search and seizure exclusionary rule. The full importance of the rationales of the exclusionary rule cannot come into sight if one sticks to an internal viewpoint. I argue that no specific rationale is perfect, absolutely better than the others; furthermore there is a trend to combine both internal and external rationale.

2.2.1 The Reliability Rationale

An important aim of the criminal justice is to ensure the accuracy of criminal proceedings. "Reliability" refers to the propensity of the criminal justice system to produce a factually correct verdict. At first, the confession exclusionary rule was designed primarily to guard against the introduction of unreliable evidence. Society's abhorrence at the use of confessions extracted under questionable means and circumstances is mainly based on its unreliability. Such unreliable information may even lead to false convictions. The first principle, the consideration of intrinsic policy, is concerned with the promotion of reliability of confessions and the outcome of the decisions that are made.

The confession exclusionary rule is linked to the belief that certain types of evidence, such as confessions obtained through torture, are intrinsically unreliable and therefore unsuitable for the discovery of truth. The use of torture in an interrogation presupposes the "efficacy" of torture to produce "reliable" information. Conversely, it is cleared that the illegally secured confessions are inherently unreliable as under sufficient duress the victim, whether guilty or innocent, will admit to anything or say anything to avoid the pain and save himself from further torture. These statements are not trustworthy. The classic example is confessions gained through torture. Torture is unacceptable. Psychological pressure will be coupled with torture. "Confessions" may stop the physical pain and psychological pressure. In addition, vulnerable defendants, for example, juveniles and the mentally ill or handicapped, may confess falsely. Pressed by

56 How should we apply constitutional protections from the eighteenth century to today's computerized world? For instance, can the police use an infrared thermal imaging device at a suspect's home? Searching and seizing computers are common during criminal investigation nowadays. How does the exclusionary rule govern the steps that an investigator takes when retrieving evidence from a personal computer?

police, even the innocent confess.[57] The goal of this rationale is to avoid unreliable confessions. The confession exclusionary rule is an important means to weed out unreliable statements at trial.

In 1783, the first clear enunciation of the rationale appeared in *Warickshall.* Nares J. established a theory which based on the reliability of the confession in question and articulated the reason for rejecting the confession:

> Confession are received in evidence, or rejected as inadmissible, under a consideration whether they are or are not entitled credit. A free and voluntary confession is deserving of the highest credit, because it is presumed to flow from the strongest sense of guilt, and therefore it is admitted as proof of the crime to which it refers; but confessions forced from the mind by the flattery of hope, or by torture of fear, comes in so questionable a shape when it is to be considered as the evidence of guilt, that no credit ought to be given to it; and therefore it is rejected.[58]

The Criminal Law Revision Committee of 1972, the Royal Commission on Criminal Procedure of 1981 and the Royal Commission on Criminal Justice of 1993 followed this rationale. The Criminal Law Revision Committee noted that one of the reasons for the exclusionary rule is the reliability principle which says that confession obtained involuntarily may not be reliable.[59] The Royal Commission on Criminal Procedure stated that the principle behind the rule is the reliability rationale because evidence of certain kinds is or may be so unreliable as to preclude its being heard by the jury.[60] The Royal Commission on Criminal Justice noted that a confession may be excluded because of unreliability where there has been no impropriety on the police.[61]

This is important because unreliable confessions may lead to the miscarriages of justice. Torture and interrogation process have a long association that continues to the present day. Judicial torture (i.e., torture by officials authorized by the law) can be traced back in England in the sixteenth and early seventeenth centuries. The investigative process is the first and extremely important stage in the criminal process. These incriminating confessions cast a long shadow over the suspects' future in the criminal justice system and may keep them behind bars for decades.

Many police officers are under tremendous pressure to find "facts" and are only concerned with securing a statement from the defendant on which they could convict him. Zeal in finding the truth and tracking down crime is not in itself

---

57 See Chapter 5.

58 1 Leach 263, 168 Eng. Rep. 234 (Q.B. 1783).

59 The Criminal Law Revision Committee, "Eleventh Report, Evidence (General)" (Cm 4991, 1972) [55].

60 The Royal Commission on Criminal Procedure, "Report" (Cm 8092, 1981) [4.123].

61 The Royal Commission on Criminal Justice, "Report" (Cm 2263, 1993) [36].

an assurance of fairness of trial. Accordingly, many innocent suspects falsely confess to crimes they did not commit and be wrongfully convicted.[62] It produced tragedies—false confessions carrying life imprisonment or death. The common feature of these miscarriages of justice was that the police used illegal or unfair physical and psychological pressure to secure confessions. Here are some small samples from twentieth-century Britain.

From 1970 to 1990, a series of notorious wrongful convictions occurred such as that of Judith Ward, Cardiff Three, Bridgewater Four, Guildford Four, Birmingham Six and Maguire Seven. Some prompted the government to appoint official commissions.

In October 1974, bombings had taken place at public houses in Guildford, England. The police abused and threatened four suspects, known as the Guildford Four, and obtained confessions for acts of terror. The defendants, alleged Irish Republican Army (IRA) terrorists, were convicted of murders and conspiracy to murder and all four were sentenced to life sentences based completely on false confessions. One of the defendants died in prison in 1980. After 15 years of wrongful imprisonment, in 1989, the Court of Appeal quashed their convictions on the basis of new evidence showing that the defendants' confessions had been unreliable and their written statements included fabrications by the police.[63]

In November 1974, explosions occurred at two public houses in Birmingham, England. The six appellants, known as the Birmingham Six, alleged IRA terrorists, were convicted on 21 counts of murder because the police fabricated confessions and relied on faulty forensic tests. After they had served almost two decades in prison, in 1991, the Court of Appeal finally quashed their unsafe and unsatisfactory convictions on the basis of new evidence showing that the prosecution evidence at the trial was very unreliable.[64]

In 1978, four defendants, known as the Bridgewater Four, were convicted of the murder of Carl Bridgewater. All four were subjected to torture by the police, confessions were fabricated and interview evidence was forged against them. One defendant died in prison. The Court of Appeal overturned their convictions in 1997. The others served 17 years in prison for crimes they had not committed.[65]

In 1990, three defendants, known as the Cardiff Three, were convicted of the murder of a prostitute. One defendant, Miller, on the borderline of mental handicap with an IQ of 75 and a mental age of 11, was interviewed for some 13 hours over five days. Having denied involvement over 300 times, Miller was finally persuaded to make "confessions." The Court of Appeal excluded their "confessions" as oppressive and quashed their convictions in 1992. The Lord Chief Justice Taylor was appalled by the bullying and hectoring to which Miller

62 See Chapter 5.

63 *R v. Richardson; R v. Conlon; R v. Armstrong; R v. Hill*, *The Times*, Oct. 20, 1989.

64 *R v. McIlkenny and Others*, [1992] 2 All ER 417.

65 J.J. Eddleston, *Blind Justice: Miscarriages of Justice in Twentieth-Century Britain* (ABC-CLIO, Oxford, 2000) 399–408.

was subjected: "[t]he officers ... were not questioning him so much as shouting at him what they wanted him to say. Short of physical violence, it is hard to conceive of a more hostile and intimidating approach by officers to a suspect."[66] All in all, until today, the House of Lords took the view that one of the reasons that the common law against involuntary confessions is their inherent unreliability.[67]

Although originally exclusion of involuntary confessions depended primarily on the reliability of the evidence and the reliability rationale is one of the justifications for the confession exclusionary rule, it is tremendously important to note that the question of admissibility is distinct from the weight attached to a confession. These are two quite distinct issues. The exclusionary rule is not solely based on concerns about the value of the impugned evidence. That is the reason why the reliability rationale is no longer the principal and only test of admissibility in this context after the 1940s in the United States and 1980s in the United Kingdom. I argue that the reliability rationale *only* played a subordinate role.

Inherent untrustworthiness is not the question in the United States anymore. In the 1944 case of *Ashcraft v. State of Tennessee*,[68] for example, the police kept the defendant under continuous cross examination for 36 hours without rest in an effort to extract a "voluntary" confession. The Court held that even completely reliable evidence will be excluded if the method in which it was obtained is considered to be in violation of due process guarantees."[69] Justice Frankfurter, for the Court in *Rochin v. California*,[70] also declared that "[u]se of involuntary verbal confessions in State criminal trials is constitutionally obnoxious not *only because of their unreliability*. They are inadmissible under the Due Process Clause even though statements contained in them may be independently established as true."[71]

A similar analysis was employed in *Spano v. New York*.[72] The Court reversed the defendant's conviction because the trial court's admission of his involuntary confession was inconsistent with the Fourteenth Amendment in 1959. The Court concluded that the defendant's will was overcome by official pressure, fatigue, and sympathy falsely aroused in a post-indictment setting. Chief Justice Warren pointed out that "[t]he abhorrence of society to the use of involuntary confessions does not turn alone on their inherent untrustworthiness. It also turns on the deep-rooted feeling that the police must obey the law while enforcing the law."[73]

---

66 *R v. Anthony Paris; R v. Yusuf Abdullahi; R v. Stephen Wayne Miller* (1993) 97 Cr. App. R. 99.

67 *A and others v. Secretary of State for the Home Department (No 2)*, [2005] UKHL 71, [2006] 2 AC 221.

68 322 U.S. 143 (1944).

69 322 U.S. 143, 161 (1944).

70 342 U.S. 165 (1952).

71 342 U.S. 165, 173 (1952).

72 360 U.S. 315 (1959).

73 360 U.S. 315, 320 (1959).

Two years later, once again, Justice Frankfurter delivered the opinion of the Court in *Rogers v. Richmond*[74] and explained the reason why even reliable involuntary confessions should be excluded. The Court expressly rejected the notion that reliability per se was at the heart of the confession exclusionary rule and held "[t]his is so not because such confessions are unlikely to be true but because the methods used to extract them offend an underlying principle in the enforcement of our criminal law."[75] This means that whether or not the defendant in fact spoke the truth is not the key point; there is no question of weight and truth in this case. The aim of the Court is of due process and fairness, regardless whether the evidence is trustworthy or not.

In the United Kingdom,[76] Lord Hailsham stated, in *Wong Kam-Ming v. The Queen*,[77] that "[t]his is not only because of the potential unreliability of such statements, but also, and perhaps mainly, because in a civilised society it is vital that persons in custody or charged with offences should not be subjected to ill treatment or improper pressure in order to extract confessions."[78]

The Privy Council reaffirmed its position that the potential unreliability of illegally obtained statements is not the only concern and also held in *Lam Chi-ming v. R*[79] that:

> [S]ome means of excluding confessions … obtained by improper methods … is not only because of the potential unreliability of such statements, but also … because in a civilised society it is vital that persons in custody or charged with offences should not be subjected to ill treatment or improper pressure in order to extract confessions.[80]

All these decisions mentioned above herald the court's concern for the methods by which evidence obtained—a concern that is independent of the desire to prevent the admission of untrustworthy confessions.

2.2.2 The Self-Incrimination Rationale

The Latin maxim "*nemo debet prodere se ipsum*" means no one is obliged to accuse himself. The establishment of the privilege against self-incrimination can be traced to the early seventeenth European canon law.[81] From the nineteenth

74 365 U.S. 534 (1961).
75 365 U.S. 534, 541 (1961).
76 This case is from Hong Kong.
77 [1980] AC 247.
78 [1980] AC 247, 261.
79 [1991] 2 AC 212.
80 [1991] 2 AC 212, 220.
81 R.H. Helmholz, "Origins of the Privilege against Self-incrimination: The Role of the European Ius Commune" (1990) 65 *New York University Law Review* 962, 963–4.

century, the privilege started to insulate suspects from being compelled to speak in criminal trials. The privilege was historically closely linked with the abolition of judicial torture[82] and developed from the struggle to "eliminate torture as a government practice."[83] The inclusion of the privilege was expected to prevent the state from imposing judicial torture. In *Sang* both Lord Diplock and Lord Scarman gave as the justification for refusing to admit improperly obtained confessions the principle that no man is to be compelled to incriminate himself. Lord Diplock commented:

> The underlying rationale of this branch of the criminal law, though it may originally have been based on ensuring the reliability of confessions is … now to be found in the maxim, *nemo debet prodere se ipsum*, no one can be required to be his own betrayer, or in its popular English misinterpretation "the right to silence."[84]

In *Lam Chi-ming*,[85] Lord Griffiths again endorsed the rationale and stated that:

> English cases established that the rejection of an improperly obtained confession is not dependent only upon possible unreliability but also upon the principle that a man cannot be compelled to incriminate himself and upon the importance that attaches in a civilised society to proper behaviour by the police towards those in their custody.[86]

The Fifth Amendment self-incrimination clause of the United States Constitution also prohibits the police from compelling any person in a criminal case to incriminate himself. The privilege against self-incrimination is a fundamental right of criminal suspects and protects them from being forced to "testify" against themselves.

2.2.3 The Deterrence Rationale

The principle that the police should obey the law while enforcing it is a deep-rooted feeling. The third rationale, which has been coined "the disciplinary theory" or "the deterrent theory," attempts to justify the exclusion of illegally obtained evidence on the basis that the courts should remove the inducements by

---

82 Leonard Levy, *Origins of the Fifth Amendment: The Right against Self-incrimination* (Oxford University Press, New York 1968) 414–31.

83 Erwin Griswold, *The Fifth Amendment Today: Three Speeches* (Harvard University Press, Massachusetts 1955) 7.

84 [1980] AC 402, 410.

85 [1991] 2 AC 212.

86 [1991] 2 AC 212, 220.

the exclusion in order to prevent abusive interrogation practices, and deter due process violation and police misconduct.

Only by the exclusionary rule can we impress upon overzealous or ruthless officers that violation of the law will lose the very thing they retained from illegal searches and do them no good at the end. The exclusionary rule deters other law enforcement officers who may contemplate similar police misconduct. If the police know that evidence secured by their unlawful act would be inadmissible in the courts, police officers might minimize or put an end to this kind of malpractice. The rationale focuses on the *future*, i.e., present exclusion by court will defer future wrongdoing by police. As long as courts allow the evidence, police will investigate lawlessly. The goal of this rationale is to deter police misconduct.

Almost four decades ago, the Criminal Law Revision Committee of 1972 drew attention to the deterrence rationale. According to the Committee, one of the reasons for excluding involuntary confession is the disciplinary principle which means that the police must be discouraged from using illegal means to secure a confession. This discouragement takes place by depriving the police of the advantage of the confession for the purpose of obtaining a conviction. If the principle were applied, one could have expected the evidence to be excluded to prevent the prosecution from taking advantage of the impropriety. A majority of the Committee accepted the disciplinary principle. The Committee stated:

> Two reasons have been given for this rule. The first is that a confession not made voluntarily may not be reliable ... The second reason is that the police must be discouraged from using improper methods to obtain a confession. This discouragement takes place by depriving them of the advantage of the confession for the purpose of obtaining a conviction.[87] ... As to the discouragement of improper methods of interrogation, the majority think that to remove all restrictions on admissibility of confessions on account of the use of improper methods to obtain them could not but operate, human nature being what it is, to encourage the police to resort on occasions to at least small improprieties.[88]

The disciplinary principle proposed by the Criminal Law Revision Committee would have been *very* unique in the United Kingdom (except Scotland). The House of Lords, as well as the Court of Appeal, have rejected this kind of principle to be a goal of the country's limited exclusionary rule.

Here is a collection of *obiter dicta* in the House of Lords and the Court of Appeal.

In *Sang*,[89] Lord Diplock observed that "[i]t is no part of a judge's function to exercise disciplinary powers over the police or prosecution as respects the way

87 The Criminal Law Revision Committee, "Eleventh Report, Evidence (General)" (Cm 4991, 1972) [55].

88 Ibid. [64].

89 [1980] AC 402.

in which evidence to be used at the trial is obtained by them."[90] Lord Scarman pointed out that "[t]he role of the judge is confined to the forensic process. He controls neither the police nor the prosecuting authority.[91] Likewise, in *Fox v. Chief Constable of Gwent*,[92] Lord Fraser endorsed that "[t]he duty of the court is to decide whether the appellant has committed the offence with which he is charged, and not to discipline the police for exceeding their powers."[93]

In the later case of *R v. Mason*,[94] Mason was arrested and questioned regarding an offence of arson. The police hoodwinked both him and his solicitor that they had found a fragment of a bottle which had contained inflammable liquid and that his fingerprint was on the fragment. Although the Court of Appeal noted that a deceit practiced by the police was a most reprehensible thing, quashed the conviction and hoped never again to hear of deceit such as this being practiced, Lord Justice Watkins also mentioned that the court is "not the place to discipline the police. That has been make clear here on a number of previous occasions."[95]

In *R v. Oliphant*, Lord Justice Woolf approved this concept and said that "[i]t is not my job or the function of the court to educate and discipline police officers."[96] In *R v. Hughes*, Lord Taylor emphasized that "[i]t has been said more than once in this court that the object of a judge in considering the application of section 78 is not to discipline or punish police officers or customs officers for breaches of the code."[97]

As Dawson observed that "[t]he English judiciary are to exercise no control over the police and the ability of the alternative remedies to deter in fact is not ever discussed."[98] There is no denying that "policing" the police is a tremendously difficult task. However, something had to be done; if not by the judge, then by whom? It is impossible for the legislature to control police conduct directly. In the United Kingdom, the Royal Commission on Criminal Procedure of 1981 envisaged that the Crown Prosecution Service (CPS) would supervise the work of the police but this does not happen in practice.[99] In the United States, it is impractical to expect the Department of Justice to supervise local police activity and prosecute police officers.[100] The same reason in both countries is simply the lack of resources.

---

90 [1980] AC 402, 436.

91 [1980] AC 402, 454–5.

92 [1985] 3 All ER 392.

93 [1985] 3 All ER 392, 396–7.

94 [1988] 1 WLR 139 (Eng. C.A. 1987).

95 [1988] 1 WLR 139, 144 (Eng. C.A. 1987).

96 [1992] Crim LR 40.

97 [1994] 1 WLR 876.

98 J.B. Dawson, "The Exclusion of Unlawfully Obtained Evidence: A Comparative Study" (1982) 31 *International and Comparative Law Quarterly* 513, 536.

99 Michael Zander, *Cases and Materials on the English Legal System* (10th edn, Cambridge University Press, Cambridge 2007) 264.

100 *Irvine v. California*, 347 U.S. 128, 141 (1954) (Douglas J., dissenting).

Nothing can destroy a government more quickly than its disregard of the constitution of its own existence for the purpose of getting ignoble convictions of its people. I argue that it is the duty and obligation of the judicial branch to uphold the constitutional guarantees. The courts exist to see that these principles are faithfully enforced. Whether illegally obtained evidence is admissible in court will definitely have a huge impact on the manner in which investigations are conducted by the police. The heavy burden falls right upon the shoulders of judges and from which judges should not shrink.

In the United States, the deterrence principle, adopted by the Supreme Court in 1914, has emerged and stood as the prime, if not the sole, rationale for exclusion since 1961. Over the next several decades until now, the Court has clearly recognized that the exclusionary rule's prime purpose is to deter future lawless enforcement of the law by the police. The Court has gradually assigned increasing significance to deterrence. The express purpose of the rule is deterrence. The focus on the exclusionary rule's deterrent effects first surfaced in *Wolf v. Colorado*,[101] in which the court stated that "in practice the exclusion of evidence may be an effective way of deterring unreasonable searches."[102]

Eleven years later, as the Court explained in a series of cases, for example, in *Elkins v. United States*:[103] "The [exclusionary] rule is calculated to prevent, not to repair. Its purpose is to deter—to compel respect for the constitutional guaranty in the only effectively available way—by removing the incentive to disregard it."[104] The deterrence rationale was also explained in *Linkletter v. Walker*,[105] Justice Clark stated that:

> [The exclusionary rule], it was found, was the only effective deterrent to lawless police action. Indeed, all of the cases since Wolf requiring the exclusion of illegal evidence have been based on the necessity for an effective deterrent to illegal police action.[106]

Shortly thereafter, in *Terry v. Ohio*,[107] Chief Justice Warren Burger also stated that "its major thrust is a deterrent one … and experience has taught that it is the *only* effective deterrent to police misconduct in the criminal context."[108] There followed *Alderman v. United States*,[109] in which Justice White asserted:

---

101 338 U.S. 25 (1949).
102 338 U.S. 25, 31 (1949).
103 364 U.S. 206 (1960).
104 364 U.S. 206, 217 (1960).
105 381 U.S. 618 (1965).
106 381 U.S. 618, 636–7 (1965).
107 392 U.S. 1 (1967).
108 392 U.S. 1, 12 (1967) (emphasis added).
109 394 U.S. 165 (1969).

> The deterrent values of preventing the incrimination of those whose rights the police have violated have been considered sufficient to justify the suppression of probative evidence even though the case against the defendant is weakened or destroyed.[110]

The prime purpose of the exclusionary rule, therefore, is to deter future unlawful police conduct.[111] Once again in *United States v. Calandra,*[112] Chief Justice Warren Burger wrote:

> [T]he exclusionary rule has rested on the deterrent rationale—the hope that law enforcement officials would be deterred from unlawful searches and seizures if the illegally seized, albeit trustworthy, evidence was suppressed often enough and the courts persistently enough deprived them of any benefits they might have gained from their illegal conduct … [T]he rule's prime purpose is to deter future police conduct …[113]

The *Leon*[114] Court relied on the deterrence rationale explained: "The exclusionary rule … operates as a 'judicially created remedy' designed to safeguard Fourth Amendment rights generally through its deterrent effect."[115] The exclusionary rule "is designed to deter police misconduct rather than punish the errors of judges and legislators."[116] An echo of this principle was played out in the *Herring*[117] decision. The Court declared that:

> [T]he exclusionary rule … applies only where it results in appreciable deterrence … we have focused on the efficacy of the [exclusionary] rule in deterring Fourth Amendment violations in the future … To trigger the exclusionary rule, police conduct must be sufficiently deliberate that exclusion can meaningfully deter it, and sufficiently culpable that such deterrence is worth the price paid by the justice system.[118]

The exclusionary rule was historically intended to deter police misconduct.[119] It would be unrealistic to believe that the exclusionary rule has had no deterrent effect on police conduct. The American exclusionary rule is perceived as necessary

---

110 394 U.S. 165, 174 (1969).
111 414 U.S. 338, 347 (1974) (Burger, C.J., dissenting).
112 414 U.S. 338 (1974).
113 414 U.S. 338, 347 (1974) (Burger, C.J., dissenting).
114 *United States v. Leon*, 468 US 897 (1984).
115 468 U.S. 897, 906 (1984).
116 Ibid.
117 *Herring v. United States*, 129 S. Ct. 695, 700, 702 (2009).
118 129 S. Ct. 695, 700, 702 (2009).
119 *Arizona v. Evans*, 514 U.S. 1, 12 (1995).

to deter police from excesses. The search and seizure exclusionary rule is "a judicially created means of deterring illegal searches and seizures,"[120] designed to protect Fourth Amendment rights.

2.2.4 The Protective Rationale

It is the function of the court to uphold the propriety of the criminal process in order to protect the suspect dealt with by that process. In *Director of Public Prosecutions v. Ping Ling*,[121] the protective rationale compensates the defendant for detriment he suffered as a result of police conduct by excluding the use of what was obtained as a result of the conduct. Lord Hailsham stated that:

> [W]hen the savage code of the eighteenth century was in full force ... There was no legal aid. There was no system of appeal. To crown it all the accused was unable to give evidence on his own behalf and was therefore largely at the mercy of any evidence, either perjured or oppressively obtained, that might be brought against him. The judiciary were therefore compelled to devise artificial rules designed to *protect* him against dangers now avoided by other and more rational means.[122]

The protective rationale was also adopted by the Criminal Law Revision Committee. The Committee admitted that the strict rules of evidence may have been necessary to give the accused some protection against injustice.[123]

More specifically, the impetus for this rationale explicitly came in the form of an article by Andrew Ashworth in 1977.[124] The principle argues that certain standards are set for the conduct of criminal investigation. Citizens expect to be treated in accordance with these standards and not to be treated in certain ways. Courts have the responsibility for protecting the citizens' rights from disadvantages, which means illegally secured evidence should not be used against them, resulting from infringement of their rights. It argues that the violation of citizens' rights supplies "a prima facie justification for the exclusion of evidence obtained as a result of that infringement."[125]

The Royal Commission on Criminal Procedure of 1981 followed this rationale and abandoned the disciplinary principle adopted in 1972 by the Criminal Law Revision Committee. The Committee argues that the courts have the responsibility

---

120 *Pennsylvania Board of Probation and Parole v. Scott*, 524 U.S. 357, 363 (1998).

121 *Director of Public Prosecutions v. Ping Ling*, [1976] AC 574.

122 [1976] AC 574, 600 (emphasis added).

123 The Criminal Law Revision Committee, "Eleventh Report, Evidence (General)" (Cm 4991, 1972) [21].

124 Andrew Ashworth, "Excluding Evidence as Protecting Rights" [1977] *Criminal Law Review* 723, 725.

125 Ibid.

for protecting the citizen's rights. The best way to do so in these circumstances is to remove from the investigator his source of advantage which is to exclude the evidence. If the principle is applied, exclusion of good evidence irregularly obtained is the price to be paid for securing confidence in the rules of criminal procedure and ensuring that the public sees the system as fair.[126]

In 1977, Ashworth argued that both the reliability and disciplinary principle are not based on sound premises. However, the protective rationale provides a stronger justification for the exclusionary rule.[127] It seems that protective rationale is better than the reliability and disciplinary principles according to Ashworth. Almost three decades later, however, he changed his mind and said "[i]t is probably a mistake to think that one is necessarily better, more logical, than the others."[128]

It is important to remember that the protective rationale is rather different from the disciplinary rationale because (a) it is backward-looking and (b) focuses on the person wronged while the disciplinary rationale is (a) forward-looking and (b) focuses on the wrongdoer. The protective rationale is a remedy for the victim of someone wronged by the police or other state agencies and is not principally concerned with controlling the latter.

2.3 Conclusion

The object of the exclusionary rule is to protect the individual against arbitrary public authorities' interference. History shows that when governments trade defendants' rights with "truth-finding," most often they get neither. It has been demonstrated in this chapter that the exclusionary rule can be justified by internal and external rationales. The reliability rationale is neither the central nor the exclusive concern of the rule. Reliability has not been treated as the sole test of admissibility in this context. Although one important purpose of the rule is to prevent future police misconduct, deterrence alone is not the sole justification for the exclusionary rule's existence. The role of the exclusionary rule is much greater than mere deterrence. In addition to deterrence, the exclusionary rule may limit governmental power, protect individual privacy, "enables the judiciary to avoid the taint of partnership in official lawlessness,"[129] and minimize[s] the risk of seriously undermining popular trust in government."[130] The court should not limit the exclusionary rule only to deterrent purposes.

---

126 The Royal Commission on Criminal Procedure, "Report" (Cm 8092, 1981) [4.130].

127 Andrew Ashworth, "Excluding Evidence as Protecting Rights" 723, 723.

128 Andrew Ashworth and Mike Redmayne, *The Criminal Process* (3rd edn, Oxford University Press, Oxford 2005) 328. In addition, Ashworth's whole emphasis now is on human rights.

129 *United States v. Calandra*, 414 U.S. 338, 357 (1974) (Brennan, J., dissenting).

130 Ibid.

The failure of courts to scrutinize the precise rationales underlying the exclusionary rule is the significant factor for the unsatisfactory state of the substantive law on the topic. It is therefore of very great importance that the courts should explicitly explain the principles behind the rule. To deter violation of the right to be free from illegal searches and seizures is only one goal of the exclusionary rule. The rule should have a broader purpose, for example, promoting judicial integrity. Every court has an inherent power and duty to sustain constitutional principles against lawless government intrusions and a recurrence of highhanded investigation measures. In order to maintain the vitality of the constitutional process, both the Supreme Court of the United Kingdom and United States Supreme Court must shoulder their responsibilities. By recourse to the exclusionary rule, courts ensure that executive agents do not misuse their powers. The exclusionary rule is a construct based on common law and constitutions. The primary rationale of the rule is to protect the constitutional right of the suspects. The rejection of torture and illegal search is characterized as a constitutional principle and *not* merely a criminal procedure or evidence rule. We will explore much of the detail of this theme in the succeeding chapters.

Chapter 3
The Exclusionary Rule Debates

The acrimonious debate between supporters and critics of the exclusionary rule indicates that the rule is still the vexing question even today. The exclusionary rule remains one of the most controversial rules in evidence law of this era. In the succeeding sections of this chapter, I attempt to address the debates on the exclusionary rule. The chapter begins with the controversy over whether the exclusionary rule causes criminals to go free. I then turn to argue that although the exclusionary rule is not explicitly mentioned in the constitution, the need to enforce the constitution's limits on the executive requires the rule. I next examine the question of whether the exclusionary rule should not apply to suspects who committed some serious offenses, for example, murder, career armed robbery, rape and terrorism? The second section analyzes the "alternatives" to the exclusionary rule, and explains how they do not function in practice. Ample intrinsic and extrinsic evidence supports the conclusion that the exclusionary rule is the most effective means to enforce the prohibition against illegal police conduct. The exclusionary rule works better than any other alternative that has been tried. The third section offers critical analysis of the cost-benefit balancing of the exclusionary rule. Finally, the fourth section addresses the myths of the exclusionary rule.

3.1 Arguments against and for the Exclusionary Rule

The intense debate of the exclusionary rule has lasted for almost one century. Jeremy Bentham (1748–1832) and John Henry Wigmore (1863–1943) were two prominent early critics. Both were committed to the view that the pursuit of truth is the overriding objective in a trial.[1] In 1922, Dean Wigmore, the authority on the law of evidence for the first half of the twentieth century, best known for his *Treatise on the Law of Evidence*, criticized bluntly:

> [The exclusionary rule] puts [courts] in the position of assisting to undermine the foundations of the very institutions they are set there to protect. It regards the over-zealous officer of the law as a greater danger to the community than the unpunished murderer or embezzler or panderer.[2]

---

1 William Twining, *Theories of Evidence: Bentham and Wigmore* (Weidenfeld & Nicolson, London 1985) 117.

2 J.H. Wigmore, "Using Evidence Obtained by Illegal Search and Seizure" (1922) 8 *The American Bar Association Journal* 479, 482.

The search and seizure exclusionary rule, according to Wigmore, may lead to an "unnatural type of justice."[3]

Although evidence law is not the subject for which Bentham is best known, he wrote on the use of torture and the law of evidence in two manuscripts.[4] He defined torture as instances "where a person is made to suffer any violent pain of body in order to compel him to do something or to desist from doing something which done or desisted from the penal application is made to cease."[5] Under two circumstances, according to Bentham, torture may be allowed: (1) if a person is required to do something that the public has an interest in his doing, and which is without doubt in his power to do; and (2) where that which the person is required to do is not a certainty within his power:

> but which the public has so great an interest in his doing that the danger of what may ensure from his not doing it is a greater danger than even that of an innocent person's suffering the greatest degree of pain that can be suffered by torture, of the kind and in the quantity permitted to be employed.[6]

He wrote that "[e]vidence is the basis of justice: exclude evidence, you exclude justice"[7] in his writings some two centuries ago.[8] He believed that accuracy (his term was "rectitude") is the primary objective of criminal procedure. It was critical of technical systems of proof and recognized that all evidence should be included unless it is "irrelevant or superfluous or its production would involve preponderant vexation, expense or delay."[9] Therefore, excluding relevant evidence is unnecessary as a safeguard and is likely to result in the loss of useful information. He believed that one of the major obstacles to the discovery of truth in the courtroom was the exclusionary rule.[10]

It is clear that the assertion of Bentham was much too simple and imprecise since the pursuit of truth is by no means the *sole* task of adjudication. The achievement of accurate outcomes should not be the primary aim of criminal procedure and the laws of evidence. It seems axiomatic that there are other values in play. The criminal justice system should not value truth above all other considerations,

---

3 Ibid., 484.

4 "Of Torture" and "Of Compulsion and herein of Torture". See W.L. Twining and P.E. Twining, "Bentham on Torture" (1973) 24 *The Northern Ireland Legal Quarterly* 305, 308, 320.

5 W.L. Twining and P.E. Twining, "Bentham on Torture" 305, 309.

6 Ibid., 312–13.

7 Jeremy Bentham, *Rationale of Judicial Evidence: Specially Applied to English Practice* (Hunt & Clarke, London 1827) 1.

8 Jeremy Bentham, *Rationale of Judicial Evidence*.

9 Ibid., 42.

10 James Oldham, "Truth-telling in the Eighteenth-century English Courtroom" (1994) 12 *Law and History Review* 95, 97.

otherwise the system will eventually collapse. In addition, the exclusionary rule will not hinder the search for truth. This is a completely irrelevant criticism.

There are at least two important goals of the criminal process: the first is to bring suspected offenders to trial so as to produce accurate determinations through establishing the truth; the second is to ensure that fundamental rights are protected in those processes.[11] Langbein, an eminent leading Anglo-American legal historian at Yale University, reminded us that "too much truth meant too much death."[12] That is the reason why there are some obvious restrictions on the methods by which the truth is to be pursued.

There are at least five common objections to the exclusionary rule. Some of the arguments have superficial appeal and attractions, but close scrutiny and analysis will reveal weaknesses and something unsatisfactory. The disadvantages of the rule are worth the price which must be paid. Some of the criticisms are oblivious to law enforcement practices in the real world. Some suggested alternatives from the ivory tower are unrealistic and impractical. If one wants to advocate reforms to specific police practice one would have to understand how they act in reality, the police culture in their community and then consider how that can be done.

3.1.1 The Exclusionary Rule Causes Criminals to Go Free?

The primary concern of the anti-exclusionary rule camp is that the exclusionary rule exacts a huge toll in lost convictions. Justice Cardozo of the New York Court of Appeals criticized that "[t]he criminal is to go free because the constable has blundered."[13] Chief Justice Burger argued that "[s]ome clear demonstration of the benefits and effectiveness of the exclusionary rule is required to justify it in view of the high price it exacts from society—the release of countless guilty criminals."[14] In 2009, the United States Supreme Court argued that "the principal cost of applying any exclusionary rule is, of course, letting guilty and possibly dangerous criminals go free."[15]

This critique is mistaken and has two fundamental flaws. Furthermore, by accepting their illegally obtained evidence, we may condone a steady course of illegal police practice that deliberately and flagrantly violated the constitution so that the guilty would not go free.

First, empirical evidence demonstrates that few convictions are lost.

---

11 Andrew Ashworth and Mike Redmayne, *The Criminal Process* (3rd edn, Oxford University Press, Oxford 2005) 55.

12 J.H. Langbein, *The Origins of Adversary Criminal Trial* (Oxford University Press, Oxford 2003) 6.

13 *People v. Defore*, 150 N.E. 585 (NY App. Ct. 1926).

14 *Bivens v. Six Unknown Federal Narcotics Agents*, 403 U.S. 388, 416 (1971) (Burger, C.J., dissenting).

15 *Montejo v. Louisiana*, 129 S. Ct. 2079, 2090 (2009).

From the 1980s, almost all empirical research in the United States confirms that the exclusionary rule has had a very limited impact in freeing the guilty. In other words, few suspects are acquitted in court because of the exclusionary rule. The exclusionary rule rarely changes the outcome of a criminal trial. Here are some examples. A five-year study of California data by Thomas Davis in 1983 found that illegal search problems were given as the reason for the rejection of only 13 of more than 14,000 forcible rape arrests (0.09 percent), and eight of approximately 12,000 homicide arrests (0.06 percent) where evidence was excluded because of Fourth Amendment problems.[16] The study indicated that the cumulative loss in felony cases due to prosecutor screening, police releases and court dismissals because evidence had been illegally seized is between 0.6 percent and 0.8 percent to 2.35 percent.[17] In addition, defendants do not receive lesser sentences as a result of plea bargaining because of the exclusionary rule.[18] Further, according to Charles Silberman, except for "victimless crimes" few convictions are lost due to the exclusionary rule.[19]

Second, the exclusionary rule should not be blamed for losing convictions.

The criminal is to go free, but it is the constitution or law that sets him free, not the exclusionary rule per se. If the police possess an unrestrained power to search without suspicion anywhere they desire to look, they ensure that many more criminals will be caught. Instead, if the police apply the constitution at all, then they ensure that they will discover fewer crimes and some criminals could not be convicted, including murderers and rapists. This is undesirable; however, what matters here is that the Fourth Amendment was set down by the legislature. Framers of the United States Constitution presumably thought it an appropriate price to pay for maintaining fundamental rights, which is the very thing the Fourth Amendment was designed to prevent. It is the necessary price we have to pay for compliance with the constitution.

3.1.2 Without Textual Basis

One argument that might be advanced by the anti-exclusionary rule camp is that the exclusionary rule is not legitimate because it is nowhere explicitly authorized in the United States Constitution and ECHR. My response is that this critique is far from accurate.

First, true, the Constitution and Convention do not contain a proviso stating the confession exclusionary rule, or search and seizure exclusionary rule. There was

16 Thomas Davies, "A Hard Look at What We Know (and Still Need to Learn) about the 'Costs' of the Exclusionary Rule: The NIJ Study and Other Studies of 'Lost' Arrests" (1983) 8 *American Bar Foundation Research Journal* 611, 640, 645.

17 Ibid., 680.

18 Ibid., 668.

19 Charles Silberman, *Criminal Violence, Criminal Justice* (Random House, New York 1978) 263–5.

no provision in the Constitution and Convention precluding the use of evidence obtained in violation of its commands. The exclusionary rule is not mandated by the Constitution and Convention. They do not explicitly state that confessions obtained by torture, violent, coercive, threat, oppressive, inhuman or degrading conduct shall not be admissible (the confession exclusionary rule). No evidence obtained in violation of one's right to be free from illegal searches and seizures shall be admissible (the search and seizure exclusionary rule). But neither does the Constitution and ECHR add that evidence obtained by torture or by illegal searches is admissible.

Second, decisions of the United States Supreme Court and ECtHR constitute an important part of the living constitution and ECHR. Both the Constitution and Convention, for instance, the Bill of Rights, do not provide solutions to the violation of constitutional principles. They list certain rights guaranteed to the people. Most guarantees themselves offer little guidance as to how these rights should be preserved and do not provide for explicit remedies. For example, the Fourth Amendment prohibits illegal searches and seizures, and provides that the right to be free from unreasonable searches and seizures "shall not be violated," but the text is silent with respect to the consequences of a violation of this constitutional command. Thus, except in the rarest of circumstances, the framers meant the Constitution to mean more than they say. The judges should take their responsibilities to protect our fundamental rights by filling the empty crevices of the constitution. Perhaps Justice Brennan said it best that "many of the Constitution's most vital imperatives are stated in general terms and the task or giving meaning to these precepts is therefore left to subsequent judicial decision-making in the context of concrete cases."[20]

Article 3 of the ECHR, the first example, provides that "[n]o one shall be subjected to torture or to inhuman or degrading treatment or punishment." It says nothing about what should happen or how this guarantee would be enforced. The admissibility of evidence obtained by torture is not mentioned in ECHR. I argue that the Convention's prohibition on torture could be interpreted as implicitly prohibiting the use of evidence secured under torture. The House of Lords has also held that "[t]he exclusionary rule is inherent in the prohibition of torture and other ill-treatment."[21] The second example is the Fifth Amendment of the United States Constitution which mandates that "[n]o person … shall be compelled in any criminal case to be a witness against himself …" It does not mention the admissibility of the compelled confessional statements. As noted earlier, involuntary confessions will be excluded. Similarly, the exclusionary rule, even though not mentioned in the Constitution and Convention provisions, is the appropriate way to protect against abuse of power, according to the United States Supreme Court and ECtHR.

20 *United States v. Leon*, 468 U.S. 897, 932 (1984) (Brennan, J., dissenting); *Massachusetts v. Sheppard*, 468 U.S. 981 (1984) (Brennan, J., dissenting).

21 *A and others v. Secretary of State for the Home Department (No 2)*, [2005] UKHL 71, 2 AC 221, 239.

In sum, although the Constitution and Convention do not explicitly provide for exclusion, the need to enforce the Constitution's and Convention's limits on the executive requires the exclusionary rule.

3.1.3 Serious Crimes Exception?

In this section, I examine the question of whether we should establish a serious crime exception to the exclusionary rule in the criminal justice process. John Kaplan believed that the exclusionary rule should not apply in most serious cases unless the police conduct shocked the conscience. Kaplan carved out an exception for "treason, espionage, murder, armed robbery, and kidnapping by organized groups."[22] Cameron and Lustiger also argued that the exclusionary rule should not apply in most serious cases or where the reprehensible nature of the crime is greater than seriousness of the police malfeasance.[23] On the question of whether we should establish a serious crime exception to the exclusionary rule, I find as follows: there could be nothing worse than a serious crimes exception to the exclusionary rule. The government owes the same respect to every citizen whether suspected or accused of a crime or not. Judge Tymkovich emphasized that: "The purpose of the Fourth Amendment and the associated exclusionary rule is not to grant certain guilty defendants a windfall by letting them go free … The objective is rather to protect *all* citizens, particularly the innocent, by deterring overzealous police behavior."[24] It would be inconsistent with the constitution to permit confession extracted by torture, regardless of whether the suspect was involved in serious cases or non-serious cases. The objection includes three flaws. I have never been convinced by that argument because of three reasons.

First, an obvious one is that a court may never exclude illegally obtained evidence in some categories of cases.

The Fourth Amendment was designed to protect both the guilty and the innocent from illegal searches and seizures.[25] Likewise, it is fair to say that the exclusionary rule protect both the serious cases and non-serious cases. In applying the "serious crime" test, a court might *never* exclude illegally obtained (confessions and physical) evidence in the "serious" crimes cases. If we limit the exclusion of evidence to only those non-serious cases or allow the accused to invoke the exclusionary rule only where the illegality committed against him is graver than the crime he has committed against others, the efficacy of the exclusionary rule

---

22 John Kaplan, "The Limits of the Exclusionary Rule" (1974) 26 *Stanford Law Review* 1027, 1046.

23 James Cameron and Richard Lustiger, "The Exclusionary Rule: A Cost Benefit Analysis" (1984) 101 *Federal Rules Decisions* 109, 110.

24 *United States v. Johnson*, 364 F.3d 1185, 1190 (10th Cir. 2004) (emphasis added).

25 Amy Codagnone, "Good-Faith Exception to Exclusionary Rule Extends to Illegal Searches Based on Police Recordkeeping Errors—*Herring v. United States*, 129 S. Ct. 695 (2009)" (2009) 43 *Suffolk University Law Review* 265, 269.

will diminish for three reasons: (1) the gravity of these "serious" crime cases *always* will by definition exceed the gravity of any constitutional violation. As Cameron claimed: "it is worse to be murdered or raped than to have one's house searched without a warrant, no matter how aggravated the latter violation";[26] (2) the defendant's conduct in such cases will always be more reprehensible than the police officer's; (3) many law enforcement officers often use illegal methods to get evidence in serious crime cases as they might be under tremendous pressure from the public.[27] The serious crime exception will create the vicious circle in the criminal process. In a sensitive and sometimes high-profile case, a more serious crime has been committed; the law enforcement officer's pressure to find the "truth" is greater. Hence, the result could be more and more police misconduct in serious crime cases. This exemption will be wholly independent of any police misconduct, no matter how serious they are.

Secondly, limited categories of serious offenses may expand to unlimited.

Suppose, for example, that homicide was one of the specified serious crimes exempted from the exclusionary rule and that the police obtained evidence of the homicide by violating the right to be free from torture, or the right to be free from illegal searches and seizures. Why should illegally obtained evidence of a rape, a robbery, or a burglary not be inadmissible? Should the exclusionary rule apply in murders, armed robber, or terrorists? In addition, the United States Supreme Court has never adopted this exception, presumably because this approach would raise grave problems of admissibility. Limited categories of serious offenses may expand to unlimited. For example, in 1974, for Kaplan, the short list of serious crimes that should be free from the exclusionary rule is "treason, espionage, murder, armed robbery, and kidnapping by organized groups."[28] One decade later, Arizona Supreme Court expanded upon Kaplan's short list, adding rape and arson to the list.[29]

Thirdly, the serious crime exception sends the wrong message to law enforcement officers.

Governments should send a clear signal to law enforcement agencies that police torture will not be tolerated. Establishing the exclusionary rule is powerful in that this sends a clear message to law enforcement officers that courts will not condone the use of illegal investigatory methods that ride roughshod over constitutional rights. The serious crime exception, however, sends the wrong message to law enforcement officers that breaching constitutionally protected rights is acceptable as long as the ends justify the means in a serious case. To my mind, the constitution violation is the constitution violation. There is no distinction between the slight and substantial constitution violations. We should not give judicial imprimatur

---

26 *State v. Bolt*, 689 P. 2d, 519, 530 (Ariz. 1984) (Cameron, J.).

27 See Chapter 5.

28 John Kaplan, "The Limits of the Exclusionary Rule" (1974) 26 *Stanford Law Review* 1027, 1046.

29 *State v. Bolt*, 689 P. 2d 519, 530 (Ariz. 1984) (Cameron, J.).

to constitutional violations whatsoever. It cannot be compatible with the spirit of the constitution that varying degrees of fairness apply to different categories of accused in criminal trials. The right to be free from illegal searches and seizures, contained in the guarantees of the Fourth Amendment, must apply so equally to those accused of other types of rape, murder or terrorist offenses.

3.1.4 The Exclusionary Rule Deters Police Misconduct

There are two kinds of deterrent effect of the exclusionary rule: (1) general deterrent, which discourages a class of enforcement officers from illegal police conduct; and (2) specific deterrent, which discourages individual enforcement officers from illegal police conduct.

There is debate over whether the exclusionary rule deters the police from wrongdoing, especially from committing future illegal searches and seizures. Critics claim that the exclusionary rule is not an effective deterrent. For example, Chief Justice Burger argued that there is no reliable evidence that the exclusionary rule deters unlawful police behavior.[30] A number of empirical studies in the United States, however, indicated that the exclusionary rule deters illegal law enforcement conduct, serves as an effective deterrent, and encourages compliance with constitutional requirements. These studies concluded that the exclusionary rule has had a deterrent effect upon the police.[31] In addition, the rule continues to deter illegal police wrongdoing.

After conducting 90 interviews with New York City police commanders on all levels, according to Loewenthal's 1980 study, the exclusionary rule works as a significant deterrent.[32] In 1987, Orfield interviewed police officers in the Narcotics Section of the Organized Crime Division of the Chicago Police Department; the officers reported that the exclusionary rule has significant deterrent effects.[33] In addition, in the empirical study of the Chicago criminal court system, including police, prosecutors, public defenders and judges, Orfield concludes that the exclusionary rule does deter abuse, particularly in important cases.[34]

In a separate 1997 study, the empirical study in California sought to determine whether the exclusionary rule deters individual police officers from violating

30 *Bivens v. Six Unknown Federal Narcotics Agents*, 403 U.S. 388, 416 (1971) (Burger, C.J., dissenting).

31 Michael Katz, "The Supreme Court and the States: An Inquiry into *Mapp v. Ohio* in North Carolina: The Model, the Study, and the Implication" (1966) 45 *North Carolina Law Review* 119, 134.

32 M.A. Loewenthal, "Evaluating the Exclusionary Rule in Search and Seizure" (1980) 49 *University of Missouri-Kansas City Law Review* 29, 35.

33 Myron Orfield, Jr., "The Exclusionary Rule and Deterrence: An Empirical Study of Chicago Narcotics Officers" (1987) 54 *University of Chicago Law Review* 1016, 1019–22.

34 Myron Orfield, Jr., "Deterrence, Perjury and the Heater Factor: An Exclusionary Rule in Chicago Criminal Courts" (1992) 63 *University of Colorado Law Review* 75, 85–94.

the Fourth Amendment.[35] Significantly, the study further reported that most law enforcement officers considered the potential exclusion of evidence to be an important concern. Furthermore, about 20 percent indicated that it was a primary concern in their investigative work.[36]

3.1.5 Limited to the United States and Common Law Countries?

The views that the exclusionary rule is only limited to the United States[37] and common law countries, and the rule does not exist in continental European countries are far from accurate. Chief Justice Burger's observation that the exclusionary rule is unique to American jurisprudence in 1971[38] is a misconception. The French courts, for instance, as early as 1672, excluded evidence obtained by means of an illegal search. In the twentieth century, the first French exclusionary rule case occurred in 1910, four years before *Weeks* in the United States.[39] In Germany, evidence obtained from an illegal search and seizure was excluded in 1889,[40] although it was sporadically applied in practice. Obviously, the exclusionary rule is not unique to the United States.

There has been a remarkable increasing trend toward convergence in the development of the exclusionary rule since the twentieth century. A number of countries have some form of an exclusionary rule. One of the important global legal developments is the growing recognition that the suspect will be given the exclusionary rule in both domestic and international law. In the last several decades, the exclusionary rule has been found not only within Anglo-American jurisprudence, but also within many domestic and international systems. It is truly an inspiration to the rest of the world.[41]

At a national level, Ireland, Italy, Germany, Greece, Spain, Russia, Hungary and Turkey, among other countries, have adopted a version of the exclusionary rule. These countries had begun to accept the exclusionary rule as the proper response to violations of the right to be free from torture, and the right to be free from illegal searches and seizures. In Ireland, the judgment in *Kenny*[42] is of interest because, for the first time, a supreme court anywhere in the world considered the exclusionary rule in its own country as stricter than its United States counterpart,

---

35 L.T. Perrin and others, "If It's Broken, Fix It: Moving beyond the Exclusionary Rule" (1998) 83 *Iowa Law Review* 669, 670.

36 Ibid., 678.

37 403 U.S. 388 (1971) (Burger, C.J., dissenting).

38 Ibid.

39 Walter Pakter, "Exclusionary Rules in France, Germany, and Italy" (1985), 9 *Hastings International and Comparative Law Review* 1, 4–5.

40 Ibid., 5, 17.

41 The Chinese regime should bring its criminal justice system into line with international human rights standards.

42 *People v. Kenny* (1990) 2 I.R. 110.

which is well known for its relative strictness. The Supreme Court of Ireland made it clear that the rule differs from that in the United States. The latter is subjected to a range of exceptions and founded on a desire to deter unlawful police conduct. But the Irish rule is "the absolute protection test."[43]

Italy has developed the exclusionary rule to implement provisions in its 1948 Constitution protecting the civil rights of citizens against unlawful police activity. In 1988, Article 191(1) of the Italian Code of Criminal Procedure declares that "[e]vidence acquired in violation of prohibitions established by the law may not be used."[44]

In Germany, according to Para. 136a Section 3 of the Code of Criminal Procedure, when police or other interrogators have used prohibited means any ensuing statement is inadmissible, and information from protected private conversations obtained through hidden microphones must not be used as evidence.[45] Next, in Greece, according to Article 179 of the Code of Criminal Procedure, evidence obtained unlawfully must not be taken into account in deciding on the defendant's guilt.[46] Also, in Spain, Article 11 of the Code of Criminal Procedure lays down the principle that "evidence obtained either directly or indirectly in contravention of fundamental rights and liberties will be of no effect."[47]

Furthermore, in 2002, the new Russian Code of Criminal Procedure became effective. Article 7(3) declares that "a violation of the rules of this Code by a court, procurator, investigator, inquiry agency, or inquiring officer in the course of criminal proceedings shall cause the evidence thus obtained to be inadmissible," while Article 75(1) reinforces the rule that "evidence obtained in violation of the requirements of this Code shall be inadmissible."[48]

Turning to the international arena, in international criminal proceedings, although more flexible with regard to the introduction of evidence, tribunals also exclude evidence gathered in breach of fundamental human rights standards.

In Nuremberg trial, for example, Sauckel claimed that his interrogations had been taken under duress and the International Military Tribunal for the Major War Criminals, Nuremberg (IMT) excluded it.[49] In *Greifelt and others*,[50] allegations of misconduct by the interrogator against defendants, including threats and coercion,

43 Ibid.

44 Codice Di Procedura Penale, Article 191(1).

45 §100c § 5, 3rd sent. CCP.

46 Ed Cape and others (eds), *Suspects in Europe: Procedural Rights at the Investigative Stage of the Criminal Process in the European Union* (Intersentia Antwerpen, Oxford 2007) 122–4.

47 Article 11 of the Spanish Code of Criminal Procedure.

48 Leonard Orland, "A Russian Legal Revolution: The 2002 Criminal Procedure Code" (2002) 18 *Connecticut Journal of International Law* 133, 150.

49 XV IMT Proceedings, 64–8.

50 *United States of America v. Ulrich Greifelt and Others (RuSHA)*, United States Military Tribunal I, Judgment of March 10, 1948, in 5 Trials of War Criminals before the Nuremberg Military Tribunals under Control Council Law No. 1088 (U.S. 1951).

the United States Military Tribunal, Nuremberg excluded the affidavits.[51] The exclusionary rule is laid down in Rule 95 of the 1996 Statute of the International Criminal Tribunal for the Former Yugoslavia (ICTY) Rules of Procedure and Evidence (RPE) and in Article 69(7) of the 1998 Rome Statute of the International Criminal Court (ICC Statute). Rule 95 of the ICTY RPE states: "No evidence should be admissible if obtained by methods which cast substantial doubt on its reliability or if its admission is antithetical to, and would seriously damage, the integrity of the proceedings." According to Ho, in the spirit of Article 19 of the International Criminal Tribunal for Rwanda (ICTR), the evidence must be excluded if its admission undermines the fairness of the trial.[52]

Article 69(7) of the ICC Statute provides that evidence obtained by means of a violation of the Statute or internationally recognized human rights shall not be admissible if: (a) the violation casts substantial doubt on the reliability of the evidence; or (b) the admission of the evidence would be antithetical to and would seriously damage the integrity of the proceedings.

Moreover, similar provisions are also in international human rights treaty agreements which impose an obligation on states to ensure that an effective procedure exists in national law for the exclusion of evidence obtained by torture. For example, Article 15 of the 1984 United Nations Convention against Torture and other Cruel, Inhuman or Degrading Treatment or Punishment (UNCAT) states: "Each State Party shall ensure that any statement which is established to have been made as a result of torture shall not be invoked as evidence in any proceedings." It requires the exclusion of statements made as a result of torture as evidence in any proceedings. Further, Article 10 of the 1985 Inter-American Convention to Prevent and Punish Torture provides that no statement that is verified as having been obtained through torture shall be admissible as evidence in a legal proceeding.

3.2 Are There Alternatives to Exclusion?

Some commentators may maintain that any remedy other than the rule is equally effective, i.e., the alternatives are as capable of ensuring that suspects are not tortured, and deterring illegal searches and seizures. Others may paint a misleading picture by intimating that there are sensible methods better than exclusion. If a more appropriate remedy can amend or replace the rule then the dilemmas of the rule can be solved.

At first glance, some jurists' opinions regarding the remedies of the rule seem attractive, so that many might accept these remedies as the replacement. This would be unfortunate. Neither theory and practice nor perception and reality always match, and the general conception of "alternative remedies" is exaggerated.

---

51 XV NMT, 879.

52 H.L. Ho, *A Philosophy of Evidence Law—Justice in the Search of Evidence Law* (Oxford University Press, Oxford 2008) 313.

In theory there are at least three "alternative remedies" available of enforcing the deterrent of due process violations during police interrogation and investigation. In practice, however, these alternatives afford very limited protection against promiscuous intrusion and sadly cannot adequately achieve these goals. We should not work in an intellectual vacuum.

The usual theoretical alternatives can be grouped under three heads:

1. The criminal remedy: criminal prosecution;
2. The civil remedy: tort suits;
3. The administrative remedy: disciplinary measures.

Unfortunately, there are significant flaws in all three types of remedies. In real life there is often a disparity between theory and practice. The rich potential of criminal, civil and administrative responses to police misconduct has never been fully exploited. In addition, an available remedy does not necessarily make an effective remedy. These alternatives are unrealistic, impractical and not much of a deterrent. Each of these alternatives will now be considered.

3.2.1 Criminal Prosecution

Any public official or agent who uses torture to extract evidence from an accused commits a crime. Penal sanctions may also apply to officers who have illegally searched private dwellings in most countries and the misbehaving police can therefore be punished. Most states have penal provisions which are applicable to cases of torture or illegal search practices. In the United Kingdom, under Sections 90–104 of PACE, an offending police officer may face criminal sanction. In the United States, 18 U.S.C. § 2236 holds that officers involved in illegal searches shall be fined or guilty of a misdemeanor, or both.[53] Justice Cardozo said that "[t]he [offending] officer might be … prosecuted for oppression."[54]

However, it is far from sufficient for the implementation of the exclusionary rule to prohibit torture and illegal search or to make it a crime. Penal sanctions only play a marginal role in preventing police misconduct because there are many profound impediments for those wishing to pursue charges against the police. Almost no criminal prosecutions of illegal search and seizure can be found in the reported cases. Sanders and Young expressed the same sentiment that "there have been no

53 18 U.S.C. § 2236 provides that: Whoever, being an officer, agent, or employee of the United States or any department or agency thereof, engaged in the enforcement of any law of the United States, searches any private dwelling used and occupied as such dwelling without a warrant directing such search, or maliciously and without reasonable cause searches any other building or property without a search warrant, shall be fined under this title for a first offense; and, for a subsequent offense, shall be fined under this title or imprisoned not more than one year, or both.

54 *People v. Defore* 150 NE 585, 586–7 (NY App. Ct. 1926).

reported cases of this."[55] Chief Justice Roger Traynor, the most respected state judge in the United States, explained why the California Supreme Court had overruled its precedent and adopted the exclusionary rule in *People v. Cahan*:[56] "without fear of criminal punishment or other discipline, law enforcement officers … casually regard [illegal searches and seizures] as nothing more than the performance of their ordinary duties for which the city employs and pays them."[57] There are four reasons why so few prosecutions are brought against police officers and why most of the law enforcement officers do not worry about criminal punishment.

First, prosecutors are reluctant to indict police.

Prosecutors have an extensive liaison with the police because of the nature of their duties. In situations where the officers become the accused, some prosecutors are disinclined to prosecute the front-line police who are in daily cooperation, and endure the hostility of the law enforcement personnel. It may generate tensions between the two agencies. Prosecutors hope to maintain good working relationships with police in the future. Nevertheless prosecution of police will not be vigorously pursued. We may share the opinion of Justice Carter in *White v. Towers*[58] that:

> I should like to have brought to my attention any such case where a plaintiff has been successful, or even where a prosecution has been instituted. It is absurd to suggest that any district attorney, or superior officer, is going to take criminal action against one of his subordinates at the request of one injured by an unwarranted prosecution, especially where the prosecutor has relied upon the testimony of the subordinate as a basis for the prosecution.[59]

Even if prosecutors wanted to investigate such cases, investigation with limited police assistance can be difficult.

Secondly, police may cover up their colleagues' wrongdoing.[60]

In most of the cases the only witnesses will be the victim and the police. Police officers are often the most important witnesses called in the presentation of illegal search and torture cases. If there are other witnesses, they may be reluctant to testify, fearing retaliation and trouble. Many police officers usually follow their abuse of power with the charge that the citizen was assaulting an officer and resisting arrest.[61]

---

55 Andrew Sanders and Richard Young, *Criminal Justice* (3rd edn, Oxford University Press, Oxford 2007) 94.

56 282 P.2d 905 (Cal. 1955).

57 Ibid., 907 (Cal. 1955).

58 37 Cal. 2d 727 (1951).

59 Ibid., 737 (1951).

60 Joycelyn Pollock, *Ethical Dilemmas and Decisions in Criminal Justice* (6th edn, Cengage Learning, Australia 2008) 288.

61 Monroe Freedman, "The Professional Responsibility of the Prosecuting Attorney" (1967) 55 *Georgetown Law Journal* 1030, 1037–8.

Thirdly, the code of silence prevents police from telling the truth.

The police community is a closed society similar to the military. The police code of silence is part of the police culture. The members of community are required to be loyal to the group. Once someone betrays the group, he betrays himself, destroys his identity and may change his career forever. In order to maintain the honor of the police community, those who do not want to perjure themselves but are eyewitness will choose to keep silent in the court instead of testifying against their comrades as to what is actually happening. Sanders and Young found that in the United Kingdom "the 'code of silence' operated by senior as well as junior officers to cover it up; and the failure to discipline adequately most of those few officers who are found to have broken the rules."[62]

In the United States, for example, in 1991, the Christopher Commission identified a pervasive officer code of silence.[63] Its investigation into the Los Angeles Police Department noted that "the greatest single barrier to the effective investigation and adjudication of complaints is the officers' unwritten 'code of silence' ... [which] consists of one simple rule: an officer does not provide adverse information against a fellow officer."[64]

Lastly, jurors are reluctant to convict officers.

Because an officer's job is dangerous and difficult, the juries usually see the police sympathetically and may intentionally ignore the facts and law. After all, they became involved in the incident as part of their duties, i.e., combating crime. It is very doubtful whether many juries will convict a law enforcement officer who has violated the civil rights of "bad guys."

For a variety of psychological reasons, juries prefer to believe that their police officers are not liars and would not perjure themselves. Instead, criminal records may destroy victims' credibility. Most jurors are more likely to believe the officer's version of the "facts" than the victim's. I do not think many jurors will convict policemen who illegally searched the gangsters. It seems that penal sanctions will never have significance as a deterrent. These seemingly lenient treatments by the jurors would undermine faith in the criminal justice system.

3.2.2 Civil Damage Actions

At common law, when a police officer uses excessive force against an individual, that individual can bring tort suits and need not await the government's decision to go forward for trespassing[65] or maliciously procuring a search warrant against the offending party.

---

62 Andrew Sanders and Richard Young, *Criminal Justice* (3rd edn, Oxford University Press, Oxford) 643.

63 Report of the Independent Commission on the Los Angeles Police Department (1991).

64 Ibid., 168–71.

65 *Commonwealth v. Elisha W. Dana*, 43 Mass. 329 (1841).

In the United Kingdom, under the Police Act 1996, people can sue a police officer and the chief officer of the department for damages. The Royal Commission on Criminal Procedure of 1981 recommended that "the civil courts may therefore prove to have a useful role to play in the application of the statutory rules."[66] Lord Diplock maintained that "[i]f it was obtained illegally there will be a remedy in civil law."[67]

In the United States, tort suits were the remedy of choice from the middle of the eighteenth century for official wrongdoing such as unlawful searches.[68] Victims of police misbehavior can sue the officer for violating their civil rights under 42 U.S.C. 1983.[69] The plaintiff in a 1983 case may sue the police officer individually for unconstitutional searches. Judge Cardozo said that "[t]he [offending] officer might have ... sued for damages."[70] Amar has argued that civil damage can handle law enforcement abuses.[71] He hopes to replace the exclusionary rule with tort actions.

However, very few civil actions are pursued in the area of illegal search and seizure. Furthermore, rare tort actions against the police have succeeded, except in clear cases of physical coercion and brutality. Research by the United States Department of Justice[72] discovered that plaintiffs filed 12,000 actions related the Fourth Amendment between 1971 and 1986. Only in five cases have the defendants actually paid damages. With regard to 42 U.S.C. 1983, there were fewer than three dozen reported Fourth Amendment cases between 1966 and 1986.[73]

Civil litigations cannot fulfill their potential as deterrents to police illegality. Instead, civil processes per se are full of deterrents to suit. In the past, tort systems provided legal impediments to shield officers from suit. In the 1700s, under the

---

66 The Royal Commission on Criminal Procedure, *Report* (Cmnd. 8092) (1981) [4.122].

67 *R v. Sang*, [1980] AC 402, 436.

68 *Entick v. Carrington*, 95 Eng. Rep. 807 (KB 1765).

69 This provision provides that: Every person who, under color of any statute, ordinance, regulation, custom, or usage, of any State or Territory or the District of Columbia, subjects, or causes to be subjected, any citizen of the United States or other person within the jurisdiction thereof to the deprivation of any rights, privileges, or immunities secured by the Constitution and laws, shall be liable to the party injured in an action at law, suit in equity, or other proper proceeding for redress, except that in any action brought against a judicial officer for an act or omission taken in such officer's judicial capacity, injunctive relief shall not be granted unless a declaratory decree was violated or declaratory relief was unavailable ...

70 *People v. Defore*, 150 NE 585, 586–7 (NY App. Ct. 1926).

71 A.R. Amar, *The Constitution and Criminal Procedure: First Principle* (Yale University Press, New Haven 1997) 40–45.

72 Office of Legal Policy, the United States Department of Justice, *Truth in Criminal Justice* (Report No.2) (1986) reprinted in (1989) 22 *University of Michigan Journal of Law Reform* 437, 573–660.

73 Ibid., 626, 630.

Collection Act of 1789 in the United States, which discouraged lawsuits against custom collectors, if plaintiffs sued for wrongful seizures, they would forfeit twice the amount for which they sued.[74] Because of four formidable obstacles, their paucity and low likelihood of success, it is not surprising to find that victims are deterred from filing civil suits against police.

First, the cost of litigation may deter victims from bringing suit.

These actions are difficult, costly and time consuming to pursue. The great majority of those aggrieved come from the lowest economic levels of society, for example, minorities, and may be least able to bear the burden. Victims of torturous conduct may probably be unable to afford the expense of litigation. Legal aid may not be available because of eligibility requirements. If victims are fortunate enough to be able to afford attorneys, because of the small chances to win and limited profit, solicitors may be reluctant to take their cases.

Secondly, proving malice is too onerous a hurdle for victims.

In civil litigation, the plaintiff bears the legal burden of proof in relation to the issue. Unless the victim can demonstrate and prove real ill will or malice by the officer, the claim of maliciously procuring a search warrant and trespass will fail; negligence of this kind[75] does not qualify.[76] It seems reasonable to presume that the responsible law enforcement officers' pursuit of crime bears no ill will towards the suspect. The onerous hurdle is set in favor of protection of the police in such cases.

Thirdly, the jury may think criminals deserved what they got.

Some of the plaintiffs have criminal records, or are suspected of criminality. In most of the cases, jurors are naturally unsympathetic to victims of unlawful searches and prefer to trust policemen instead of civil plaintiffs with criminal records.

The pervasive attitude among jurors is that even if these people have not committed a crime, they are suspected criminals. The jurors do not want to reward criminals or suspected criminals by giving damages award in tort actions. Even if the victims are not criminals, unsympathetic juries have been reluctant to grant damages awards.[77]

Fourthly, actual reparation may be an insignificant amount.

Even if the victims overcome all the above impediments, then after enduring a long and arduous litigation process, compensatory damages will be an insignificant amount—inadequate to encourage the plaintiffs to bring tort suits. It is hard to quantify the value of awards in these cases. It is likely to be limited to injuries to property and to be very small even in the serious cases. Punitive damages are very hard to recover. In order to obtain punitive damages the plaintiff in Pennsylvania,

---

74 Collection Act of 1789, ch. 5, § 27, 1 Stat. 29.

75 Maliciously procuring a search warrant and trespass.

76 *Keegan and others v. Chief Constable of Merseyside Police*, [2003] EWCA Civ 936.

77 Guido Calabresi, "The Exclusionary Rule" (2003) 26 *Harvard Journal of Law and Public Policy* 111, 114.

for instance, must (1) prove real malice,[78] (2) establish actual physical damage,[79] and (3) show that the claim bears a reasonable proportion to the actual damages.[80]

Moreover, the individual officer will *not* suffer direct financial loss. In the United States, the police officer rarely pays any damages awarded. Cities usually indemnify law enforcement officers in § 1983 cases.[81] In England, the practice was established by Section 48 of the Police Act 1964. Money will not be taken from officers' pockets and the taxpayer will pay the bill. At the De Menezes case,[82] for instance, English taxpayers had to pay £560,000 (fining the force £175,000 and ordering it to pay £385,000 in costs).[83] It is hard to deter officers' illegality because of their financial irresponsibility. Under this circumstance, civil damages action itself may provide very little deterrent effect to the law enforcement officer who will not actually have pay damages.

Prior 1961, as Powe, a leading historian of the United States Supreme Court, has aptly pointed out, "[n]either criminal nor civil sanctions were ever brought against police who did not get warrants, and there was ample reason to believe that the practice of illegal searches was widespread."[84] Tort suits cannot prevent the misconduct of the police.

3.2.3 Complaints and Disciplinary Procedures

Internal disciplinary machinery, in both the United Kingdom and United States, exists within police forces for disciplining a law enforcement officer who engages in illegal or improper conduct. The internal discipline is a less severe sanction than criminal sanctions. These measures include fines, pay cuts, undesirable transfers, and removal from the force. Lord Diplock has suggested that "[i]f it was obtained illegally but in breach of the rules of conduct for the police, it is a matter for the appropriate disciplinary authority to deal with."[85] However, there are long-standing problems with this approach. An interior administrative investigation of a complaint may have form, but lack substance. On the one hand, the lack of independent mechanism of citizen complaints against police has long been

---

78 *McCarthy v. DeArmit*, 99 Pa. 63, 72 (1881).

79 *Mitchell v. Randall*, 288 Pa. 518, 137 Atl. 171 (1927).

80 *Rider v. York Haven Water Co.*, 251 Pa. 18, 95 Atl. 803 (1915).

81 M.A. Schwartz, "Should Juries be Informed that Municipality Will Indemnify Officer's § 1983 Liability for Constitutional Wrongdoing" (2001) 86 *Iowa Law Review* 1209, 1211.

82 After Jean Charles De Menezes was mistaken by the London Metropolitan police for a possible suicide bomber, he was killed by the police in a London subway station in 2005.

83 Vikram Dodd, "Guilty, but Blair Refuses to Go" *The Guardian*, London, Nov. 2, 2007, at 1.

84 L.A. Powe, Jr., *The Warren Court and American Politics* (Belknap Press of Harvard University Press, Cambridge 2000) 198.

85 [1980] AC 402, 436.

a significant deficit. On the other hand, police superiors may have a hard time punishing hard-working cops for minor mistakes.

In Britain, the Home Secretary set up a committee to consider whether the application of five techniques in Northern Ireland require amendment. Lord Gardiner published the Northern Ireland Interrogation Methods Minority Report in 1972 as part of the Parker Report (Report of the Committee of Privy Counselors appointed to consider authorized procedures for the interrogations of persons suspected of terrorism).[86] Between 1971 and 1974, there were 2,615 complaints against the police; only 6 were fined.[87] The minority report by Lord Gardiner found a widespread belief that complaints against members of the security forces were not taken seriously. It then recommended the establishment of an independent means of investigating complaints.[88]

Three decades ago Lord Scarman already acknowledged that the impartial and unfair complaints process does not command the confidence of the public and complainants would risk being subjected to intimidation by the police as a result.[89] He also warned that unless a system of independent investigation was available for all complaints to be introduced the complaints procedure would fall into disrepute.[90]

The Police Complaints Authority (PCA), established under the statutory authority of Section 83 of PACE in 1985, is empowered to supervise the investigation of complaints against the police. Although the PCA is obligated, under the Police Act 1996, Section 70 (1)(a), to review any cases in which there has been a death or serious injury to a civilian, very limited complaints are substantiated. In 2000/1, only 903 complaints were substantiated—9.1 percent of the complaints which were investigated, but only 2.9 percent of those initially made.[91] The Police Reform Act 2002 established the Independent Police Complaints Commission to investigate complaints against the police.

The Royal Commission on Criminal Justice of 1993 pointed out the failings with police disciplinary measures: "They appear to be both lengthy and uncertain and frequently result, when they lead to a finding against the officer concerned, in the imposition of penalties less than the offence would seem to require."[92]

---

86 Committee of Privy Counselors, *Report of* the Committee of Privy Counselors Appointed to Consider Authorized Procedures for the Interrogations of Persons Suspected of Terrorism (Cmnd. 4901) (1972) [9]; also available at: http://cain.ulst.ac.uk/hmso/parker.htm (accessed January 1, 2011).

87 *Ireland v. United Kingdom* (App 5310/71) (1978) 2 EHRR 25 at [140].

88 Ibid., at [138].

89 Lord Scarman, The Brixton Disorders April 10–12, 1981, *Report of an Inquiry* (Cmnd. 8427) (1981), at para. 7.11.

90 Ibid., para. 7.21.

91 J. Cotton and D. Povey, "*Police Complaints and Discipline: England and Wales, April 1999 to March 2000* (Home Office Statistical Bulletin, Issue 14/00, London, Home Office Research and Statistics Directorate, 2000).

92 The Royal Commission on Criminal Procedure, *Report* (Cmnd. 8092) (1981) [96].

In Scotland in 2000 a report by the HM Inspectorate of Constabulary for Scotland revealed that the police do not count all of their complaints as statistics. There are many more complaints than those in the official statistics.[93]

At the same time, the European Committee for the Prevention of Torture or Degrading Treatment or Punishment (CPT), an international treaty body falling under the auspices of the Council of Europe,[94] commented in the report[95] on its visit to the United Kingdom and the Isle of Man that:

> [S]tatistically few criminal prosecutions and disciplinary proceedings which were brought, and identified certain aspects of the procedures which cast doubt on their effectiveness: The chief officers appointed officers from the same force to conduct the investigations ... the majority of investigations were unsupervised by the Police Complaints Authority.[96]

In *Hugh Jordan v. United Kingdom*, the ECtHR determined that the officers investigating the incident were insufficiently independent from the officers implicated in the incident.[97]

Despite the Police Complaints Authority having power to refer charges of criminal offenses to the Director of Public Prosecutions and itself to bring disciplinary charges, it is insufficiently independent from the police and does not provide an effective remedy to police misconduct as required under Article 13 of the ECHR.[98]

In the United States, although most large police departments had procedures for dealing with charges of misconduct by their members from the 1960s, too few forces had adequate procedures for dealing with complaints. In Philadelphia, in 1952 for example, it was said that the machinery "has not been used in the case of an illegal search or arrest."[99] The United States Department of Justice Report

---

93 HM Inspectorate of Constabulary for Scotland, *Fair Cop?: The Investigation of Complaints against the Police in Scotland* (2000).

94 The Committee comprises one representative from each European country, and delegations make visits to selected prison facilities in every country every few years. See Morgan Evans and Malcolm Evans, *Combating Torture in Europe: The Work and Standards of the European Committee for the Prevention of Torture* (Council of Europe, Strasbourg 2001) 23, 29.

95 Council of Europe, *Report to the Government of the United Kingdom on the Visit to the United Kingdom and the Isle of Man Carried out by the European Committee for the Prevention of Torture or Degrading Treatment or Punishment (CPT) from 12 to 23 May 2003* (Doc. No. CPT/Inf 1) (2005). Available at: http://www.cpt.coe.int/documents/gbr/2005-01-inf-eng.htm (accessed January 1, 2011).

96 Ibid.

97 *Hugh Jordan v. United Kingdom* (App. 24746/94), Judgment of May 4, 2001.

98 *Khan v. United Kingdom* (App. 35394/97), Judgment of 4 Oct. 2001.

99 Paula Markowitz and Walter Summerfield, Jr., "Philadelphia Police Practice and the Law of Arrest" (1952) 100 *University of Philadelphia Law Review* 1182, 1211.

discovered only seven investigations into Fourth Amendment violations between 1981 and 1986. No police officer was internally sanctioned and two defendants were pardoned by the President.[100]

Before 1961, state courts were free to adopt or reject the exclusionary rule. In 1955, Roger Traynor, then Chief Justice of the California Supreme Court, the most respected mid-century state court jurist, adopted the exclusionary rule and eloquently asserted that:

> [O]ther remedies have completely failed to secure compliance with the constitutional provisions on the part of police officers with the attendant result that the courts under the old rule have been constantly required to participate in, and in effect condone, the lawless activities of law enforcement officers.[101]

The Court's analysis in *Mapp* reflects the same concern. The *Mapp* Court found that "[t]he experience of California that such other remedies have been worthless and futile is buttressed by the experience of other States."[102] Until the Court created the exclusionary rule, there was simply no institutional brake on illegal searches. As Jerome Skolnick puts it, "[s]uperiors within the police organization will … be in sympathy with an officer, provided the search was administratively reasonable, even if the officer did not have legal 'reasonable' cause to make an arrest."[103] When the illegality is not egregious, police chiefs are more likely to protect the police as protecting the police means protecting themselves, instead of sanctioning the police.

As Chambliss and Seidman pointed out in 1971, there are two reasons why internal control by the police has not achieved the desired results.[104] First, there are inherent obstacles to a useful complaint procedure. Secondly, there are insufficiently independent inherent contradictions in the position of the police force as an institution when presented by a complaint against an individual officer. In 1968 the National Advisory Committee on Civil Disorders (The Kerner Commission) reported:

> In Milwaukee, Wisconsin and Plainfield, New Jersey … ghetto residents complained that police chiefs reject all complaints out of hand. In New Haven, a Negro citizens' group characterized a police review board as "worthless."

100 Office of Legal Policy, the United States Department of Justice, *Truth in Criminal Justice* (Report No.2) (1986) reprinted in (1989) 22 *University of Michigan Journal of Law Reform* 621, 623.

101 *People v. Cahan*, 282 P.2d 905, 911–12 (Cal. 1955).

102 367 U.S. 643, 652 (1961).

103 Jerome Skolnick, *Justice without Trial: Law Enforcement in Democratic Society* (John Wiley and Sons Inc., New Jersey 1975) 223.

104 William Chambliss and Robert Seidman, *Law, Order and Power* (Addison-Wesley Publishing, Reading 1971) 370.

> In Detroit, the Michigan Civil Rights Commission found that, despite well-intentioned leadership, no real sanctions are imposed on offending officers. In Newark, the Mayor referred complaints to the FBI, which had limited jurisdiction over them ...[105]

Overall, for lessons set out above it is easy to envision that there are substantial institutional difficulties in using these so-called alternative remedies as methods for achieving the ends for which we strive. The obstacles to achieving such a result are far too great through these remedies. The remedies to the exclusionary rule are mainly illusory and of no practical avail. The truth is that no other remedy can adequately achieve these goals.

People adopting actions mentioned above encounter numerous legal hurdles that prevented these alternatives from becoming effective methods to illegal intrusions. The *Irvine*[106] Court also took the view that other remedies for Fourth Amendment violations are "of no practical avail," since "the police are unlikely to inform on themselves or each other"[107] and hence any claim against the police will probably be brought by convicted criminals.[108] Thus, I argue that the exclusionary rule has the most powerful influence on police investigation practices and can reduce police misconduct at least in some situations. Absent the rule, I profoundly believe that there is no other effective method to stop the police from invading fundamental rights.

3.3 Cost-Benefit Balancing of the Exclusionary Rule

> The purpose of the Bill of Rights ... was to place certain subjects beyond the reach of cost-benefit analysis.
>
> Yale Kamisar[109]

Balancing is a process of measuring competing interests to determine which is "weightier." By a "balancing opinion," I mean a judicial opinion that analyzes a criminal procedure question by identifying interests implicated by the case, and measuring competing interests. Sometimes the United States Supreme Court talks about one interest outweighing another. In *Payton v. New York*,[110] for instance, Justice Blackmun declared that "a suspect's interest in the sanctity of

---

105 National Advisory Commission, "Report of the National Advisory Commission on Civil Disorders" (New York 1968) 310.

106 *Irvine v. California*, 347 U.S. 128, 137 (1954) (Jackson, J.).

107 Ibid.; See also *People v. Cahan*, 282 P.2d 905, 913 (Cal. 1955).

108 367 U.S. 643 (1961).

109 Yale Kamisar, "Does (Did) (Should) the Exclusionary Rule Rest on a 'Principled Basis' Rather than an 'Empirical Proposition'?" (1983) 16 *Creighton Law Review* 565, 653.

110 *Payton v. New York*, 445 U.S. 573 (1980).

his home … outweighs the governmental interests" so as to require a warrant.[111] Further, decisions whether to exclude illegally obtained evidence may involve an economic calculation of costs against benefits.[112]

More specifically, in the context of the search and seizure exclusionary rule, after considering the costs and benefits of the application of the rule, and measuring competing interests to determine which is "weightier," judges decide whether or not to exclude evidence obtained through illegal methods. The inquiry goes something like this: are the costs of excluding valuable illegally obtained evidence outweighed by the deterrent benefits gained? Under such a balancing test, the exclusionary rule will not be permitted where the costs outweighed the benefits. No one, however, seems to pause and ask, in the context of the exclusionary rule, whether every problem can and should be solved through balancing conflicting considerations.

Does this balancing approach matter? Some might argue that balancing may make the exclusionary rule more flexible. According to Richard Posner, for example, all Fourth Amendment issues should be resolved through cost-benefit balancing.[113] However, this author asserts that there is danger in applying the narrow deterrence-oriented cost-benefit balancing approach in the context of the exclusionary rule. I will develop the proposition that the cost-benefit balancing approach is not doable and even threatens the very life of the exclusionary rule itself. Not every exclusionary rule decision can be solved through cost-benefit balancing. In cases involving the confession exclusionary rule, for example, torture, the court does not, and moreover should not, engage in balancing at all. Instead, it should utilize a stringent form of the exclusionary rule. The right to be free from illegal searches and seizures should receive the more certain protection from categorical rules, rather than the less certain protection resulting from the cost-benefit balancing.

This section is divided into two parts. By using the cost-benefit balancing approach, the most notable limitation created is the good faith exception announced in *United States v. Leon*.[114] To begin with, I will explore the *Leon* decision and critically examine *Leon*'s good faith exception to the exclusionary rule and explore *Leon*'s flawed reasoning. There is a startling disjunction between the cost-benefit balancing and "factors" imposed by the Court in the name of the cost-benefit balancing.

Second, while balancing has emerged in criminal justice,[115] few commentators have analyzed what goes on within the "black box" in the context of the exclusionary rule. I reject to the balancing approach adopted by the United States

111 Ibid., 603 (1980).

112 Richard Posner, "Rethinking the Fourth Amendment" (1981) *The Supreme Court Review* 49, 50.

113 Ibid., 74.

114 *United States v. Leon*, 468 U.S. 897 (1984).

115 Royal Commission on Criminal Justice, *Report* (1993).

Supreme Court as this abstract balancing metaphor is not helpful in understanding which interests get weighed, how weights are assigned, how judges decide which interest should prevail, or how balance was struck. The courts simply employed the rhetorical device (the weighing and balancing) and arguments to justify their conclusions. The current cost-benefit analysis of the exclusionary rule tends to focus on the "cost" and minimize the "benefit." The Court did not fully analyze, for balancing, what the objective methodology is. Instead the balancing approach has hindered the development of the exclusionary rule. I contend that cost-benefit balancing in the context of the exclusionary rule is an illusion. In addition, the courts have taken an unnecessarily narrow view of one or more aspects of the exclusionary rule.

3.3.1 The Cost-Benefit Approach: United States v. Leon

Cost-benefit balancing has governed search and seizure exclusionary rule analysis. In *United States v. Leon,*[116] for instance, the Court created the "good faith" exception, which allows unconstitutionally seized evidence to be admitted in a trial when the police officer act in good faith reliance on a facially valid warrant later found to be invalid. *Leon* involved an anonymous informant of unproven reliability who told the police that two suspects were selling narcotics from their residence, and a motion was raised to exclude evidence seized pursuant to a warrant-authorized search of several residences. The Court held that evidence obtained by police officers acting in reasonable reliance on a search warrant later found to be illegal is admissible.[117]

To assess the deterrent value of the exclusionary rule, the majority opinion, written by Justice White,[118] held that there exists a three-part argument analysis for establishing the *Leon* good faith exception. First, the exclusionary rule is designed to deter only police conduct and not that of non-police government actors. Second, there is no evidence which suggests that judges are inclined to ignore the Fourth Amendment. Third, the exclusion would not have serve as a deterrent effect on court officials.[119]

Applying the cost-benefit approach, the Court went on to argue that the issue of whether to exclude illegally obtained evidence would be resolved "by weighing the costs and benefits of preventing the use in the prosecution's case in chief of inherently trustworthy tangible evidence obtained in reliance on a search warrant issued by a detached and neutral magistrate that ultimately is found to be defective."[120] The Court concluded that since the officer relying in good faith on a

---

116 *United States v. Leon*, 468 U.S. 897 (1984).

117 Ibid., 922 (1984).

118 Ibid., 916 (1984).

119 Ibid. (1984).

120 *United States v. Leon*, 468 U.S. 897, 906–7 (1984).

facially valid warrant could not be deterred by exclusion, the benefits of exclusion are marginal or non-existent while the costs to society remain unbearably high.[121]

The reasoning in *Leon* is vulnerable on several different perspectives. Close analysis of the cost-benefit approach and the assumptions apparently underlying it serves to demonstrate further what is wrong with the *Leon* rationale.

First, the Court exaggerated the costs of the exclusionary rule.

The Court did not accurately identify the relevant "cost" and "benefit" of the exclusionary rule. Referring to the costs incurred in the application of the exclusionary rule, the Court exaggerated the costs of the rule. Writing for the Court in *Leon*, Justice White has characterized them as "substantial."[122] Considering the costs of the rule, the Court noted that the costs were two-sided because by excluding certain evidence, first the Court suggested that the exclusion impedes the "truth-finding" process of the criminal justice system.[123] Second, some guilty defendants may go free and thus indiscriminate application of the rule generates disrespect for the law and the justice system.[124] However, there exists inconsistency between the "substantial" costs and the "insubstantial" benefit of the rule. As noted in 3.1.1 above, empirical evidence demonstrates that few convictions are lost. Only about one percent of felony prosecutions were "lost" due to suppression of physical evidence.[125] In Davies's study, he concluded that "the general level of the rule's effects on criminal prosecutions is marginal at most."[126]

Moreover, balance has not really existed the way it ought to. There is too much weight on the side of the "cost." The *Leon* holding itself is an example of such misdirection. The Court has never offered any systematic explanation of the principles that guided its assessment of "costs."

Secondly, the Court undervalued the benefits of the exclusionary rule.

The *Leon* Court not only exaggerated the costs of the exclusionary rule but also underestimated the benefits of the rule. The Court commonly bypasses the "benefit" of the rule and proceeds directly to the "cost" of the rule. In fact, there exists no assessment of the "benefit" of the rule at all. As Justice Brennan observed in his *Leon* dissent, a group of magicians (i.e., the *Leon* majority) made the benefits of the exclusionary rule disappear "with a mere wave of the hand."[127]

The exclusionary rule is a forward-looking device for discouraging government actors from engaging in torture, illegal searches or seizures by removing the

121 Ibid., 922 (1984).

122 Ibid., 909 (1984).

123 Ibid., 907 (1984).

124 Ibid.; see also *Stone v. Powell*, 428 U.S. 465, 490 (1976).

125 Thomas Davies, "A Hard Look at What We Know (and Still Need to Learn) about the 'Cost' of the Exclusionary Rule: The NIJ Study and Other Studies of 'Lost' Arrest" (1983) *American Bar Foundation Research Journal* 611, 617.

126 Ibid., 622.

127 *United States v. Leon*, 468 U.S. 897, 929 (1984) (Brennan, J., dissenting).

evidentiary profits. Therefore, a major benefit of the exclusionary rule is the deterrence of future crime. In addition, society may have a general interest in preventing illegal governmental intrusions and it is difficult to measure the deterrent effect of the rule.

Finally, the exclusionary rule deters the government's misconduct.

Leon stands for the proposition that the exclusionary rule is designed to act as a deterrent against future violations of the Fourth Amendment. By distinguishing the two types of government officials—those in law enforcement and those in the judiciary, *Leon* merely focuses on the identity of the wrongdoer. Under the narrow *Leon* approach, the identity of the offending actor is the dominant factor. The Court pondered the impact of deterrence on two separate groups in the criminal justice system: the police and non-police government actors. The Court relied heavily on this "police officer versus nonpolice government actor" distinction.[128] The application of the exclusionary rule is measured mainly according to whether the offending actor is a law enforcement officer or a judicial officer.

If the mistake was made by non-police government actors, the exclusionary rule would not apply and the evidence would be allowed. In the Court's assumption, the exclusionary rule is designed only to deter police misconduct rather than to punish the errors of judges.[129] However, the Court provided no answer as to why the rule should target only law enforcement instead of the judiciary or any other non-police government actors. As a matter of fact, it is evident that the true purpose of the exclusionary rule is to deter the government's misconduct, including the courts. The Constitution's framers were not merely concerned with unreasonable searches and seizures by police, but by *the government* as a whole.[130] The prohibition against unreasonable search and seizure is directed at the government as a whole. As Justice Brennan noted in his *Leon* dissent:

> The [Fourth] Amendment, like other provisions of the Bill of Rights, restrains the power of the government as a whole; it does not specify only a particular agency and exempt all others. The judiciary is responsible, no less than the executive, for ensuring that constitutional rights are respected.[131]

This artificial distinction should be abolished. All government actors, both the police and non-police government actors, are obliged to honor the constitution. People should obey its constitution. By the same token, officers of that government were bound by the same constitution. Officers of the government, not limited to law enforcement officers, were restrained by the same constitution. The deterrent function of the exclusionary rule is its tendency to promote institutional compliance

---

128 In *Leon*, the form was "judge versus police officer."

129 *United States v. Leon*, 468 U.S. 897, 906 (1984).

130 Ibid., 929–30.

131 Ibid., 932 (1984) (Brennan, J., dissenting).

with constitutional requirements. Within the "one-government" conception, there should be no distinction between government actions, whether it happens to be a police mistake or a non-police government actors' mistake under the exclusionary rule. Therefore, the Court should not exempt non-police government actors, including judges, magistrates and court personnel, from the exclusionary rule.

Leon's flawed foundation poses a triple threat: it undermines the cost-benefit approach, calls into question the current structure of the Fourth Amendment itself, gutting the Fourth Amendment's substantial protections. The majority's use of the cost-benefit balancing test disregards Court's responsibilities to enforce constitutional guarantees. The exclusionary rule is inseparable from the underlying substantive guarantee. As will be discussed in more detail in 3.3.2, however, it indicates that the scales of the cost-benefit balancing test are initially tilted against the constitutional substantive guarantee.

3.3.2 The Metaphor of Balancing: Rhetorical Device

The United States judiciary is familiar with using balancing tests and balancing seems become the metaphor for procedural due process analysis. In *Lopez-Mendoza*,[132] for example, the Court found that the government's interest in preserving probative evidence under current procedure outweigh the benefit of applying the procedure.[133] Balancing was again adopted in *Pennsylvania Board of Probation and Parole v. Scott*;[134] the Court held the application of the exclusionary rule in parole revocation hearings would impair the functioning of state parole systems.[135] Against this cost, the Court held no deterrence could be gained through the application of the exclusionary rule.[136] However, the Court has examined "cost-benefit balancing test" from a somewhat skewed and unrealistic perspective. This metaphor is potentially problematic in three major ways.

First, the approach lacks an objective methodology.

According to the Court, there are at least two competing interests: the cost of exclusion (the fact that probative evidence cannot be considered by the trier of fact, impediment of the truth-finding process in court proceedings,[137] the guilty go free[138] and community safety cannot be enhanced) and the deterrent benefit (i.e.,

---

132 *Immigration and Naturalization Service v. Lopez-Mendoza*, 468 U.S. 1032 (1984).

133 Ibid., 1050–51.

134 *Pennsylvania Board of Probation and Parole v. Scott*, 524 U.S. 357 (1998).

135 Ibid., 364–7.

136 Ibid., 364–9.

137 *United States v. Leon*, 468 U.S. 897, 907 (1984).

138 *Immigration and Naturalization Service v. Lopez-Mendoza*, 468 U.S. 1032, 1050 (1984) (including as a cost of exclusion of illegal evidence from a deportation proceeding the fact that a person who was committing a crime at the time of the proceeding could go free); *United States v. Leon*, 468 U.S. 897, 907 (1984).

the deterrent effect of the exclusionary rule). Accordingly, the exclusionary rule will not apply when the cost to society of losing probative evidence outweighs the deterrent effect of the rule.

The exercise of judgment, however, pervades the creation and application of legal rules and standards in a way that is not true of economics. There are indisputably correct answers in economics, but not in law. The concept of "balancing" is itself a metaphor and this metaphor is abstract and ambiguous. The trouble with the current balancing approach is that this approach is a vague method of measuring imponderable interests against each other.

While the Court has increasingly relied on a cost-benefit balancing approach, under such approach, judges often fail to employ an objective standard and thus create the danger of arbitrary or biased results. This cost-benefit balancing is meaningless without some pre-existing objective criteria for valuing or comparing the interest at stake. Justice Brennan stressed that "placing the burden of proof on the proponents of the exclusionary rule's effectiveness becomes outcome determinative because measurement of costs and benefits is impossible."[139]

Furthermore, perhaps most problematic is the difficulty of comparing incommensurables in law. It is impossible for us to shut our eyes to the fact that some interests are simply incommensurable with others. How does one balance the "competing interests" and weigh incommensurable values without objective methodology? How does one balance a suspect's "right to be free from torture" against the state's interest in securing confessions through police investigation? How does one balance a suspect's "right to be free from illegal searches and seizures" against the state's interest in securing physical evidence through police searches? It is very difficult for a judge to compare apples with oranges. Listen once more to a sentence from Justice Scalia: "The scale analogy is not really appropriate, since the interests on both sides are incommensurate. It is more like judging whether a particular line is longer than a particular rock is heavy."[140] Since the court cannot compare them, as a consequence, they just simply choose between them.

For the reasons mentioned above, the deterrence and balancing approaches appear to be constitutionally irrelevant factors in determining the scope of the exclusionary rule; I instead deem the illegality of the means used to obtain the evidence to be constitutionally sufficient, by itself, to require exclusion.

Secondly, the outcome is predictable.

I am distrustful of the cost-benefit balancing approach in the Criminal Procedure Law. When the question of whether to admit or exclude illegally seized evidence is considered, a balancing test is employed in many cases.[141] Although

---

139 *United States v. Leon*, 468 U.S. 897, 942–3 (1984) (Brennan, J., dissenting).

140 *Bendix Autolite Corp. v. Midwesco Enters. Inc.*, 486 U.S. 888, 897 (1988) (Scalia, J., concurring).

141 *United States v. Calandra*, 414 U.S. 338 (1974); *United States v. Janis*, 428 U.S. 433 (1976); *Stones v. Powell*, 428 U.S. 465 (1976); *Rakas v. Illinois*, 439 U.S. 128

I have no doubt that the Court has tried to balance conflicting interests in the criminal process, I am also disappointed to find that the cost-benefit balancing approach as it stands contains no such balance. It seems make no sense to apply the "cost-benefit balancing approach"; so long as the Court adopted the approach, the outcome is predictable: costs will outweigh benefits. In other words, in the calculus employed by the Court, the highly emotional and nebulous "cost" of enforcing the Fourth Amendment always exceeds the "benefit" of vindicating the exclusionary rule. Since 1974, the Supreme Court has increasingly employed the "cost-benefit balancing test" to determine whether to apply the exclusionary rule[142] and decide the scope of exclusionary rule. The Court, under the balancing test, held the exclusionary rule inapplicable in:

1. grand jury proceedings;[143]
2. tax assessment proceedings;[144]
3. habeas corpus proceedings;[145]
4. where the evidence is offered against a person who had no expectation of privacy in the place things seized;[146]
5. deportation proceedings;[147]
6. where officers conducted the search based on a warrant that a reasonable officer could have believed to be valid;[148]
7. parole revocation proceedings;[149] and
8. sentencing hearings.[150]

In all these cases mentioned above,[151] without exception, once the Court applies the cost-benefit "balancing" approach, the evidence would be admissible. The courts have thought that because exclusion would not provide a significant deterrent effect in these circumstances, the rule should not be applied. The narrow cost-benefit balancing approach almost *always* concludes that the exclusionary

---

(1978); *Immigration and Naturalization Service v. Lopez-Mendoza*, 468 U.S. 1032 (1984).

142 *United States v. Calandra*, 414 U.S. 338, 349–50 (1974).

143 Ibid.

144 *United States v. Janis*, 428 U.S. 433, 453–4 (1976).

145 *Stones v. Powell*, 428 U.S. 465, 487–9 (1976).

146 *Rakas v. Illinois*, 439 U.S. 128 (1978).

147 *Immigration and Naturalization Service v. Lopez-Mendoza*, 468 U.S. 1032, 1050–51 (1984). (The Court addressed the issue of whether the exclusionary rule should apply in a deportation hearing, so as to exclude evidence illegally seized by INS officers).

148 *United States v. Leon*, 468 U.S. 897, 922 (1984).

149 *Pennsylvania Board of Probation and Parole v Scott*, 524 US 357, 359 (1998).

150 *United States v. Torres*, 926 F.2d 321, 324–5 (3d Cir. 1991); *United States v. Brimah*, 214 F.3d 854, 859 (7th Cir. 2000).

151 I have selected these cases from the United States Supreme Court decisions (in which the Court employed the deterrence-oriented cost-benefit balancing test) decided from 1970 to 2010.

rule's costs outweigh its benefits, especially considering that the perceived costs of undermining the truth-finding goal of the criminal trial are great. Under these circumstances, there exists no so-called balance at all.

The results have been predictable. The biased result is the costs of exclusion *always* outweigh the deterrent and the Court has routinely opted for admission rather than exclusion—as correctly noted by Kamisar: "perhaps even more so than in the First Amendment area, because the crime may be so heinous and the relevance of the evidence so overwhelming."[152] As a result, the cost-benefit balancing approach undermines the checking function of constitutional law.

Thirdly, the Court has taken a narrow view of the exclusionary rule.

The Court has taken an unnecessarily narrow view of the rule. As discussed below, it is illogical and unreasonable to limit the exclusionary rule to cases involving the police, criminal cases and intentional misconduct.

(1) The exclusionary rule is limited in the police. Under the narrow deterrence-oriented cost-benefit balancing, the identity of the offending actor (whether he is a police officer or a non-police government actor) becomes the dominant factor because of the inapplicability of the exclusionary rule if offending actors are "not adjuncts to the law enforcement team."[153] The Court generally suspends its operation of the exclusionary rule against non-police government actors. The Court's reasoning appears to include the notion that exclusion is not necessary to deter judicial officers, for example, judges, magistrates,[154] and clerks,[155] because they have "no stake in the outcome of particular criminal prosecutions,"[156] and there is nothing to deter. (2) The exclusionary rule is limited to criminal cases. The Court has consistently applied the exclusionary rule in criminal trials and has refused to extend it to civil proceedings and administrative contexts.[157] (3) The exclusionary rule is limited in intentional misconduct. *Leon* refused to apply the exclusionary rule where the purpose of the rule (i.e., where police officers act in good faith) would not be served.

But the identity of the offending actor is too limited. The *Leon* Court mistakenly assumed that the deterrence function can operate only when the offending actor is a law enforcement officer. Historical evidence shows that the exclusionary rule was *not* designed merely to deter police misconduct.[158] Although, one of the rationales behind the exclusionary rule is intended to deter police misconduct, it is

---

152 Yale Kamisar, "Does (Did) (Should) the Exclusionary Rule Rest on a 'Principled Basis' Rather than an 'Empirical Proposition'?" 565, 649.

153 *Arizona v. Evans*, 514 U.S. 1, 15 (1995).

154 *United States v. Leon*, 468 U.S. 897 (1984).

155 *Arizona v. Evans*, 514 U.S. 1, 15 (1995).

156 Ibid.

157 *United States v. Calandra*, 414 U.S. 338, 349–50 (1974); *United States v. Janis*, 428 U.S. 433, 447 (1976); *Immigration and Naturalization Service v. Lopez-Mendoza*, 468 U.S. 1032, 1050–51 (1984).

158 See 2.1.2.

not necessarily meant that the rule cannot deter non-police government actors in the future. Compared to the police, although non-police government actors do not have much stake in the outcome of searches and seizures, it does not necessarily mean that the exclusion of the evidence would not have any deterrent effect on them. It is still necessary for courts to deter judicial misconduct by applying the rule. The point is simply this: under the exclusionary rule, the judiciary may learn that it was not enough that they serve as "rubber stamp," and then devote greater care and attention during the warrant-issuing process. Because that warrant was subject to challenge at the later motion to exclude, it was important to the magistrates that the warrant be properly and carefully issued. If the overall educational effect of the exclusionary rule is considered, application of the rule to non-police government actors can still be expected to deter future non-police government actors' misconduct and have a considerable long-term deterrent effect.

To take another example, court clerks are responsible for inputting warrant information in the database and are essential actors in the criminal justice system in spite of whether their position is characterized as being part of law enforcement. It is reasonable to believe that court clerks responsible for updating information into the criminal justice system have an interest in its functioning, and the exclusionary rule would have a deterrent effect on them whose mistakes might result in evidence being excluded. It is also reasonable to presume that the judiciary are in the best position to monitor such errors and to apply the exclusionary rule to prevent their occurrence.

In addition, the job realities of the judiciary and the law enforcement are different. The *Leon* Court simply ignored the job realities of the former. Operation of the exclusionary rule would create deterrence to the judiciary, including judges, from improperly issuing warrants. I am skeptical that exclusion would not affect judicial behavior at all. In terms of systematic deterrence there is good reason to exclude evidence. The exclusionary rule can affect both intentional misconduct and carelessness as the rule may create an incentive for both law enforcement officers and judicial officers to act with greater care. Thus the exclusionary rule can be an appropriate tool for preventing carelessness by non-police government actors.

The problem with cost-benefit balancing is illustrated by *United States v. Leon*.[159] *Leon* is unnecessary and confusing. Severe problems beset the deterrence-oriented cost-benefit balancing approach to the exclusionary rule. The basic error in this approach is that the United States Supreme Court has taken an unnecessarily narrow view of the exclusionary rule's deterrence function. The exclusionary rule may shape the behavior of government institutions, not just police departments. The Court failed to appreciate that the exclusionary rule is necessary to remove effectively the incentive for *all* officers violating the Fourth Amendment rather than focusing on specific deterrence of the individual law enforcement officer who conducted the illegal searches and seizures. By applying the exclusionary rule to government officials, including both police and judicial, the court would afford

159 *United States v. Leon*, 468 U.S. 897 (1984).

more protection to its citizens. Neither the judges nor court personnel should be exempt from the exclusionary rule. From the foregoing it is clear that the narrow balancing approach could transform the exclusionary rule by making the exclusion of evidence the exception rather than the rule.

3.4 Ending the Myths of the Exclusionary Rule

There are at least three myths and misconceptions about the exclusionary rule.[160] These key myths of the rule are producing many problematic and sometimes controversial laws, policies and decisions.

Myth one: The exclusionary rule is the "fruit of the poisonous tree" doctrine It is a misunderstanding of the concepts of the exclusionary rule and the fruit of the poisonous tree doctrine. The exclusionary rule deals with the evidence which is the direct or primary result of a violation of the defendant's constitutional rights. For example, confession obtained by torture. Or a murder weapon found during the illegal search of a suspect's house.

By contrast, the fruit of the poisonous tree doctrine copes with the evidence which is derivative, or secondary in character.[161] For instance, a tortured confession may reveal the location where the suspect hid a gun used in a murder. Or an illegal search may turn up a key to an airport locker where stolen diamond rings are being kept. The poisonous tree doctrine deals with whether the gun and stolen diamond rings mentioned above are admissible.[162]

Myth two: The exclusionary rule excludes every single piece of evidence obtained, directly and indirectly, by any illegal method The important core of this myth about the rule holds that the exclusionary rule suppresses every single piece of illegally obtained evidence. Let me be clear that I am not saying the exclusionary rule should apply to all kinds of police misconduct and thus every single piece of illegally obtained evidence should be excluded. I do not mean to suggest that we exclude evidence every time the police err. Nor do I argue that any other evidence derived from police wrongdoing will be excluded. But I do contend that

160 These myths were believed by some lawyers, judges and scholars I discussed the exclusionary rule with, especially in China.

161 *Wong Sun v. United States*, 371 U.S. 471 (1963) (discussing the fruit of the poisonous tree doctrine).

162 China does not establish an explicit exclusionary rule, let alone follow the poisonous tree doctrine, such that courts may use evidence obtained as a result of excluded statements or physical evidence.

courts generally should exclude evidence obtained through illegal means from consideration at trial.

In addition, not every Fourth Amendment violation resulting in discovery of evidence mandates use of the search and seizure exclusionary rule. This has been recognized by the United States Supreme Court in its decision in *United States v. Calandra*[163] and *Herring v. United States*.[164] The *Calandra* Court argued that "the exclusionary rule has never been interpreted to proscribe the use of illegally seized evidence in all proceedings or against all persons."[165] The *Herring* Court explained: "We have never suggested that the exclusionary rule must apply in every circumstance in which it might provide marginal deterrence."[166]

Myth three: The exclusionary rule is the "monster" Some people might think that the exclusionary rule is "flood and the monster." The consequence of establishing the exclusionary rule is like letting the monster out of the cage. The costs of the exclusionary rule are usually overstated.[167] When the judge actually possesses the illegally obtained evidence and cannot use it to support its decision, this appears to be a cost of the rule. It must be remembered, however, that the police obtained the evidence in the first place only because they violated the Constitution or the Code of Criminal Procedure. Hence, loss of "evidence" is often a cost of the Constitution (in the United States, the Fourth Amendment) or the Code of Criminal Procedure (in China, Article 54 of the Code of Criminal Procedure) itself rather than of the means of enforcement—the exclusionary rule. Limited judicial resources and the nation's high crime rate situation should not be excuses not to establish the exclusionary rule in China. It is clear that the exclusion of illegally obtained evidence does affect some police some of the time. To protect freedom from torture and advance the administration of the criminal justice system, I call upon China to maintain the exclusionary rule immediately and to ensure that the right to be free from torture is safeguarded.

The exclusionary rule is not monstrous. According to an empirical study in the United States, all of the narcotics officers interviewed opposed elimination of the exclusionary rule.[168] In another study, 90 percent of the respondents in the survey which interviewed judges, prosecutors, and public defenders from Cook County, Illinois believe the exclusionary rule to be the best possible remedy, or could think of no better alternative.[169]

---

163 *United States v. Calandra*, 414 U.S. 338 (1974).

164 *Herring v. United States*, 129 S. Ct. 695 (2009).

165 *United States v. Calandra*, 414 U.S. 338, 348 (1974).

166 *Herring v. United States*, 129 S. Ct. 695, 700 (2009).

167 See 3.3.

168 Myron Orfield, Jr., "The Exclusionary Rule and Deterrence: An Empirical Study of Chicago Narcotics Officers" 1016, 1051.

169 Myron Orfield, Jr., "Deterrence, Perjury, and the Heater Factor: An Exclusionary Rule in the Chicago Criminal Courts" 75, 126.

3.5 Conclusion

No one wants criminals to go unpunished, but this was in fact an inevitable consequence the executive branch anticipated when enforcing the constitution and law. Everyone prefers more law and order, but this goal must be pursed with constitutional and legal limits. Indeed, the exclusionary rule is a construct based on common law, constitutions and human rights law. The rejection of torture and illegal search is characterized as a constitutional principle and *not* merely a criminal procedure or evidence rule.[170] In addition, there is reliable evidence that the exclusionary rule deters unlawful behavior. In brief, these empirical studies[171] support the conclusion that the exclusionary rule is an effective means of deterring police misconduct. The rule works better than any other alternatives that have been tried. Application of the exclusionary rule would deter the occurrence of future mistakes.

The deterrence-oriented cost-benefit balancing approach created in the Court represents a limitation on the exclusionary rule. This approach is an attractive but unworkable idea. The search and seizure exclusionary rule read, essentially, "if real evidence is obtained by illegal search, then exclude it." With the cost-benefit balancing approach, according to the Court, the rule should be, "if real evidence is obtained by illegal search, then exclude it *if* doing so will deter police misconduct." In practice, however, the exclusionary rule became "once the Court applies the cost-benefit balancing approach, costs will always outweigh benefits. Therefore, real evidence obtained by illegal search would be admissible." It introduces uncertainty about when the exclusionary rule will apply. The exclusionary rule is suffering in the age of deterrence-oriented cost-benefit balancing. Given the importance of the right to be free from torture, and the right to be free from illegal searches and seizures, the potential erosion through this balancing approach is particularly problematic.

But surely the search and seizure exclusionary rule should not be so limited, as many more violations of the Fourth Amendment are the result of carelessness than of deliberate misconduct. To further the purpose of the exclusionary rule (deterring the government's misconduct), the court needs to take a stand that will force government officials, both police and non-police government actors, to act in a way which more carefully safeguards the Fourth Amendment.

---

170 We will explore much of the detail of this theme in the succeeding chapters.

171 See 3.1.4.

Chapter 4
Theoretical Constitutional Foundation

The main focus of this chapter is to explore the theoretical constitutional foundation of the exclusionary rule. This is not merely a matter of the law of evidence. I argue that the existing functional approach to the exclusionary rule cannot be squared with constitutional theory. The exclusionary rule is one of the most crucial principles in constitutional criminal procedure which is an area long neglected in evidence law in England. Books on criminal procedure and evidence law in the United Kingdom find almost nothing to say about the rule from a constitutional perspective.

I propose to develop the rule in the context of constitutional law. I will introduce the cornerstone of the exclusionary rule at a constitutional level: the *separation of powers*. The rule is fundamentally based on the separation of powers, and it is not a castle in the air. It is particularly appropriate to rely upon the separation of powers doctrine to develop an understanding of the theoretical foundations of the rule. This is a central part of this book.

My discussion is divided into three parts. To set the stage for advancing this claim, it is necessary to understand how the separation of powers doctrine works. The first section introduces the crucial building block of the exclusionary rule—the separation of powers doctrine and then analyzes how the doctrine works in the criminal justice system and identifies its key aspects.

Another issue in this section is whether policing the police should be the responsibility of the judiciary or another branch of government. It is necessary for the judiciary to exercise supervision to preserve legality. The exclusionary rule will exercise its indirect control over police behavior in the field and exercise its indirect disciplinary authority over the police. Additionally, it is important to add that the right to a fair trial is directly connected to the exclusionary rule at the constitutional level.

The second section offers a basis for rethinking the relationship between the courts, the exclusionary rule and the police, and that it explains that this relationship is triadic and multi-directional. The primary idea behind this approach involves the recognition of the dynamic relationship among these three spheres.

The third section deals with the question of what will happen to investigative powers with no checks and balances. I argue that a right without checks and balances is no right at all. This section argues that the ECtHR's rejection of exclusion of evidence obtained by interception represents a step in its limitation of the Article 6 of the ECHR.

4.1 The Crucial Building Block: Separation of Powers

As early as 1748, Baron de Montesquieu (1689–1755), a French judge, and one of the most influential political thinkers, noted that "constant experience shows us that every man invested with power is apt to abuse it, and to carry his authority as far as it will go … To prevent this abuse, it is necessary from the very nature of things that power should be a check to powers."[1] According to Montesquieu, political power should be divided among legislative, executive, and judicial branches of government so as to ensure the people's liberty. He had shown the necessity of separating the three branches. The Declaration of the Rights of Man and the Citizen of 1789 (The French Declaration of 1789) also stated that "any society in which the guarantee of rights is not assured or the separation of powers not settled has no constitution."[2] Montesquieu's theory of the separation of powers had tremendous influence on the framers of the United States Constitution.

In determining the shape of a new government, the framers believed that three coordinate branches should strike a balance between a workable government and the protection of individual liberty. James Madison, the leading theoretician among the framers on the subject of separation of powers, explained that:

> If men were angels, no government would be necessary. If angels were to govern men, neither external nor internal controls on government would be necessary. In framing a government which is to be administered by men over men, the great difficulty lies in this: you must first enable the government to control the governed; and in the next place oblige it to control itself. A dependence on the people is, no doubt, the primary control on the government; but experience has taught mankind the necessity of auxiliary precautions.[3]

The framers' intent was to establish a system whereby the necessary separation of powers could be accomplished through a system of checks and balances. The Constitution provides the structure and functions of government as well as protecting individual rights. As Henry Scheiber has pointed out: "The first structural element that the framers regarded … as the more fundamental with regard to the defense of rights and liberties was the separation of powers."[4] The most pointed declaration of the separation of powers was drafted by John Adams, the American Founding's most sophisticated political theorist, in the 1780 Massachusetts Constitution. Adams' Article reads:

---

1 B.D. Montesquieu, *The Spirit of the Laws* (Hafner Publishing, New York 1975) 150.

2 Article 16 of the French Declaration of 1789.

3 J.E. Cooke (ed.), *The Federalist* (Wesleyan University Press, Middletown 1961) 349.

4 Harry Scheiber, "Constitutional Structure and the Protection of Rights" in A.E. Howard (ed.), *The United States Constitution: Roots, Rights, and Responsibilities* (Smithsonian Institution Press, Washington and London 1992) 183, 184.

> In the government of this Commonwealth, the legislative department shall never exercise the executive and judicial powers, or either of them; the executive shall never exercise the legislative and judicial powers, or either of them; the judicial shall never exercise the legislative and executive powers, or either of them; to the end it may be a government of laws and not of men.[5]

The United States Constitution is a written constitution based on the separation of powers. Federalism divides power vertically between the government and the states. The Constitution divides separate primary powers and functions of the government horizontally into three separate and distinct branches—legislative, executive, and judicial. The doctrine is grounded in the notion that all government powers should *not* rest in one branch. The accumulation of whole power in the hand of a single branch was something the framers feared would lead to tyranny.

The doctrine is expressed in the Constitution in the first three Articles. Article I, § 1, provides that "[a]ll legislative powers herein granted shall be vested in a Congress of the United States, which shall consist of a Senate and House of Representatives." Art. II, § 1, provides that "[t]he executive power shall be vested in a President of the United States of America." Article III, § 1, provides that "[t]he judicial power of the United States, shall be vested in one Supreme Court, and in such inferior courts as the Congress may from time to time ordain and establish."

The separation of powers doctrine is the absolutely structural safeguard centered on the Constitution. The major objective of the doctrine is to prevent governmental tyranny and protect liberty. In order to preclude a liberty-endangering concentration of power in one hand, the government decided to disperse power among three branches and preserve a balance among the branches. The President has a veto over congressional bills and the power to nominate federal judges. Congress has the power to override presidential vetoes and control over the size of the federal courts, as well as the power to impeach the federal officials. As Chief Justice Burger pointed out in *Nixon v. Fitzgerald*:[6]

> The essential purpose of the separation of powers is to allow for independent functioning of each coequal branch of government within its assigned sphere of responsibility, free from risk of control, interference, or intimidation by other branches.[7]

In the United Kingdom, we may argue that the British constitution consists of limited checks and balances and a partial separation of powers, but we *cannot* deny that the concept of separation of powers underlies the United Kingdom

---

5 Massachusetts Constitution Article XXX cited in *Morrison v. Olson*, 487 U.S. 654, 697 (1988) (Scalia J., dissenting).

6 457 U.S. 731 (1982).

7 457 U.S. 731, 760–61(1983) (Burger, C.J., concurring).

constitution.[8] There is a long history of checks and balances in the British constitution, although close ties exist between the executive and the legislative.

The separation of powers doctrine underlies the English constitution and plays an important part in British law. In *Entick v. Carrington*,[9] the Court of Common Pleas held that the executive could not seize books and papers without clear statutory authority. In *Duport Steels v. Sirs*,[10] Lord Diplock asserted that the British constitution is firmly based upon the separation of powers.

Again, in *Regina v. Her Majesty's Treasury, Ex parte Smedley*,[11] Sir John Donaldson M.R. emphasized that "[a]lthough the United Kingdom has no written constitution, it is a constitutional convention of the highest importance that the legislature and the judicature are separate and independent of one another, subject to certain ultimate rights of Parliament over the judicature."[12]

4.1.1 The Separation of Powers in the Criminal Context

Constitutional law and criminal procedure law have a long association that continues to the present day. The separation of powers doctrine is the most important element in the constitution's structural provision. At the level of theory, my exclusionary rule framework is grounded in the separation of powers.

Previous research about the separation of powers doctrine has focused almost entirely on constitutional law[13] and political theory.[14] They completely ignored the special role that the doctrine plays in the criminal justice system, a role consisting of the exercise of a reviewing function to ensure executive compliance with the criminal law. The doctrine in the context of criminal justice system is not some abstract political science theory. The Anglo-American separation of powers in this

8 It mainly refers to England and Wales.

9 19 How. St. Tr. 1030, 95 Eng. Rep. 807 (1765).

10 [1980] 1 WLR 142, 157.

11 [1985] 2 QB 657.

12 Ibid., 666.

13 See Burt Neuborne, "Judicial Review and Separation of Powers in France and the United States" (1982) 57 *New York University Law Review* 363; R.A. Schapiro, "Contingency and Universalism in State Separation of Powers Discourse" (1998) 4 *Roger Williams University Law Review* 79, and B.G. Peabody and J.D. Nugent, "Toward a Unifying Theory of the Separation of Powers" (2003) 53 *The American University Law Review* 1.

14 See M.H. Redish and E.J. Cisar, "'If Angels were to Govern': The Need for Pragmatic Formalism in Separation of Powers Theory" (1991) 41 *Duke Law Journal* 449; M.S. Paulsen, "The Most Dangerous Branch: Executive Power to Say What the Law is" (1994) 83 *Georgetown Law Journal* 217 and James Hyre, "The United Kingdom's Declaration of Judicial Independence: Creating a Supreme Court to Secure Individual Rights under the Human Rights Act of 1998" (2004) 73 *Fordham Law Review* 423.

context was designed to prevent the concentration of power in the hands of the executive or legislative, especially the executive.[15]

In the United Kingdom, the Human Rights Act 1998 gives a legal force and recognition to most of the fundamental rights for suspects and defendants in the criminal process of the ECHR. In the United States, there is plentiful constitutional regulation of many aspects of the criminal process, and in a similar vein, the exclusionary rule occurs in the arena of constitutional criminal procedure. For example, the Fourth Amendment acts as a check on police powers by prohibiting illegal searches and seizures.[16] The exclusionary rule forbids the introduction at criminal trials of evidence seized by an illegal search and seizure.[17] The Fifth Amendment regulates executive power by prohibiting prosecuting individuals twice for the same offense.[18] The exclusionary rule excluded statements elicited by means violating this amendment.[19] The Six Amendment provides the right to a speedy and public trial, the right to notice of criminal charges, the right to confrontation, and the right to assistance of counsel.[20] These powers are strictly defined. The exclusionary rule excluded statements elicited in violation of this amendment at criminal trials.[21]

There is a distinction between legislative, executive and judicial functions. In the realm of criminal process, the legislature is responsible for creating criminal law and criminal procedure law; the executive is limited to administering and enforcing these laws; the judiciary is to interpret the laws. Under the separation of powers scheme, each segment of the criminal justice system (for example, the legislature, police and court) is given both its own authority and the means to check the potential excess of other units. The criminal justice system of separate branches with independent powers that check and balance each other imposes on each branch specific structural responsibilities. If any branch fails to fulfill its responsibility, the function of the criminal justice system cannot exert. Each branch, especially the executive, cannot reach beyond the limits of the Constitution that created it. When controversy arises, the judiciary should enforce adherence to legislative standards by policing enforcement agents' obedience to legislative commands.

The reasons for the separation of powers between the judge (the judiciary) and police (the executive) go to the foundation of the exclusionary rule. As Justice Jackson so well stated in *Johnson v. United States*:[22]

---

15 See 2.1.
16 United States Constitution the Fourth Amendment.
17 *Weeks v. United States*, 232 U.S. 383 (1914).
18 United States Constitution the Fifth Amendment.
19 *Miranda v. Arizona*, 384 U.S. 436 (1966).
20 United States Constitution the Sixth Amendment.
21 *Massiah v. United States*, 377 U.S. 201 (1964).
22 333 U.S. 10 (1948).

> The point of the Fourth Amendment, which often is not grasped by zealous officers, is not that it denies law enforcement the support of the usual inferences which reasonable men draw from evidence. Its protection consists in requiring that those inferences be drawn by a neutral and detached magistrate instead of being judged by the officer engaged in the often competitive enterprise of ferreting out crime.[23]

It is decisive that the exclusionary rule is consistent with separation of powers in the criminal justice system. In this respect, the separation of powers principle is the foundation of the exclusionary rule.

4.1.2 Checks and Balances: Search Warrants

The whole point of the separation of powers is to ensure the checks and balances of each branch. The three separate branches of government need a system of checks over each other to keep them in their proper places. Because no branch possesses all of the powers of government, the actions of each are checked by the others. The Fourth Amendment gives the guarantee that a man's home is his castle beyond invasion by the government. The phrase "a man's home is his castle" originated from Justinian's Code.[24] The framers of the American Constitution constitutionalized the search and seizure principles of thc English common law.

Unreasonable searches and seizures are constitutionally prohibited. As I will discuss below, the criminal procedure law originally was designed to prevent any single branch in the criminal justice system from dominating the criminal process by dividing authority among three offices. The Anglo-American legal system has developed a procedure that is dependent on the issue of judicial warrant prior to execution of the search. The normal procedure should require a judicial warrant and only in exceptional circumstances should prior judicial authorization be unnecessary.[25] In addition, only the judiciary is constitutionally empowered to issue search warrants.

The warrant is the best way to ensure that privacy is not arbitrarily invaded. The search warrant is a method of checks and balances for the judiciary to oversee the executive. The legislative establish a procedure by which the police seek a neutral's determination as to whether probable cause for a search or seizure exists. As Justice William Douglas noted, the Fourth Amendment requires a neutral fact-

23 333 U.S. 10, 13-14 (1948).

24 Robert McWhirter, "Molasses and the Sticky Origins of the Fourth Amendment" (2007) 43 *Arizona Attorney* 16, 18.

25 In Canada, for instance, the lack of a search warrant makes a search prima facie unreasonable and the onus is the prosecution to establish that it is reasonable. See *R v. Collins* (1987) 33 CCC (3d)1, 38 DLR (4th) 508.

finder to issue search warrants.[26] The clear purpose of a warrant is to allow a neutral judge to assess whether the police have probable cause to conduct a search.

In order to discover physical evidence, the police may wish to search the suspect's premises. A police officer searching a dwelling house should have some valid basis in law for the intrusion. In the United Kingdom, for example, Section 8 of PACE requires an individual judicial authorization for entry into private premises and empowers a justice of the peace to issue a search warrant. It provides:

> If on an application made by a constable a justice of the peace is satisfied that there are reasonable grounds for believing—(a) that [an indictable offence] has been committed; and (b) that there is material on premises [mentioned in subsection (1A) below] which is likely to be of substantial value (whether by itself or together with other material) to the investigation of the offence; and (c) that the material is likely to be relevant evidence; and (d) that it does not consist of or include items subject to legal privilege, excluded material or special procedure material; and (e) that any of the conditions specified in subsection (3) below applies [in relation to each set of premises specified in the application], he may issue a warrant authorizing a constable to enter and search the premises.[27]

Furthermore, in connection with firearms, theft and drugs cases, there are several statutes under which search warrants may be issued. Section 46(1) of the Firearms Act 1968 empowers a magistrate to issue a search warrant where he is satisfied by information provided on oath that there are reasonable grounds for suspecting that an offense under the Act has been, is being, or is about to be committed.[28]

Under Section 26(1) of the Theft Act 1968, a search warrant may be issued by a justice of the peace in respect of premises where he is satisfied by information that there are reasonable causes for suspecting that stolen goods are on the premises.[29] Moreover, under Section 23(3) of the Misuse of the Drugs Act 1971, a search warrant may be issued by a magistrate in respect of premises where he is satisfied by information by the police that there are reasonable grounds for suspecting

---

26 *Katz v. United States*, 389 U.S. 347, 359 (1967).

27 Section 8 of the Police and Criminal Evidence Act 1984.

28 Section 46 (1) of the Firearms Act 1968 provides: If a justice of the peace or, in Scotland, the sheriff, is satisfied by information on oath that there is reasonable ground for suspecting—(a) that an offence relevant for the purposes of this section has been, is being, or is about to be committed; or (b) that, in connection with a firearm or ammunition, there is a danger to the public safety or to the peace, he may grant a warrant for any of the purposes mentioned in subsection (2) below.

29 Section 26(1) of the Theft Act 1968 provides: (1) If it is made to appear by information on oath before a justice of the peace that there is reasonable cause to believe that any person has in his custody or possession or on his premises any stolen goods, the justice may grant a warrant to search for and seize the same…

that controlled drugs are on the premises.[30] Of course, in some situations, the requirement of a judicial warrant may be dispensed with, for example, "emergency searches" or "searches by consent."

In the United States, the Fourth Amendment requires the courts to issue warrants[31] and protects people from illegal searches and seizures. The amendment commands that a warrant should be issued not only upon probable cause supported by oath, but also specify the place to be searched, and the persons or things to be seized. Searches and seizures must be grounded in probable cause; police officers should have probable cause before acting and they should obtain a warrant before acting or run the risk of suppression of evidence obtained thereby. This requirement repudiates general warrants and makes general searches impossible and prevents the search of one place under a warrant describing another. The purpose of this amendment is to let a neutral judge decide whether a search or seizure is appropriate and necessary as opposed to a potentially biased police officer engaged in the enterprise of ferreting out crime.

Obtaining a warrant requires the police officer to justify the arrest or the search before it is made. When the police would like to search a place, they must present materials to apply search warrants to support their application. The affidavit, for instance, might allege that "[a]ffiants have received reliable information from a credible person and do believe that heroin, marijuana, barbiturates and other narcotics and narcotic paraphernalia are being kept at the above described premises for the purpose of sale and use contrary to the provisions of the law."[32]

Magistrates or judges are empowered to issue warrants. The Fourth Amendment allows only the judiciary to issue warrants, and that illegal searches emanating from the executive are a violation of its legal territory. The judiciary will screen warrant requests and decide whether the materials presented establish probable cause to believe that specific items related to the crime will be found at the designated location.

---

30 Section 23 (3) of the Misuse of the Drugs Act 1971 provides: If a justice of the peace (or in Scotland a justice of the peace, a magistrate or a sheriff) is satisfied by information on oath that there is reasonable ground for suspecting—(a) that any controlled drugs are, in contravention of this Act or of any regulations made thereunder, in the possession of a person on any premises; or (b) that a document directly or indirectly relating to, or connected with, a transaction or dealing which was, or an intended transaction or dealing which would if carried out be, an offence under this Act, or in the case of a transaction or dealing carried out or intended to be carried out in a place outside the United Kingdom, an offence against the provisions of a corresponding law in force in that place, is in the possession of a person on any premises, he may grant a warrant authorising any constable acting for the police area in which the premises are situated at any time or times within one month from the date of the warrant, to enter, if need be by force, the premises named in the warrant, and to search the premises …

31 *Katz v. United States*, 389 U.S. 347 (1967).

32 *Aguilar v. Texas*, 378 U.S. 108, 109 (1964).

The police have to provide a sufficient basis for a finding of probable cause; otherwise, the search warrant will not be issued and that the evidence obtained as a result of the warrant will be inadmissible. The purpose served by this mechanism of checks and balances for obtaining a judicial warrant is that it provides the detached scrutiny of a neutral judge, which is a more reliable safeguard against improper searches. If the executive branch fails to respect the Fourth Amendment or law, then the most effective remedy at the court's disposal is to exclude the evidence uncovered by those illegal investigative methods.

The right to privacy is attached to prohibitions on illegal searches and illegal interception.[33] The exclusionary rule safeguards privacy and protection from government intrusion and manifests a preference for privacy over the level of law enforcement efficiency which could be achieved if police were permitted to search without probable cause or to intercept private conversation without judicial authorization.

4.1.3 The Enforcement of Constitutional Rights

The people have the right to be secure in their persons, houses and other possessions against illegal searches, seizures, invasions of privacy or interceptions of communications by eavesdropping devices or other methods. The mere existence of these rights is insufficient to ensure realization. These rights should be constitutional rights, which the sole question on the table is how these rights should be enforced.

The primary means of enforcing these rights is the exclusionary rule. The rule serves as the critical safety valve against malpractice by the executive branch. The separation of powers requires an independent judiciary armed with judicial review. The judiciary should have independent power to oversee the executive's adherence to constitutional and statutory standards. Judicial review of the police investigation methods is necessary to maintain proper checks and balances. Courts should concern themselves with how evidence is obtained. Some responsibility for control over police misconduct must rest with on the court.

The role of the judiciary is to ensure that government is conducted according to the law. The judiciary should strike down the unconstitutional actions of the other two branches. Judges should not act as "rubber stamps" in the review of warrant applications as the judiciary is not as part of the executive. Judge Kaufman accurately argued that:

> Judicial independence is not a cliché conjured up by those who seek to prevent encroachments by the other branches of government. The term is one of art,

---

33 See 4.3.3.

> defined to achieve the essential objective of the separation of powers that justice be rendered without fear or bias, and free of prejudice.[34]

The courts, when a case arises, can always step in when officers violate the law. Brock CJ explained that:

> Enforcement of the [exclusionary] rule places the parties in the position they would have been in had there been … no violation of the defendant's constitutional right to be free of searches made pursuant to warrants issued without probable cause. In so doing, the rule also preserves the integrity of the judiciary and the warrant issuing process.[35]

The exclusionary rule is an effective judicial response to illegal investigative methods used by the executive branch. Once the police have got used to unchecked authority, limits on their powers are unlikely to be respected.

As regards the United Kingdom, it is quite easy for the ECtHR to argue that "[i]t is not the role of the Court to determine … whether unlawfully obtained evidence … may be admissible"[36] and that its admissibility is a matter for regulation under national law. In a similar vein, the House of Lords can also argue that supervision of the police is not its judicial function.[37]

However, interposing the judge between the police and the individual strikes the right balance between the constitutional rights of the defendant and the powers of the government. Enforcement of the right to be free from torture, and the right to be free from illegal searches and seizures will encourage fair police practices. It would be wrong for the courts to rely on illegally obtained evidence.

4.1.4 The Fair Trial Doctrine

There are two goals of regulating the criminal process: first is to bring suspected offenders to trial so as to produce accurate determinations, and to ensure that fundamental rights are protected in those processes.[38] Justice is often perceived as procedural fairness.[39] Fairness is absolutely essential in order to produce an accurate verdict. The court's main duty is to hold a fair trial. One of the most

---

34 I.R. Kaufman, "The Essence of Judicial Independence" (1980) 80 *Columbia Law Review* 671, 701.

35 *The State of New Hampshire v. Rafael Canelo a/k/a Rafael Canelo Valdez*, 139 NH 376, 1105 (1995).

36 *Khan v. United Kingdom* (App no 35394/97) (2001) 31 EHRR 45 [34].

37 *R v. Sang*, [1980] AC 402, 436.

38 Andrew Ashworth and Mike Redmayne, *The Criminal Process* (3rd edn, Oxford University Press, Oxford, 2005) 55.

39 Cf. John Rawls, *Political Liberalism* (Columbia University Press, New York, 1996).

important global legal developments is the growing recognition that the suspect will be given a right to a fair trial in both international and domestic law. For example, the Universal Declaration of Human Rights (UDHR) Articles 10 and 11,[40] the International Covenant on Civil and Political Rights (ICCPR) Article 14[41] and the Police and Criminal Evidence Act (PACE) 1984 Section 78(1).[42] In the criminal justice context the most important Articles of the European Convention

---

40 Article 10 of the Universal Declaration of Human Rights provides: Everyone is entitled in full equality to a fair and public hearing by an independent and impartial tribunal, in the determination of his rights and obligations and of any criminal charge against him. Article 11 of the Universal Declaration of Human Rights provides: Everyone charged with a penal offence has the right to be presumed innocent until proved guilty according to law in a public trial at which he has had all the guarantees necessary for his defence …

41 Article 14 of the International Covenant on Civil and Political Rights provides: 1. All persons shall be equal before the courts and tribunals. In the determination of any criminal charge against him, or of his rights and obligations in a suit at law, everyone shall be entitled to a fair and public hearing by a competent, independent and impartial tribunal established by law … 2. Everyone charged with a criminal offence shall have the right to be presumed innocent until proved guilty according to the law. 3. To have adequate time and facilities for the preparation of his defense and to communicate with counsel of his own choosing; (a) To be informed promptly and in detail in a language which he under stands of the nature and cause of the charge against him; (b) To have adequate time and facilities for the preparation of his defense and to communicate with counsel of his own choosing; (c) To be tried without undue delay; (d) To be tried in his presence, and to defend himself in person or through legal assistance of his own choosing; to be informed, if he does not have legal assistance, of this right; and to have legal assistance assigned to him, in any case where the interests of justice so require, and without payment by him in any such case if he does not have sufficient means to pay for it; (e) To examine, or have examined, the witnesses against him and to obtain the attendance and examination of witnesses on his behalf under the same conditions as witnesses against him; (f) To have the free assistance of an interpreter if he cannot understand or speak the language used in court; (g) Not to be compelled to testify against himself or to confess guilt. 4. In the case of juvenile persons, the procedure shall be such as will take account of their age and the desirability of promoting their rehabilitation. 5. Everyone convicted of a crime shall have the right to his conviction and sentence being reviewed by a higher tribunal according to law. 6. When a person has by a final decision been convicted of a criminal offence and when subsequently his conviction has been reversed or he has been pardoned on the ground that a new or newly discovered fact shows conclusively that there has been a miscarriage of justice, the person who has suffered punishment as a result of such conviction shall be compensated according to law, unless it is proved that the non-disclosure of the unknown fact in time is wholly or partly attributable to him. 7. No one shall be liable to be tried or punished again for an offence for which he has already been finally convicted or acquitted in accordance with the law and penal procedure of each country.

42 Section 78(1) of the Police and Criminal Evidence Act the provides: In any proceedings the court may refuse to allow evidence on which the prosecution proposes to rely to be given if it appears to be the court that, having regard to all the circumstances, including the circumstances in which the evidence was obtained, the admission of the

for the Protection of Human Rights and Fundamental Rights (ECHR) are Articles 5, 6 and 7. Article 6 guarantees the right to a fair trial.[43] The essence of Articles 6 is the right to a fair trial.

The right to a fair trial applies in civil and criminal proceedings. This study concentrates on the latter. It refers to the right to be free from arbitrary arrest and coerced confessions, the right to silence, the presumption of innocence, the privilege against self-incrimination, the right to be tried within a reasonable time and the right to an independent and impartial tribunal. The guarantee of fairness under the ECHR is not limited to the trial, but underpins the whole criminal process including "the way in which evidence was taken."[44]

It is important to add that the right to fair trial is directly connected to the exclusionary rule at the constitutional level. The connection between the right to fair trial and the exclusionary rule is that the use of illegally obtained evidence against defendants is intrinsically antithetical to the concept of fundamental fairness. Take for example, the confession exclusionary rule; tortured confessions generate unfairness in three basic senses. First, the unreliable statements result from illegal methods that civilized society abhors. These methods threaten the dignity and autonomy of the individual. Secondly, the unreliable statements threaten to produce unreliable outcomes and thus the conviction of innocents. Thirdly, the right to a fair trial encompasses the entitlement to fair play to established rules and procedures in criminal process. Even though these products of such "unfair play" by law enforcement officials are "reliable," once the criminal justice system relies

---

evidence would have such an adverse effect on the fairness of the proceedings that the court ought not to admit it.

43 Article 6 of the European Convention for the Protection of Human Rights and Fundamental Rights provides: 1. In the determination of his civil rights and obligations or of any criminal charge against him, everyone is entitled to a fair and public hearing within a reasonable time by an independent and impartial tribunal established by law. Judgment shall be pronounced publicly but the press and public may be excluded from all or part of the trial in the interests of morals, public order or national security in a democratic society, where the interests of juveniles or the protection of the private life of the parties so require, or to the extent strictly necessary in the opinion of the court in special circumstances where publicity would prejudice the interests of justice. 2. Everyone charged with a criminal offence shall be presumed innocent until proved guilty according to law. 3. Everyone charged with a criminal offence has the following minimum rights: (a) to be informed promptly, in a language which he understands and in detail, of the nature and cause of the accusation against him; (b) to have adequate time and facilities for the preparation of his defence; (c) to defend himself in person or through legal assistance of his own choosing or, if he has not sufficient means to pay for legal assistance, to be given it free when the interests of justice so require; (d) to examine or have examined witnesses against him and to obtain the attendance and examination of witness on his behalf under the same conditions as witnesses against him; (e) to have the free assistance of an interpreter if he cannot understand or speak the language used in court.

44 *Teixeira de Castro v. Portugal* (App no 25829/94) (1998) 28 EHRR 101 [34].

on these products, the resulting convictions are inevitably infected with unfairness. The concept of "fairness" influences the criminal justice system from the start of the investigation to the release of the offender. This illegally obtained evidence is naturally inconsistent with a criminal justice system devoted to due process. That is why, in England, for example, if any question of the exclusion of physical evidence on the ground that the circumstances in which it has been obtained would make it unfair to admit it, then the judge should exercise his discretion under Section 78 of PACE to exclude it. The criterion under Section 78 is the effect which the admission of the evidence would have on the fairness of the proceedings.

4.2 The Court, Exclusionary Rule and Police

The exclusionary rule has three essential characteristics: the first, for the court, is the protection of constitutional rights; the second, for the rule per se, is preventing arbitrary governmental invasion and the third, for the police, is adherence to the constitution law and criminal procedure law. Without these, courts and the police may readily become engines and tools of tyranny. I will offer a fresh perspective on this argument from the perspective of comparative criminal procedure.

In this section I am going to explore the complicated and constantly shifting interplay between the court (the judiciary branch), exclusionary rule and police (the executive branch) in the criminal justice system. The basic objective is to provide a broader way of thinking about the role of the exclusionary rule in the context of the criminal process. The role of the rule in the criminal justice system is a difficult issue. The rule is not an independent variable in the system. The criminal justice system is not static. The relationship is dynamic and interactive. Therefore, legal reasoning should respond to a variety of interrelated concerns.

4.2.1 The Court and Exclusionary Rule: Judicial Discretion?

> The most significant role for judges is to protect the individual criminal defendant against the occasional excesses of the popular will, and to preserve the checks and balances within our constitutional system that are precisely designed to inhibit swift and complete accomplishment of popular will.
>
> Justice Scalia[45]

The first matter to be examined here is whether an English trial judge should have the discretion to exclude physical evidence discovered as a result of an illegal search. I will use the House of Lords' landmark decision in *R v. Sang*[46] as a basis for discussion of this issue. The House of Lords' puzzling and opaque decision

---

45 Antonin Scalia, "The Rule of Law as a Law of Rules" (1989) 56 *University of Chicago Law Review* 1175, 1180.

46 [1980] AC 402.

is not satisfying from the practical point of view, especially in the twenty-first century. *Sang* is a confusing case; deeper consideration of this issue reveals the fallacy of the reasoning employed in *Sang*. Although the House of Lords tried to clarify the position concerning the exclusionary rule, I argue that it leaves many questions unanswered.

The House of Lords failed to reach a consensus as to whether the court has the discretion to exclude illegally obtained real evidence. The Court split 3:2 on the issue of whether discretion to exclude evidence existed as a consequence of "fairness" to the defendant. Two of their Lordships, Lord Diplock and Viscount Dilhorne, took the most restrictive interpretation of discretion of the court. Lord Diplock asserted that the judge has no discretion to refuse to admit relevant and otherwise admissible evidence on the ground that it was obtained improperly or by unfair means. Therefore, the House of Lords is not concerned with how the evidence was obtained.[47] With respect to real, reliable, physical evidence, according to the House of Lords, supervision of the police is not a judicial function. In addition, Viscount Dilhorne claimed that previous cases were wrong, because he had not been able to find any authority for the general principle for the exclusionary rule. I argue that both of their opinions were far from accurate. I reach that opinion on two grounds.

First, there are many reported cases in which the House of Lords have expressed that there is judicial discretion.

In England, before *Sang* the general rule was that criminal judges had discretion to decline to admit evidence on the ground that operation of the rule of admissibility would operate unfairly against the accused. Police trickery, bribery, threats, or other oppressive behavior to an accused could trigger the discretion.[48]

As early as 1955, *Kuruma*[49] was the first case regarded as establishing the existence of this kind of judicial discretion. Lord Goddard stated that:

> No doubt in a criminal case the judge always has a discretion to disallow evidence if the strict rules of admissibility would operate unfairly against the accused … If, for instance, some admission of some piece of evidence … had been obtained from a defendant by a trick, no doubt the judge might properly rule it out.[50]

A number of subsequent decisions re-affirmed the discretion recognized in *Kuruma.* Returning to the words of Lord Denning in 1970:

> The common law does not permit police officers … to ransack anyone's house, or to search for papers or articles therein, or to search his person, simply to see if

47 [1980] AC 402, 436.

48 *Callis v. Gunn* [1964] 1 QB 495 (QB) 501.

49 *Kuruma Son of Kaniu v. Reginam* [1955] 1 All ER 236 (PC) 239.

50 [1955] 1 All ER 236 (PC) 239.

> he may have committed some crime or other. If police officers should so do, they would be guilty of a trespass. Even if they should find something incriminating against him, I should have thought that the court would *not* allow it to be used in evidence against him, if the conduct of the police officers was so oppressive that it would not be right to allow the Crown to rely on it.[51]

In the 1978 case of *Jeffrey v. Black*,[52] Lord Widgery CJ once again emphasized:

> [I]f the case is such that not only have the police officers entered without authority, but they have been guilty of trickery or they have misled someone, or they have been oppressive or they have been unfair, or in other respects they have behaved in a manner which is morally reprehensible, then it is open to the justices to apply their discretion and decline to allow the particular evidence to be let in as part of the trial.[53]

Courts play the most important role in administering the criminal justice system. They are there to do justice according to the constitution and law. Judges should enhance their roles as citizens' protectors against the arbitrary actions of those in authority. If the executive branch attempts to erode the judiciary's power, for example, to issue judicial warrants, the appropriate judicial response is to exclude evidence produced by unlawful searches. The exclusionary rule is the device for judges to administer criminal justice.

Furthermore, in *Sang*, Lord Diplock claimed that the judge at the trial has no discretion to disallow illegally retained physical evidence.[54] I argue that judges do have discretion to exclude illegally retained evidence. Undoubtedly the judiciary has discretion to determine the admissibility of criminal evidence. The discretion applies to evidence obtained not only by coercive interrogations but also by illegal searches. In the administration of criminal justice, judicial supervision is becoming increasingly important. It is hard to imagine that judges could say it is *not* their concern at any stage of the criminal process.

From the very beginning of the investigative stage of the criminal process, before issuing a warrant, judges have to evaluate evidence and then decide whether the police establish that probable cause exists for a particular search and seizure.[55] Additionally, judges have to decide on detention orders and issue warrants for

---

51 *Ghani and Others v. Jones*, [1970] 1 QB 693 (QB) 706 (emphasis added).

52 [1978] 1 All ER 555.

53 Ibid., 559.

54 *R v. Sang*, [1980] AC 402, 437.

55 Probable cause is an indispensable element of the Fourth Amendment. It requires "reasonably trustworthy information ... sufficient ... to warrant a man of reasonable caution in the belief that an offense has been or is being committed" or certain evidence of a crime will be located in the specific place to be searched. See *Brinegar v. United States*, 338 U.S. 160, 175-176 (1949).

telephone taps. Otherwise, magistrates will become rubberstamps for police. Accordingly, the judiciary plays a crucial role in checking police power.

Next, at the trial stage, for judges, the power and duty to exclude illegally obtained evidence is the *necessary* tool to enforce constitutional protections. It is the role of the judge to determine whether unlawfully obtained evidence should be inadmissible. Lord Justice-General Cooper, one of Scotland's greatest judges, expressed the same view in *Chalmers v. HM Advocate*,[56] saying that judges have "the power and duty to exclude from the cognizance of a jury evidence which … is inadmissible."[57] The power and duty from judges acts as a direct check against the abuse of power in executive branch.

If the trial judge were not given discretion to suppress illegally obtained evidence, would that mean the police could use any illegal methods they prefer to collect evidence, and that judges would have no choice but to accept all of them? The answer is definitely no. Except for judges, I cannot imagine any other participants in the criminal justice system have the ability to check the arbitrary police power. Indirect supervision from the court is not replaceable by legislation and internal regulation.

While the exclusionary rule is historically limited to involuntary confessions in England, the rule should not only be limited to cases where the evidence was unreliable. Judges should not consider the probative weight of the evidence prior to ruling upon its admissibility. The probative weight of the evidence and admissibility of evidence are *completely* two different issues. According to English law, a confession must not have been by torture. If it was, it is excluded, and the question of reliability need not be addressed.[58] We should focus on the examination of the manner in which the evidence was obtained instead of whether the prejudicial effect outweighed its probative value.

Only five years after *Sang*, Parliament promulgated the Police and Criminal Evidence Act 1984, which rejected the opinion of Lord Diplock and Viscount Dilhorne. Under Section 78, judges *have* discretion to exclude evidence where admission of evidence "would have such an adverse effect on the fairness of the proceedings that the court ought not to admit it." One of PACE's significant functions is that it clearly directs the judiciary to police the police.

The issue in England is whether excluding unlawfully obtained evidence would avoid unfairness to the accused at his trial. Under this premise, illegal evidence is excluded not because such evidence was unfairly obtained, but because it is unfair to prosecute the accused based on this illegally obtained evidence.

It is the role of the court to determine whether unlawfully obtained evidence should be admissible. All judges have discretion to exclude illegally obtained evidence. This discretion should not limited to the evidence were unreliable and

56 1954 JC 66.

57 Ibid.

58 J.A. Andrews and Michael Hirst, *Andrews and Hirst on Criminal Evidence* (4th edn, Jordan, Bristol 2001) 19, 24.

should not be exercised in a manner that compromises the defendant's right to be free from torture. Judges should exercise their discretion to exclude illegally obtained evidence rather stick to the stereotypical passive attitude of the traditional search and seizure exclusionary rule.

4.2.2 The Exclusionary Rule and Police: Tremendous Impact

Prior to 1961, the United States Supreme Court had not interpreted the Constitution to require application of the exclusionary rule in state criminal proceedings. The states had the option to adopt or reject the exclusionary rule. The Court landmark decision in *Mapp v. Ohio*[59] reversed *Wolf*[60] and required all states to exclude evidence procured by means of an illegal search and seizure from criminal proceedings through the due process clause of the Fourteenth Amendment. *Mapp* closed "the only courtroom door remaining open to evidence secured by official lawlessness"[61] in violation of the constitutional guarantee against unreasonable illegal searches and seizures. The impact of the exclusionary rule and *Mapp* were manifold.

First, the issuance of search warrants sharply increased.

As Leonard Reisman, the head of the New York City Police Department's legal bureau, observed that "before [*Mapp*], nobody bothered to take out search warrants."[62] The primary result of the exclusionary rule was a sharp increase in the number of search warrants issued.[63] History tells us that the police seldom applied for search warrants prior to *Mapp* in cities where the exclusionary rule was not adopted. The use of search warrants by the Boston police prior 1961 was negligible, but afterward, about 950 warrants were issued in 1963. In Cincinnati—another city whose courts had admitted illegally obtained evidence prior to *Mapp*—only three warrants were obtained by the police in 1958. The police obtained none in 1959. Only seven warrants were obtained in 1960. However, in 1964 the issuance of search warrants increased to 113.[64] Similarly, according to the New York report, in the New York City the issuance of search warrants increased from virtually zero in 1961 to about 17,900 in 1966.[65]

Secondly, the police began to take the Fourth Amendment seriously.

---

59 367 U.S. 643 (1961).

60 *Wolf v. Colorado*, 338 U.S. 25 (1949).

61 *Mapp v. Ohio*, 367 U.S. 643, 654–5 (1961).

62 S.E. Zion, "Detectives Get a Course in Law: They Return to Classroom to Study Court Decisions" *The New York Times* (New York April 28, 1965) at 50.

63 B.C. Canon, "Is the Exclusionary Rule in Failing Health?: Some New Data and a Plea against a Precipitous Conclusion" (1974) 62 *Kentucky Law Journal* 681, 709.

64 Ibid.

65 Lawrence Tiffany, Donald Mclntyre, and Daniel Rotenberg, *Detection of Crime: Stopping and Questioning, Search and Seizure, Encouragement and Entrapment* (Little, Brown, Boston 1967) 87; See also Arlen Specter, "*Mapp v. Ohio*: Pandora's Problems for the Prosecutor" (1962) 111 *University of Pennsylvania Law Review* 4.

Prior to the adoption of the exclusionary rule law enforcement agents were under no substantial pressure to seek clarification of the Fourth Amendment. California Supreme Court Chief Justice Roger Traynor, one of the most respected jurists, expressed his concern about the issue of the admissibility of illegally obtained evidence and observed that:

> [T]ime after time [illegally obtained evidence] was being offered and admitted as a routine procedure. It became impossible to ignore the corollary that illegal searches and seizures were also a routine procedure subject to no effective deterrent; else how could illegally obtained evidence come into court with such regularity.[66]

That is the reason why California converted to the exclusionary rule in 1955. Justice Traynor authored the California opinion adopting the rule in *People v. Cahan*.[67] Illuminating in this regard is this quote by Leonard Reisman, after *Mapp* decision: "Although the U.S. Constitution requires warrants in most cases, the U.S. Supreme Court had ruled that evidence obtained without a warrant—illegally if you will—was admissible in state courts. So the feeling was, why bother?"[68]

Thirdly, the response from the law enforcement officials was that the rule caused "tidal waves and earthquakes."

The conclusion about the exclusionary rule's huge impact in the United States is the prevailing view among many law enforcement officials, especially police professionals in the field. Ervin, J. of the Superior Court of Pennsylvania compared the *Mapp* case to a "hurricane" which "swept over our fair land."[69] Arlen Specter, assistant district attorney in Pennsylvania, likened it to a "revolution":

> Police practices and prosecution procedures were revolutionized in many states by the holding in … *Mapp v. Ohio* that evidence obtained from an illegal search and seizure cannot be used in a criminal proceeding … [There are indications] that the imposition of the exclusionary rule upon the states is the most significant event in criminal law since the adoption of the Fourteenth Amendment … *Mapp* has rewritten the criminal law treatise for states which had admitted evidence regardless of law it was obtained.[70]

---

66 Roger Traynor, "*Mapp v. Ohio* at Large in the Fifty States" (1962) 1962 *Duke Law Journal* 319, 321–2.

67 282 P2d 905 (Cal. 1955).

68 S.E. Zion, 'Detectives Get a Course in Law: They Return to Classroom to Study Court Decisions' *The New York Times* (New York 28 April 1965) 50.

69 *Common v. One 1955 Buick Sedan*, 198 Pa. Super. 133 (1962).

70 Arlen Specter, "*Mapp v. Ohio*: Pandora's Problems for the Prosecutor" (1962) 111 *University of Pennsylvania Law Review* 4, 4.

Michael Murphy, the former Police Commissioner of the City of New York, described the effects of the *Mapp* case and observed that:

> I can think of no decision in recent times in the field of law enforcement which had such a dramatic and traumatic effect as this … [*Mapp] create tidal waves and earthquakes* which require rebuilding of our institutions sometimes from their very foundations upward. Retraining sessions had to be held from the very top administrators down to each of the thousands of foot patrolmen and detectives engaged in the daily basic enforcement function.[71]

4.2.3 The Court and Police: Judicial Supervision

The judiciary and the executive have different functions and responsibilities. The court, acting in the name of the Constitution, should have the constitutional authority to police the police and ensure that the government acts within the bounds set by the Constitution and legislature. This function could *not* be better exercised by other governmental agencies. The executive branch is not neutral and disinterested under the separation of powers doctrine. The powers of the executive are vast but not unlimited. The judiciary, separated from other branches of government, is in a position to check and balance the legislature and executive and ensure that they respect the constitutional rights of individuals, for example, the right to be free from illegal searches and seizures, the right to remain silent and the right to an attorney. The courts should not abandon their judicial role. There are two central elements of the judicial role, as President of the Supreme Court of Israel Abaron Barak acknowledged in 2006, "One element is bridging the gap between law and society … The second major task is to protect the constitution and democracy."[72] A vital role of courts is to protect citizens from oppressive police conduct.[73] The duty of the judge is to administer justice according to law. It is the courts that are the chief guarantors against torture and illegal searches. It is the role of courts to prevent executive usurpation and guard constitutional and legal rights.

A supreme court for the protection of fundamental rights is, without question, an essential component of the modern exclusionary rule. Every court has not only the inherent power but also the duty to oversee execution action and ensure that the police do not misuse their power to oppress citizens. The role of the courts is to stand between the state and its citizens to make sure that the police anticrime efforts conform to the Constitution.

---

71 Michael Murphy, "Judicial Review of Police Methods in Law Enforcement" (1966) 44 *Texas Law Review* 939, 941.

72 Abaron Barak, *The Judge in a Democracy* (Princeton University Press, Princeton 2006) xvii, xviii.

73 *Terry v. Ohio*, 392 US 1, 15 (1968).

The judiciary should refuse to condone brutalized extraction of confessions or other illegal acts committed in obtaining evidence of guilt. Otherwise, it will indirectly encourage wrongful acts carried out by agents of the executive. The use of illegal evidence is "denied in order to maintain respect of law; in order to promote confidence in administration of justice; in order to preserve the judicial process from contamination."[74] Therefore, evidence obtained by illegal means which risks the conviction of the innocent should be rejected. The court should provide the guiding jurisprudence in these areas.

4.3 Powers without Checks and Balances?

In this section, I will show that history has proven when courts do not step in by employing the exclusionary rule, the problem of police wrongdoing may get worse; the privacy of individual citizens will be more frequently infringed by the government. I will use three illustrations: the Judges' Rule, unlawfully retained DNA evidence, and interception, to show that without the checks and balances in the criminal context some rights of the defendant would be a mere form of words.

4.3.1 Judges' Rules

The first and a classic example is the Judges' Rules in England. From 1912 to 1984, the treatment of suspects in England was governed by the Judges' Rules. The Rules originated from the then Lord Chief Justice Alverstone's letter to the Chief Constable of Birmingham in response to the question whether it was correct to caution after there had been two contradictory cases on this point. On the same circuit one judge had censured a member of his force for having cautioned a prisoner, while another judge had censured a constable for having omitted to do so.[75] These guidelines, promulgated in 1912, amended and revised in 1918, 1930, 1947, 1948 and 1964,[76] had become the main guidelines for the police officers on methods of interrogation.

Rule I asked the police to state the following caution before questioning a suspect, "Do you wish to say anything? You are not obliged to say anything unless you wish to do so but whatever you say will be taken down in writing and may be given in evidence."[77] Principle (e) of the preamble to the 1964 version of the Judges' Rules, derived from *Ibrahim*[78] and *Gunn*,[79] stated that:

74 *Olmstead v. United States*, 277 U.S. 438, 485 (1928) (Brandeis, J, dissenting).

75 Mark Berger, "Rethinking Self-Incrimination in Great Britain" (1984) 61 *Denver Law Journal* 507, 519.

76 Practice Note [1964] 1 WLR 152.

77 Rule IIIof the Judges' Rules.

78 *Ibrahim v. The King*, [1914] AC 599 (PC).

79 *Callis v. Gunn*, [1964] 1 QB.

> It is a fundamental condition of the admissibility in evidence against any person, equally of any oral answer given by that person to a question put by a police officer and of any statement made by that person, that it shall have been voluntary, in the sense that it has not been obtained from him by *fear of prejudice* or *hope of advantage*, exercised or held out by a person in authority, or by *oppression*.[80]

These Rules also required police investigators to inform and caution suspects of their right to keep silent and to consult a lawyer. Pursuant to Rule II:

> As soon as a police officer has evidence which would afford reasonable grounds for suspecting that a person has committed an offence, he shall caution that person or cause him to be cautioned before putting to him any questions, or further questions, relating to that offence.[81]

In addition, Rule III of the Rules reads:

> (a) Where a person is charged with or informed that he may be prosecuted for an offence he shall be cautioned in the following terms … (b) It is only in exceptional cases that questions relating to the offence should be put to the accused person after he has been charged or informed that he may be prosecuted …[82]

However, the Rules were not legally binding. They had no legal force whatsoever. In effect, they were *merely* administrative guidelines for interrogation procedure and not viewed as having the status of law. In *R v. Voisin*,[83] where the accused had written down some words at the request of the police without caution, in admitting the evidence, Lawrence J. stated that:

> These rules have not the force of law; they are administrative directions the observance of which the police authorities should enforce on their subordinates as tending to the fair administration of justice. It is important that they should do so, for *statements obtained from prisoners, contrary to the spirit of the rules, may be rejected as evidence* by the judge presiding at the trial.[84]

Without the check and balance system, it is no wonder that the Rules were frequently flouted by the police.[85] Nor did they bind the courts; breaches of the

---

80 Preamble to the Judges' Rules (emphasis added).
81 Rule II of the Judges' Rules.
82 Rule III of the Judges' Rules.
83 [1918] All ER Rep 491.
84 Ibid. (emphasis added).
85 Michael Zander, *Cases and Materials on the English Legal System* (8th edn, Butterworths, London 1999) 117.

Rules were ignored by the judges. As Zuckerman accurately observed that "before 1985 the courts tended to turn a blind eye to breaches of the Judges' Rules,"[86] the violations of the police, even if clear-cut, did not automatically result in the exclusion of evidence thus obtained. The judges were reluctant to exclude confessions only because they had been obtained in breach of the Rules. Under these circumstances, it was not surprising the Judges' Rules only had very limited impact on the police. The Rules did not provide genuine protection to suspects.[87] That is why, in 1981, the Royal Commission on Criminal Procedure recommended to "replace the vagueness of the Judges' Rules with a set of instructions which provide strengthened safeguards to the suspect and clear and workable guidelines for the police."[88]

4.3.2 Unlawfully Retained DNA Evidence

The second example is the unlawfully retained DNA evidence. DNA technology is a well-established investigative tool and is having a huge impact on the criminal justice systems both in the United Kingdom and United States. The United Kingdom was the first nation to establish the forensic DNA database, the National DNA Database (NDNAD), in the world in 1995.[89] The United States has the largest forensic DNA database in the world.[90] Police can compare traces of DNA samples collected from suspects or found at crime scenes with samples in a DNA database to prove the identity of the perpetrator of a crime without the unreliability of eyewitness. Police also can match evidence and DNA samples left at different crime scenes to find out whether there is a link between different crimes. DNA may indicate whether a defendant was present or absent at a crime scene or if a suspect committed rape.[91]

States are authorized to collect DNA samples from suspects with certain statutory limitations. PACE, for example, authorized the Forensic Science Service to retain samples from persons after an acquittal or dismissal.[92] In 2003, the Criminal Justice Act allowed police to retain samples from people arrested for a recordable offense, regardless of whether or not they are charged.[93]

---

86 Ashworth Zuckerman, "Miscarriages of Justice and Judicial Responsibility" (1991) *Criminal Law Review* 492, 498.

87 Barry Cox, *Civil Liberties in Britain* (Penguin Books, Middlesex 1975) 175.

88 The Royal Commission on Criminal Procedure, "Report" (Cm 8092, 1981) [4.109].

89 Henry Greely and others, "Family Ties: The Use of DNA Offender Databases to Catch Offenders' Kin" (2006) 34 *The Journal of Law, Medicine and Ethics* 248, 250.

90 The Forensic Use of Bioinformation: Ethical Issues, Nuffield Council Bioethics Report [1.2] (2007).

91 Kenneth Bredemeler, "In Virginia, Freedom from Fear for Crime Victims, Relief for Families" *Washington Post* (Washington July 7, 1999) A14.

92 Section 63.

93 Criminal Justice Act, United Kingdom (2003).

The retention of DNA samples is more controversial than the taking of the bioinformation. The old Section 64(1) of PACE before 2001, provided that:

> If—(a) fingerprints or samples are taken from a person in connection with the investigation of an offence; and (b) he is cleared of that offence, they must be destroyed as soon as is practicable after the conclusion of the proceedings.

In *R v. Nathaniel*,[94] the defendant was convicted of a rape committed in 1989. The primary evidence consisted of his DNA profile which was obtained from a sample taken from him in relation to offenses in respect of which he was acquitted. The issue was whether it was permissible to use in evidence a sample which should have been destroyed under the then text of Section 64 of PACE.

Under old Section 64(1) of PACE the DNA profiles should have been destroyed as soon as practicable. However, his DNA profile was not destroyed. On the contrary, four years later, in 1993 it was entered on the computer index by the police again. Then the defendant was found to be connected to another rape in 1989. The court held that the evidence should have been excluded under Section 78 of PACE and said:

> To allow that blood sample to be used in evidence at a trial four years after the alleged offences when the sample had been retained in breach of statutory duty and in breach of the undertakings to the defendant must, in our view, have had an adverse effect on the fairness of the trial. It should not in our view have been admitted.[95]

Although Section 64(3B) (b) made no provision for the consequences of a breach of the prohibition, I believe that Section 64(3B) (b) which does not provide for the exclusion of evidence is not only ineffective but also dangerous. As Her Majesty's Inspectorate of Constabulary indicated, more than 50,000 samples were being held unlawfully in 2000.[96]

If the citizenry are not willing to "pay the price" that will inevitably accompany the enforcement of the law, they should persuade the legislature to amend the law.[97] This objection leveled at the exclusionary rule is misdirected. The Royal Commission on Criminal Procedure of 1981 claimed that:

---

94 [1995] 2 Cr. App. R. 565.

95 Ibid.

96 The Forensic Use of Bioinformation: Ethical Issues, Nuffield Council Bioethics Report [4.37] (2007).

97 In 2001, Section 64(1) of PACE was substituted by Section 82 of the Criminal Justice and Police Act 2001. The Criminal Justice and Police Act removed the requirement to delete police records from those who were charged but never convicted of a recordable offence.

> We have rejected the use of an automatic exclusionary rule as a general means of securing compliance with the statutory rules we propose … the rule that we propose should be made by Parliament to control police conduct rather than to the court's exercise of a discretion to admit evidence or not.[98]

The issue here is that the law was already set down by Parliament; however, the police just ignored the law. The provisions are decided by the legislature. It is not the function of the court to reconsider them. If the police obeyed old Section 64(1) of PACE, they could not keep every DNA profile, and link many suspects to all sorts of crimes. However, this is what legislative branch decided should happen. This is the price we would have had to pay to protect people from unrestrained government power. Otherwise, the provision in question is an empty gesture.

In addition, in *S and Marper v. United Kingdom*,[99] the ECtHR also held that the indefinite retention of DNA of persons acquitted or persons having their prosecution discontinued violated Article 8 of ECHR.[100]

4.3.3 Interception

Because of technological advances, covert investigative measures have become a much more powerful, cheaper and more convenient tool for police force. On the one hand, these measures, such as interception[101] of telecommunications by post, telephone or a computer network, photographic surveillance in a public place, use of tracking devices, could be useful and effective tools to obtain evidence in prosecuting organized criminal gangs and public officials who engage in corruption. On the other hand, any given circumstances mentioned above may be illegal, not in accordance with the Regulation of Investigatory Powers Act 2000 and Article 8 of the ECHR.

The ECtHR regarded the protection for privacy as an important concern. Using the ECHR as a legal basis, ECHR, Article 8, Section 1 establishes privacy as a fundamental right: "Everyone has the right to respect for his private and family life, his home and his correspondence." This is the right which is clearly recognized and protected in the ECHR.

However, in a series of decisions issued from 1984 until now, the ECtHR held that the United Kingdom was in violation of Article 8 through police violation of individuals' rights of personal privacy by installing a listening device in a person's

---

98 The Royal Commission on Criminal Procedure, "Report" (Cm 8092, 1981) [4.131].

99 *S and Marper v. United Kingdom* (App no 30562/04 and 30566/04) (2009) 48 EHRR 50.

100 *S and Marper v. United Kingdom* (App no 30562/04 and 30566/04) (2009) 48 EHRR 50 [125].

101 The "interception" means the obtaining of information about the contents of a communication without the consent of the parties involved.

home,[102] police cell[103] or intercepting telephone calls made to or from a person's office.[104]

The first example is *Malone v. United Kingdom*[105] in 1984. Malone was prosecuted for handling stolen goods and during the trial the prosecution admitted that his telephone had been tapped on the authority of a Home Secretary's warrant. Malone argued that the tapping was unlawful and he had a right to privacy in accordance with Article 8 of the ECHR. The High Court held that the phone tapping was not illegal and Malone's case was rejected.[106] The ECtHR, however, held that the United Kingdom had not provided the minimum degree of legal protection to which citizens were entitled under the rule of law and, accordingly, there had been a violation of Article 8.[107]

Giving effect to the United Kingdom's obligation under Article 8, the Interception to Communications Act 1985 was intended to provide a clear framework for authorizing and controlling interceptions on a public telecommunication system.

Similarly, in *R v. Effick and R v. Mitchell*,[108] defendants were convicted of conspiracy to supply controlled drugs. The evidence against them was incriminating telephone conversations with a third party on a cordless telephone which had been intercepted by police. No warrant for interception had been obtained. The House of Lords held that intercepted conversations were admissible as a cordless telephone does not form part of the public telecommunications system.

Furthermore, in *Halford v. United Kingdom*,[109] Halford, a former assistant chief constable, was pursuing a case of discrimination against her chief constable. While this was proceeding her telephone at police headquarters was monitored and she argued that this infringed her privacy contrary to Article 8. However, as the Interception of Communications Act 1985 did not cover the tapping of such conversations, the United Kingdom again fell foul of Article 8. The ECtHR held that the right to private life and correspondence applied to conversations held on

---

102 *Malone v. United Kingdom* (App no 8691/79) (1984) 7 EHRR 14 [64]; *Khan v. United Kingdom* (App no 35394/97) (2001) 31 EHRR 45 [25]; *Armstrong v. United Kingdom* (App no 48521/99) (2002); *Taylor-Sabori v. United Kingdom* (App no 47114/99) (2002); *Allan v. United Kingdom* (App no 48539/99) (2002); *Chalkley v. United Kingdom* (App no 63831/00) (2003) 37 EHRR 30 [24]; *Lewis v. United Kingdom* (App no 1303/02) (2004) 39 EHRR 9 [18]; and *Elahi v. United Kingdom* (App no 30034/04) (2007) 44 EHRR 30 [18].

103 *Allan v. United Kingdom* (App no 48539/99) (2003) 36 EHRR 12 [35] and *Wood v. United Kingdom* (App no 23414/02) (2004) 36 EHRR 12 [33].

104 *Halford v. United Kingdom* (App no 20265/92) (1997) 24 EHRR 523 [51].

105 *Malone v. United Kingdom* (App no 8691/79) (1984) 7 EHRR 14.

106 *Malone v. Metropolitan Police Commissioner*, [1979] Chancery Division 344.

107 *Malone v. United Kingdom* (App no 8691/79) (1984) 7 EHRR 14.

108 [1995] AC 309.

109 *Halford v. United Kingdom* (App no 20605/92) (1997) 24 EHRR 523.

premises of an employer and the interference of Halford's telephone constituted a breach of her privacy as defined in Article 8.[110]

In *R v. Ahmed*,[111] evidence of tape-recorded conversations between defendants, which were intercepted from a police station and by the police, was admissible in their prosecution's case for conspiracy to supply controlled drugs. The Court of Appeal held that to intercept conversations within a private telephone system did not infringe the Interception of Communications Act 1985 Section 1(1) which applied only to the public system.

The main purpose of the Regulation of Investigatory Power Act 2000 was to ensure that the investigatory powers were used with the ECHR. Both making an unauthorized interception on a public[112] and private[113] system are offenses.

In *R v. Khan (Sultan)*,[114] the police were trespassing when they illegally installed the listening device in the house in 1992. At that time, as the United Kingdom lacked legal framework for the use of electronic listening devices by the police, there was no statutory authority for the installation of the device. The surveillance had been in violation of the Article 8 of the ECHR, because it was not authorized by statute. Khan was convicted of a drugs offense entirely on illegally obtained taped recordings.

This case raised issue of whether evidence of the illegally obtained taped conversation was admissible. His counsel argued that the evidence should be excluded because it was obtained illegally and in breach of Khan's right to privacy under the ECHR. The trial judge, the Court of Appeal,[115] and the House of Lords[116] all disagreed.

Khan took his case to the ECtHR. The Strasbourg Court held unanimously that there had been a violation of the right to privacy, but did not hold that this required the evidence to be excluded. The ECtHR did not see the breach of right to privacy as requiring the exclusion of the evidence.[117]

I assert that the use of evidence illegally obtained by interception conflicted with the requirement of a fair trial guaranteed by Article 6. Evidence obtained by such interference should therefore be excluded using the exclusionary rule under Section 78 of PACE. The decision by the ECtHR in *Khan* may be criticized on a variety of grounds.

First, the ECtHR mistakenly mixed up *the admissibility of evidence* and *the weight of the evidence*.

---

110 *Halford v. United Kingdom* (App no 20605/92) (1997) 24 EHRR 523 [51].

111 1994 WL 1062614.

112 Section 1(1) of the Regulation of Investigatory Power Act 2000.

113 Sections 1(2) (5), 3 and 4 of the Regulation of Investigatory Power Act 2000.

114 [1997] AC 558.

115 [1995] 1 Cr App R 242.

116 [1996] 2 Cr App R 440.

117 *Khan v. United Kingdom* (App no 35394/97) (2001) 31 EHRR 45.

The ECtHR held that "the applicant had ample opportunity to challenge both the authenticity and the use of the recording."[118] This claim overlooks the fact that the question in the present case is *not* the authenticity of the contested tape recording. It was not disputed that the recording in issue is genuine. Khan has never challenged the authenticity of the recording. It is not the point. The question must be answered is whether the proceedings as a whole, including the way in which the evidence was obtained, were fair.

Secondly, it seems that a trial cannot be described as "fair" where evidence obtained in breach of rights and freedoms protected by the Convention.

The right to a fair trial holds a prominent place in a democratic society. Article 6 includes a requirement of lawfulness. Fairness presupposes compliance with the law. The focus of Article 6 is on the right of a criminal defendant to a fair trial. It is a right to be exercised within the framework of the administration of the criminal law.

Even if the ECtHR's function was limited to deciding whether the appellant had a fair trial, I cannot imagine one can speaking of a fair trial if evidence is obtained in breach of fundamental right guaranteed by the ECHR. The ECtHR has narrowed protections in right to a fair trial, while expanding the authority of the sovereign to intrude into an individual's life.

Finally, the ECHR must be interpreted as a whole.

The case law of the ECtHR interpreting Article 3 has provided a model for Article 6. While the actual language of Article 3 prohibits torture and is silent as to the admissibility of evidence obtained by torture, the Strasbourg Court has interpreted the bar on torture to include a bar on using the evidence procured by torture.[119] The use of evidence obtained as a result of acts of violence or brutality or other forms of treatment that can be characterized as torture would be in violation of Article 6 and thus inadmissible.

With regard to Article 3, the admissibility of evidence is not merely "a matter for regulation under national law."[120] If it is not the role of the ECtHR to determine the admissibility of illegally obtained evidence, why bother the ECtHR held that the evidence obtained by torture were inadmissible. There is no reason why the admissibility of evidence becomes merely a matter for regulation under national law when it comes to Article 6.

The modern understanding of the scope of the search and seizure exclusionary rule is the prohibition of illegal searches and seizures, and interception protects reasonable expectation of privacy. If the ECtHR really wants to "ensure the observance of the engagement undertaken by the contracting states to the convention,"[121] then judicial courage is needed to recognize the right to be free

118 Ibid., [38].

119 *Jalloh v. Germany* (App no 54810/00) (2006) [105–6].

120 *Khan v. United Kingdom* (App no 35394/97) (2001) 31 EHRR 45 [34].

121 Ibid.

from illegal searches and seizures. The suppression of illegally taped material is necessary. *Khan* is rather disappointing and can be seen as lacking in courage.

4.4 Conclusion

Criminal procedure should impose procedural regulations on the criminal process by constitutional command. In this chapter, I have argued that the separation of powers principle, the constitution's central structural principle, is the crucial building block of the exclusionary rule. It is important to maintain the checks and balances of three separate and distinct branches of government in the criminal justice system. Each branch is expected to remain with its sphere and to respect the powers that the criminal justice system has assigned to the other branches. The judicial branch is intended to serve as a check on powers of the legislative and executive branches. The primary concern of the separation of powers doctrine is not to promote efficiency in the criminal justice system but to prevent the exercise of arbitrary power from the executive branch.

All government actors in the criminal justice system are obliged to honor the constitution; otherwise, without the safeguard of the exclusionary rule, the right to be free from torture, and the right to be free from illegal searches and seizures would be reduced to mere words. This view would require strict adherence to the separation of powers doctrine in criminal matters.

The exclusionary rule is tied to the separation of powers concept and can be justified on the principle of the separation of powers. The exercise of the exclusionary rule is to preserve separation of powers in criminal justice system. Without a secure structure of separated powers, the rule would be worthless. The system of checks and balances is central to a government that would not trample individual rights. The exclusionary rule exercises a reviewing function to ensure executive obedience with the constitutional commands.

The right to be free from illegal searches and seizures is one of the most important constitutional rights. Although it is a constitutionally protected interest, it is sometimes be ignored by the police. In fact, at least to some extent, the exclusionary rule helped the Anglo-American system to evolve into a system that no longer ignores illegal police activity. The exclusionary rule is a safeguard intended as an implementation of the separation of powers.

In order to take the concept of separation of powers seriously, courts should define the exact constitutional line and tell the police what they should and should not do at the same time by establishing the exclusionary rule framework. The judiciary should protect the right to be free from illegal searches and seizures. In failing to protect this constitutional liberty of the accused, the court has not fulfilled its constitutional duty.

Government agents tend to assign great weight to the interest in apprehending and convicting criminals; the danger is that the rights of defendants are often neglected. I argue that, first, the investigative techniques, used by government agents should be prescribed by law and authorized by a prosecutor or judge rather than by the executive such as the Home Secretary or chief constable. Second, these operations must be necessary and proportionate to a suspect's right to privacy. Warrantless interception seriously compromises the right to private life and the Fourth Amendment's prohibition on warrantless searches and seizures. The law should warrant and regulate the use of covert listening devices; otherwise it may constitute an interference with defendant's right of private life. Courts should consider both the lawfulness and regularity in which the evidence is obtained as well as the fairness of the trial. I contend that without exclusionary rule, there are very few instances in which evidence obtained by the use of covert listening devices has been ruled inadmissible.[122]

---

122 See 4.3.3.

PART II
Reform for the Future: The Chinese Exclusionary Rule

Introduction

The purpose of this project is to find an appropriate model for those countries that have not yet developed the exclusionary rule. This part focuses on the exclusionary rule in the People's Republic of China (PRC or China), and this is the first book to consider this specific issue in depth.

Police torture, using torture as a technique to retain evidence in the course of police interrogation, remains a very serious problem throughout China.[1] Police torture has become a topic of pressing Chinese national concern because many innocent persons have confessed to crimes that they did not commit. As the previous part argued, the exclusionary rule is a useful legal tool available to courts and the best check for regulating police coercion and violence in the Anglo-American criminal justice system. The rule can be used in a new institutional strategy of checks and balances to prevent arbitrary government. This part will shine a spotlight on the exclusionary rule in China.

In order to establish judicial control over acts by the police, constituting intrusions into constitutionally protected rights of suspects, this part will examine actual legal practices with a view to identifying the most effective means of regulating police torture and illegal searches in China. There is an urgent need to abolish torture through the exclusionary rule.

My argument is that the exclusionary rule will help China to abolish police torture in interrogation; the rule will extract the firewood from under the cauldron. If it is true that police torture is systemic, then it should be tackled at the level of the criminal justice system through structural reform. Certainly, however, the exclusionary rule is no panacea for fixing all the problems in the Chinese criminal justice system overnight. This is not, of course, to argue that the exclusionary rule alone is a "magic formula" for the problem of torture in China. To establish the rule is not the end of our task; it is the first. Other steps are needed. For example, assistance of counsel during police interrogation, mandatory videotaping or audiotaping of interrogation in custody,[2] mandatory physical examination

---

1 See 5.1.

2 For a discussion of how videotaping interrogations can be used to prevent police torture tactics in the United States, see S.A. Drizin and B.A. Colgan, "Let the Cameras

in detention centers and prisons, establishment of the privilege against self-incrimination, prompt investigation of all allegations of torture, and improvement of training courses for all practitioners in the criminal justice system. In 2005, for example, the Supreme People's Procuratorate (SPP) of China decided to experiment with videotaping police interrogations. From 2006 to 2007, over 2,800 People's Procuratorate videotaped 34,973 cases; 1,100 technicians and 5,000 investigators were trained. No torture was found in these cases.[3] I argue that if the Chinese want to prevent the future use of torture by the police, they *must* adopt criminal justice reforms that include, but go beyond, the exclusionary rule.

Roll: Mandatory Videotaping of Interrogations is the Solution to Illinois' Problem of False Confessions" (2001) 32 *Loyola University Chicago Law Journal* 337, 424.

3 Wang Xinyou, "最高檢：凡是訊問全程錄像 均未發現違法辦案" [The Supreme People's Procuratorate: No Violation is Found When the Cameras are Rolling] (2007). Availabe at: http://www.spp.gov.cn/site2006/2007-11-14/0002116095.html (accessed 10 Oct., 2013).

Chapter 5
Confessions Obtained by Police Torture

Discussion of the confession exclusionary rule would be incomplete without mention of police torture. Thus, to examine the confession exclusionary rule, one must first examine police torture. In China, police torture is at the root of many wrongful convictions, imprisonment, and executions of innocent people. In almost all cases of wrongful conviction, police torture plays a central role in the crafting of a case designed to achieve a conviction. However, to say China has no desire to solve the problem of police torture is simply untrue. Since 1996, under the external and internal pressure, China has made substantial strides in formalizing its criminal justice system by amending existing laws, enacting new laws and creating new policy agencies. Many amendments were made to the Code of Criminal Procedure and Criminal Law to ensure the protection of defendants' rights. China emphasized the right to be free from torture through frequent high-level meetings and public statements. At a conference held by the Supreme People's Procuratorate (SPP) in 2006, Wang Zhenchuan, SPP Deputy Secretary, acknowledged that the phenomenon of obtaining evidence by illegal methods is very pervasive. Some law enforcement personnel use torture regularly to coerce confessions from suspects. Almost all miscarriages of justice identified in the past few years involved illegal investigation. From 2005 to 2006, around 1,500 enforcement agents and police were convicted of having used their privileges to encroach on civil rights.[1]

In 2007 and 2009 Deputy Procurator-General Zhu Xiaoqing, regarding police torture, said that "almost all of the flawed cases discovered in recent years are closely linked to confessions extracted during interrogations."[2] The next year, the former Chief Justice of the Supreme People's Court of China, Xiao Yang, instructed Chinese judges to "strictly follow the evidence rules and ensure that innocent citizens are not prosecuted" at the First Session of the Eleventh National People's Congress.[3]

---

1 Bureau of Democracy, Human Rights and Labor, U.S. Department of State, Country Reports on Human Rights Practices—2007, China (March 11, 2008).

2 Human Rights in China, "Take Action: Put an End to Torture in China" (Sep. 10, 2008). Available at: http://www.hrichina.org/public/contents/press?revision%5f.id=84825&item%5f.id=84810 (accessed Oct. 10, 2013).

3 "最高人民法院工作報告" [Work Report of the Supreme People's Court] (Mar. 22, 2008). Available at: http://news.xinhuanet.com/newscentre/2008-03/22/content_7837838.htm (accessed Oct. 10, 2013).

In this chapter, I will argue that the current Chinese legal structure for combating police torture is not adequately armed. The fight against police torture has been plagued by many legal loopholes. Moreover, I do not accept that police torture is the unavoidable price of combating high crime rate in China. The prohibition against torture should be absolute. The exclusionary rule does not impede effective crime control; instead, it is the legal tool necessary to regulate police wrongdoing and to reduce miscarriages of justice.

The first part of this chapter describes the nature and magnitude of the problem of police torture in China, highlighting examples of proven torture cases that came to the public's attention. I will discuss the Chinese Criminal Law, the Code of Criminal Procedure, their judicial interpretations, and some of the provisions and policies that violate the spirit of the exclusionary rule. It critiques the way in which China treats a suspect who has suffered from torture.

Additionally, it identifies and analyzes barriers to (and restrictions on) effective protection of the right to be free from torture. It reflects upon the values that appear to dominate the Chinese criminal process from a lawyer's perspective.[4] In other words, it examines the crime control model[5] adopted by Chinese law enforcement officers, especially in the context of the exclusionary rule. The criminal process conforms to the crime control model, routinely granting wide latitude and discretion to the police, the prosecutors, and the judges. The Chinese criminal process can be captured by an evocative metaphor: "relay race." I found that the procedural law of China embraces the crime control values articulated by Packer[6] and argue that many of the rules which govern the criminal process are based on the principles similar to those which shape Packer's crime control model. China promotes an ordered society and an efficient judicial system at the expense of individual liberties.

This chapter next turns to the wide powers of Chinese police. There are so many cases in which the police have operated without clear and uniform standards. In these cases, the police felt they were above the law. The wide scope of police power without judicial supervision opened the door to police torture. What role do courts currently play in monitoring police torture and illegal searches? For the reasons I will discuss, very little. There was almost no judicial supervision. It violated a core component of the constitution, the separation of powers.

This chapter then challenges the proposition that the ban on police torture should be lifted. I argue that prohibition on police torture is absolute and the confessions obtained by torture cannot be justified under any circumstances. As illegally obtained confession and physical evidence can lead, and has led, to wrongful convictions, I contend that it would be a dangerous obstacle to the administration of justice if evidence obtained by illegal methods could be used against the defendants in China. The lack of an exclusionary rule is the major factor in the continuing widespread use of torture by the police.

4 See 5.2.4.
5 See 1.3.
6 See 1.3.

5.1 Causes of Police Torture

The police never have the authority to violate the law, only the incentive. The principal contribution of the confession exclusionary rule is simply to reduce that incentive. Despite official commitments to the prohibition against police torture, torture is a widespread practice in China. The routine practice of torture by political, military and judicial personnel is a long, sad history of savage barbarity. The torturers include state security agents, military personnel, the police, prison officers[7] and medical professions.[8] In 2005, Manfred Nowak, UN Special Rapporteur on Torture, visited Beijing and pointed out that the practice of torture remains widespread throughout China.[9]

In addition, according to the United States State Department's 1999 Report on Human Rights Practices, defendants frequently suffer "torture and mistreatment," "forced confessions, arbitrary arrest and detention, lengthy incommunicado detention, and denial of due process."[10] The report continued that "the judicial system denies criminal defendants basic legal safeguards and due process because authorities attach higher priority to maintaining public order and suppressing political opposition than to enforcing legal norms."[11] In 2007, the United States State Department stated that Chinese police officers used "electric shocks, beatings, shackles, and other forms of abuse."[12] Torture of suspects in China occurs during periods of incommunicado detention before a suspect is brought before a court.

Furthermore, no matter how "effective" torture is, it comes at a steep price: tens of thousands of victims suffer. From January 1979 to June 1980, over 10,000 cases of alleged police abuses were heard. Over 9,000 such persons have been found guilty.[13] The SPP statistics indicated that between 1979 and 1989 there was an average of 364 criminal cases of confessions obtained by torture, and 400 cases per year in the 1990s. The SPP reported that from 1993 to 1994 between one-third

---

7 N.D. Kristof, "Jailed Pro-Democrats in China Charge Torture" *New York Times* (New York Sep. 1, 1992), at A4.

8 In China, some Chinese psychiatrists subjected thousands of mentally healthy dissidents to psychiatric punishment; however, being in a psychiatric hospital with the mentally disordered would truly drive a mentally normal person insane. See *Human Rights Watch, Dangerous Minds: Political Psychiatry in China Today and its Origins in the Mao Era (*Human Rights Watch and Geneva Initiative on Psychiatry, New York 2002) 84–9.

9 UNCHR "Special Rapporteur on Torture Highlights Challenges at End of Visit to China" (2 Dec 2005). Available at: http://www.unhchr.ch/huricane/huricane.nsf/0/677C1943FAA14D67C12570CB0034966D?opendocument (accessed Oct. 10, 2013).

10 United State Department's 1999 Report on Human Rights Practices. Available at: http://www.state.gov/g/drl/rls/hrrpt/1999/284.htm (accessed Oct. 10, 2013).

11 Ibid.

12 United State Department's 2007 Report on Human Rights Practices. Available at: http://www.state.gov/g/drl/rls/hrrpt/2007/100518.htm (accessed Oct. 10, 2013).

13 Shao-Chuan Leng, "Criminal Justice in Post-Mao China: Some Preliminary Observations" (1982) 73 *The Journal of Criminal Law and Criminology* 204, 216.

and one-fourth of all torture cases resulted in death; 241 persons were tortured to death and 64 persons suffered severe injuries.[14] In addition, most allegations of police torture do not surface until the trial. These official numbers are only the tip of the iceberg.

Every police officer is expected to act within the law. Nevertheless, in practice, for some police officers the use of illegal investigation methods, excessive force, psychological trickery and high-pressure tactics is accepted as a necessary evil in Chinese criminal investigations.[15] Although the government's passive attitude towards torture is a tragedy, the sorrow of the victims and their families is a tragedy many times over.[16] Torture cannot be undone. Victims may never be able to return to the life they knew before being tortured.

The aim of the exclusionary rule is to avoid torture and arbitrary searches by the law enforcement officers. In order to eradicate torture, perhaps an even more important question we face is to find out why police resort to torture. Torture by law enforcement authorities is unfortunately widespread in China. Just why China displayed a disregard for the law and defendants' human rights is an intriguing question: why there was gross violation of defendants' human rights?

Not until 1996 did the People's Republic of China law guarantee the accused the right to be free from torture.[17] Both the Criminal Law and Code of Criminal Procedure forbid the use of torture to obtain confessions. The Criminal Law makes it a criminal offense to torture or ill-treatment during interrogations. Article 247 states:

> A judicial officer who extorts by torture a confession from a suspect of crime or a defendant or extorts, by means of violence, testimony from a witness shall be sentenced to fixed-term imprisonment of not more than three years or criminal detention. A judicial officer who causes another person's deformity or death shall be sentenced heavily in accordance with the provisions of Article 234 or 232 of this Law.

In the past, commentators and academics have provided a broad attack on the torture problem,[18] which cannot lead to substantial improvements. It seems that

---

14 Wang Gangping (ed.), *The Crime of Tortured Confession* (People's Procuratorate Press, Beijing 1997) 9. The information here is proven torture not the cases of alleged torture.

15 See 5.3.

16 R.F. Mollica, "The Psychosocial Impact of War Trauma and Torture on Southeast Asian Refugees" (1987) 144 *The American Journal of Psychiatry* 1567, 1571; see also Derrick Silove, "The Psychosocial Effects of Torture, Mass Human Rights Violations, and Refugee Trauma: Toward an Integrated Conceptual Framework" (1999) 187 *Journal of Nervous and Mental Disease* 200, 206.

17 In 1996, Article 247 of the Criminal Law was amended.

18 H.L. Fu, "Criminal Defense in China: The Possible Impact of the 1996 Criminal Procedure Law Reform" (1998) 153 *The China Quarterly* 31, 32; see also D.C. Turack,

China is trying to solve the problem of police torture, but why then is the problem still so serious? Why do Chinese police use torture?

The Chinese government needs to focus on the roots of the problem. The more we understand about the causes of the problem, the better we can figure out solutions to the problem. It would be a better approach to solve the problems at their root. The reasons are complex. No single factor can be singled out as determinative. Moreover, one factor may lead to another, in the long run creating a vicious circle. There are at least five reasons why Chinese government officials resort to torture: extracting confessions, the influence of historical tradition, winning convictions and then getting benefits, satisfying the "enforcement index" and a lack of investigative technology. I will explore each in turn. These are not mutually exclusive. These impetuses to torture continue.

5.1.1 Subjective Causes

There are several subjective causes why torture confessions are disproportionately likely to arise in China. First, extracting confessions. For some police officers, if they do not get confessions to find the "truth" some of the time, they probably are not doing their jobs as police. The *main* cause is the desire to obtain confessions. Torture, which usually occurs in police stations, has been widely used as a method of obtaining confession from suspects and even witnesses. The most common form of police torture is beating.[19] Confession evidence is important and powerful in the trial process. It has been called "the most potent of weapons for the prosecution."[20]

Traditionally, confessions of guilt have been the best evidence in China.[21] The Chinese criminal justice system has placed too much emphasis on confessions. Torture may yield any information, whether true or false. In order to end the pain, suspects (whether guilty or innocent), when subjected to torture, will admit anything, including a crime they did not commit. That is why it was common for suspects to be tortured in order to extract confessions.

As the police realize that these incriminating statements routinely result in convictions because of the dramatic impact of a suspect who seemingly openly admits his guilt to the police, they disregard statutory guarantees and try to get confessions at any cost.

"The New Chinese Criminal Justice System" (1999) 7 *Cardozo Journal of International and Comparative Law* 49, 72.

19 Guan Jinhua (ed.), 基本人權保護與法律實踐 [The Protection of Basic Human Rights and Legal Practice] (Xiamen University Press, Xiamen 2003) 327.

20 S.M. Kassin and Katherine Neumann, "Coerced Confessions and the Jury: An Experimental Test of the "Harmless Error" Rule" (1997) 21 *Law and Human Behavior* 27, 27.

21 Wang Min, "淺析民警刑訊逼供的心理狀態及治理對策" [Analyzing the Psychological Situations and Governance of Police Torturers] (2001) 83 *Policing Studies* 21, 22.

Secondly, there exists the influence of historical tradition. Before turning to an examination of Chinese criminal process today in the context of torture, a brief historical excursus may be useful. Our struggles with the issue of torture in China are nothing new. Judicial torture (i.e., torture by officials authorized by the law) is as old as judicial history. The earliest use of judicial torture of which we have much knowledge in China was in the Qin dynasty (221–207 B.C.). It was also used in ancient Greece and Rome. Both in China and in Rome not only the accused, but also witnesses could be tortured.[22]

Dr. Sun Yat-sen, founding Father of the Republic of China, formally outlawed judicial torture in 1912. He noted torture should not be allowed regardless of any specific context. All devices used to torture in the past must be destroyed.[23] Although we cannot rule out the possibility that deep-seated historical traditions of torture throughout Imperial China (221 B.C.—A.D. 1911) might have an impact on the current issue, it is wrong to think that in ancient China all judicial torture was desirable, atrocious and employed randomly. Most of the judicial torture was imposed by law. Law enforcement officers could not torture anybody for any reason. The judiciary in ancient China did *not* advocate judicial torture. It was never seen as the best method.

The Qin Code, for example, stated that it was better *not* use torture in the trial process. If the suspect changed his confessions many times, he might be subjected to torture. There were rules designed to prevent the unlimited application of judicial torture; these rules tried to "keep it within legally defined boundaries."[24] First, if the suspect was subjected to torture, it had to be recorded in the trial record. Second, according to Tang Lue (Code of the Tang Dynasty), promulgated in A.D. 630, confessions was required only in cases where the facts were unclear; only limited torture was permitted. The young, the old and the disabled could not be interrogated under torture.[25] That is the reason why there are few recorded cases of death by judicial torture during the Tang Dynasty.[26] In addition, according to Da Ming Lue (the Great Ming Code), promulgated in A.D. 1368, only limited torture was permitted. The young (persons of 15 years of age or less), the elderly (70 years of age or more), the disabled,[27] and pregnant women[28] should not be judicially tortured. As Klaus Muhlhahn noted, "[t]orture could be used only after enough evidence had been gathered by the investigation. Limits were set on the

---

22 Peter Reddy, *Torture: What You Need to Know* (Ginninderra Press, Charnwood 2005) 19.

23 Ye Xiaoxin (ed.), 中國法制史 [The Chinese Legal History] (Beijing University Press, Beijing 1989) 252.

24 Klaus Muhlhahn, *Criminal Justice in China: A History* (Harvard University Press, Cambridge 2009) 49.

25 Article 474 of the Tang Lue.

26 A.D. 619–907.

27 Article 428 of the Da Ming Lue.

28 Article 444 of the Da Ming Lue.

amount of torture, the instruments that could be used, and parts of the body that could be affected."[29]

Police torture is wrong even if the defendant is "really guilty"; however, it goes on around the world even in the twenty-first century. It is not only a shame of the past but also a transgression of the present. Most police officers obey the law when interrogating suspects and conducting searches. But we cannot avoid the unfortunate reality that police wrongdoing exists, particularly in the context of interrogation and search. Police torture and police coercive interrogation were rife from the 1950s until now in China.

We cannot ignore the influence of Mao Zedong's class-oriented doctrines on the judicial problem during 1949 to 1979. In the Maoist era, criminal law is merely a weapon to be used in attacking criminals and suppressing crimes. Mao drew a sharp distinction between the "people" and "enemy" of socialism. The "people" were those who favored, supported and worked for the cause of socialist construction. The "enemy" were those who resisted the socialist revolution and sabotaged socialist construction.[30] Law was the weapon used by police and courts to combat the enemy. Only "people" are entitled to human rights and those accused of crimes under the Criminal Law were considered as belonging to the "enemy." Criminals do not deserve protection. The "enemy" were not entitled to the procedural protections provided by the Code of Criminal Procedure. Therefore, according to Mao, it was reasonable to deprive the rights of criminals.

Thirdly, there is the issue of winning convictions and then getting benefits. Police have a reward structure based on the number of cases solved, while failure to solve cases could lead to reprimand or demotion.[31] There is real incentive for enforcement agents to "win" cases. By torture, law enforcement agents may get two kinds of benefits. First, the enforcement agents can get higher financial rewards. The police authority provides for bonuses to police officers who solve high profile cases quickly. Second, winning convictions will assist with career progression. In other words, the police may get promotion. Most Chinese police agencies are governed by meritorious performance with regard to promotion. For example, in the She Xianglin case, the superintendent in charge of the case was promoted to the post of chief judge in Jing Shan County.[32]

In order to pursue higher positions and bonuses, some superintendents and the upper ranks just ignored the legal standards and turned a blind eye to officers'

29 Klaus Muhlhahn, *Criminal Justice in China: A History* (Harvard University Press, Cambridge 2009) 49–50.

30 Mao Tse-tung, 毛澤東選集 [Selected Readings from the Works of Mao Tsetung] (Foreign Language Press, Beijing 1971) 433–4.

31 See 5.1.2.

32 Mao Lixin, "佘祥林冤案的偵查錯誤剖析" [The Analysis of Wrongful Conviction of She Xiang Lin Case] (2006). Available at: http://www.dffy.com/faxuejieti/ss/200601/20060109183013.htm (accessed Oct. 10, 2013).

misconduct. I found that a similar phenomenon has appeared in other national settings.[33] The impetus to police torture seems to continue.

5.1.2 Objective Causes

There are two objective causes. First, satisfying the "enforcement index."[34] One slogan in China is, "Any cat is a good cat if it catches mice." Well, any police officer is a good officer if he can satisfy enforcement criteria. And, police officers who cannot meet the enforcement criteria might be punished or removed. The primary structural basis for police torture appears to be pressure from higher authorities to meet enforcement criteria, which encourages the police to obtain confessions and evidence by torturing suspects and conducting illegal searches. The "enforcement index" exists in the Chinese police system.[35] While the criteria were set according to the crime rate and clearance rate in the specific area in the past, the predicted criteria usually cannot match the actual clearance rate.

Furthermore, the strike-hard campaign was launched in 1983 and has been an ongoing annual campaign. Law enforcement agents usually are given a quota for how many suspects should be caught for various crimes.[36] Legal constraints imposed by law would likely have less effect on police under great pressure from their bosses to make a quota.

The ability of local police force to meet these criteria is considered an important index of performance. Quantitative rather than qualitative standards determine promotion. Performance is rewarded by credits for bonuses and promotion, while failure to meet these criteria may entail the risk of disciplinary sanctions, demotion, or a reduction in salary. In 2001, for instance, Jing Aikuo, a taxi driver, was sentenced to death for the transportation of 3,600 grams of heroin in Gansu Province, but it transpired that the drugs were planted by two anti-drug "heroes" Chang Wenzhuo (the deputy chief of the Linzhao County Police

---

33 For example, in 1989, Wei En-cheng and Chen Wu-hsiung were arrested for the murder of the Yang Chun-tien family in Taiwan. According to the medical records, both suspects were subjected to beatings, electric shock and water torture by seven police officers in the Feng Yuan Police Precinct and police car; they were forced to confess to the murder. The superintendent of Feng Yuan Police Precinct immediately got promotion to the Chief Inspector in the Taichung City Police Bureau. Both suspects were completely innocent. See 79 Chungsu 1489 (The Taiwan Taichung District Court, 1990); 80 Shangsu 646 (The Taiwan High Court Taichung Branch Court, 1991); 81 Shangkengyi 120 (The Taiwan High Court Taichung Branch Court, 1992).

34 執法指標。.

35 Chang Jian, "評執法指標" [The Enforcement Index] (2003) 5 *Political Science and Law* 130, 130–32; see also Ian Jun and Yang Xiaoping, "試論公安執法指標對警察權的影響" [The Impact of the Enforcement Index towards Police Power] (2005) 2 *Journal of Adult Education of Gansu Political Science and Law Institute* 100, 100–102.

36 G. Wehrfritz and M. Laris, "Rulers are the Law" *Newsweek* Atlantic Edition (1997) 47.

Department) and Bian Weihong (top anti-narcotics officer of the Linzhao County Police Department). The enforcement criteria for each anti-narcotics officer in the county is 1,300 grams of drugs. The anti-narcotics officers who had been involved in planting drugs were awarded bonuses of 100,000 RMB (£9,400).[37]

Unrealistic expectations of enforcement criteria have resulted in police administrators pressuring police officers to solve as many cases as possible. The Ministry of Public Security, the highest police organ in China, even publicly emphasized that murder cases *must* be solved.[38]

Every country, even those countries with the most advanced investigative technology, including the United Kingdom and United States, has unsolved murder cases. It is impossible for any country, including China, to solve *every* murder case. When facing a murder case without sufficient evidence, how should Chinese police meet the "must be solved" criterion and close the case? For some of them the only way is to torture a "wretch" and allow him to be the "murderer."

There is no denying that police work is often a hazardous and frustrating task. There are five principal sources of immense pressure existing for police to solve high profile cases quickly and they must solve these cases. These are: the enforcement index, their supervisors (or senior officers), the media, victims (or the victim's family) and the public. These circumstances and significant pressure enhance the likelihood that the use of false arrests, police torture, illegal detention,[39] perjury[40] and the planting of evidence to effectively meet predicted targets will occur. However these pressures are endemic in any criminal justice system and do not excuse the police for their failure to abide by the law. The point is that all relevant actors in the criminal justice system are bound by the Criminal Law and Code of Criminal Procedure.

Illegal methods are rampant because it is easier, quicker, promising and "efficient"; they are viewed as the shortcut to clarify crimes. Police torture is viewed as the fastest way to get the result. Enforcement criteria were viewed as the "original sin" of police wrongdoing. Law became the tool of law enforcement agents who achieved the goal.

37 "公安局副局長炮制販毒大案" [Deputy Chief of the Police Department Makes the Drug Case], *Jiangnan Daily* (Aug. 26, 2002) 13.

38 "公安部：命案必破不會引發刑訊逼供" [The Ministry of Public Security: Death Cases Must Be Solved Will Not Trigger Torture]. Available at: http://news.sina.com.cn/c/l/2006-05-16/12419876496.shtml (accessed Oct. 10, 2013).

39 Suspects facing lengthy detention and interrogation often feel compelled to confess.

40 In 2002, Wang Weiqing was tortured to death by a detective in Guangdong province. In order to cover up the truth of the torture, 40 Hua Zhou police officers lied to government investigators and firmly asserted that Wang was committed suicide by hitting the tea table under oath at trial. See Cao Jingjing, "廣東化州民警刑訊逼供打死人" [Guangdong Police Tortured Suspect to Death] (2007). Available at: http://i.mop.com/ZHENGYILVSHI/blog/2007/11/22/5130711.html (accessed Oct. 10, 2013).

Secondly, China is lacking in investigative technology. A lack of new investigative technologies also is a cause of torture. According to my research, many torture cases happen in rural China or poor areas.[41] Some districts lack the judicial resources, including investigative technology and investigative personnel with adequate training. They do not have advanced forensics laboratories, modernized equipment and forensic chemists to collect and preserve evidence. Under these circumstances, some police resort to torture to investigate. These resource shortages affect police officers at least in some districts.

5.2 Barriers to the Protection of Defendants' Rights

In the last few decades, China has made progress in combating the extensive and long-standing problems with police torture. In 1996, China announced an amendment to the Criminal Law to address police torture and intensify its effort to combat torture. The Code of Criminal Procedure provided some protections by prohibiting illegal means of gathering evidence such as torture, coercion, or inducement,[42] and by prohibiting convictions based solely on the defendant's confession.[43] In addition, in 2012, the 11th National People's Congress amended the Code of Criminal Procedure during its 5th conference. The new articles introduced development in connection with the right to be free from torture. These safeguards, however, are far from enough. The government has done little to eliminate legal and social barriers to the protection of Chinese defendants. In this sense, it is crucial to understand what the barriers to effective protection of the right to be free from torture are. My goal here, then, is to identify fundamental barriers to the protection of defendant's rights. There are at least four barriers.

5.2.1 "Legal Foundation" of Torture

From the perspective of legislation, the "legal foundation" of police torture in China is Article 118 of the Code of Criminal Procedure, which provides:

> When interrogating a criminal suspect, the investigators shall first ask the criminal suspect whether or not he has committed any criminal act, and let him state the circumstances of his guilt or explain his innocence; then may ask him questions. The *criminal suspect shall answer the investigators' questions truthfully …*

The focus should be on the word "truthfully"; confessions are expected to be truthful—as judged subjectively by the interrogators and not by the suspects. A

41 See Chapter 7.
42 Article 50.
43 Article 53.

suspect who refuses to confess is generally seen as obdurate and be treated severely. On the contrary, a defendant who confesses often receives lenient punishment.[44]

In the past decades, the Chinese version of "*Miranda* warnings": the eight-character phrase "坦白從寬 抗拒從嚴" [Leniency for those who confess; severity for those who resist!] appeared on the wall of many interrogation rooms.[45] This Chinese "*Miranda* warnings"[46] assumes that the law enforcement officers *know* the suspect to be guilty, and that he is merely being stubborn when he resists their urgings that he confess. The defendants' cooperation with the police in investigations is highly expected. More importantly, suspects were legally bound to answer truthfully and unambiguously the questions asked of them. However, what is the character of this obligation? Most police regard this as a legal obligation, not merely a moral obligation. If suspects do not fulfill their obligations, police officers think they should take measures to assure the fulfillment of suspects' obligations. Hence the police often feel it justified and even legally indispensable to extract confessions.

Under existing practice, the state may penalize individuals for refusing to answer (potentially incriminating) questions. If suspects do not answer the investigators' questions "truthfully" by subjective feelings of police or refuse to answer questions, they might be treated cruelly and frequently tortured, and sometimes be tortured to death. In 2001, for instance, the police illegally arrested and detained a male who was reported as having pushed a woman down in Hubei Province. As the suspect refused to answer police questions, five police (at least one of them was under 18) beat him to death during interrogation. They buried the body under the police station in order to avoid punishment.[47]

Some police will seek confessions at virtually all costs and use whatever techniques they can to extract them. In effect, Article 118 gives police a broad license to torture and dehumanize suspects in their custody. Under such circumstances, it is not surprising that police torture is so pervasive in China. Suspects who refuse to cooperate with public officials might be subjected to torture. For example, Wang Zongxiao, a suspected drug dealer who was arrested by the Shanghai police in 1988, was subjected to torture during interrogation in an attempt to extract information from him. The police reminded Wang of the Communist Party policy repeatedly throughout the interrogation, that if he told the

44 Cai Ianbing, "論刑訊逼供屢禁不止的原因及對策" [The Reasons and Resolutions to Torture] (2000) 2 *Journal of Hunan Public Security College* 54, 55.

45 *Xiao v. Reno*, 837 F. Supp 1541 (N.D. Cal. 1993); see also Klaus Muhlhahn, *Criminal Justice in China* (Harvard University Press, Cambridge 2009) 243.

46 In other words, these are the opposite of Miranda warnings!

47 "刑訊逼供打死人埋屍工地" [Tortured to Death], *Southern Metropolis Daily* (May 28, 2004). Available at: http://news.sina.com.cn/o/2004-05-28/09272651339s.shtml (accessed Oct. 10, 2013).

officers everything, he would receive leniency; if he refused to speak, he would be treated with severity.[48]

Article 118 of the Code of Criminal Procedure destroys the very essence of the defendant's fundamental right against self-incrimination. There is no right to silence for the accused in China. Defendants are expected to answer questions in the police station, procuratorates and the courts. This is the main reason why the problem of police torture in China cannot be solved even today. Even worse, it is considered that Article 118 of the Code of Criminal Procedure should be applied at the beginning, at every stage and until the very end in the criminal process.[49]

No one shall be obliged to give incriminating evidence against himself. A defendant shall not be obligated to prove his innocence. It is undoubtedly true that anyone suspected or accused of crime should not be compelled to cooperate with any investigation authorities; otherwise miscarriages of justice will definitely occur. The agents of the state should prove their cases. For these reasons, I propose to abolish Article 118.

5.2.2 Lacking Enforcement Mechanisms

The lack of enforcement of the laws, however, is another problem. At first glance, Article 50 of the Code of Criminal Procedure prohibits torture, threat, enticement, deceit or other unlawful means:

> Judges, procurators and investigators must, in accordance with the legally prescribed process, collect various kinds of evidence that can prove the criminal suspect's or defendant's guilt or innocence and the gravity of his crime. It shall be strictly forbidden to extort confessions by torture and to collect evidence by threat, enticement, deceit or other unlawful means …

It prescribes no remedy for violation. When the Chinese Supreme People's Court (SPC) and Supreme People's Procuratorate (SPP) Interpretations made clear that the police could not torture suspects under existing law, they were trying to avoid police torture by offering a confession exclusionary rule.[50] For example, Article 61 of the Supreme People's Court's Interpretation on Several Questions for Enforcing the Chinese Criminal Procedure Law[51] provides that "[i]t shall be

48 *Xiao v. Reno*, 837 F. Supp 1541 (N.D. Cal. 1993).

49 Li Yunzhao, "刑訊逼供屢禁不止的原因及對策研究" [The Reasons and Solutions of Endless Torture] (2002) 8 *Journal of Beijing University* 154, 155.

50 Article 61 of the Supreme People's Court's Interpretation on Several Questions for Enforcing the Chinese Criminal Procedure Law and Article 65 of the Chinese People's Procuratorate's Criminal Procedure Rule 2012.

51 "最高人民法院關於執行《中華人民共和國刑事訴訟法》若干問題的解釋" [Supreme People's Court's Interpretation on Several Questions for Enforcing the Chinese Criminal Procedure Law], promulgated on June 29, 1998, effective on Sep. 8, 1998.

strictly forbidden to collect evidence by illegal methods. Evidence obtained by torture, threat, enticement and deceit or other illegal methods are inadmissible." In addition, Article 265 of the Chinese People's Procuratorate's Criminal Procedure Rule[52] provides that "[i]t shall be strictly forbidden to collect evidence by illegal methods. Confessions from suspects, victims and witnesses obtained by torture, threat, enticement and deceit cannot be used to incriminate." It indicates that evidence obtained through methods mentioned above should not be admitted into evidence in a criminal prosecution.

These laws and judicial interpretations provided by the Supreme People's Court and Supreme People's Procuratorate, however, have often failed to address crucial concerns relating to violations of the right to be free from torture and, perhaps more importantly, generally lack any mechanisms for enforcement. Courts should enforce these judicial interpretations provided by the Supreme People's Court and Supreme People's Procuratorate by barring the prosecution from using evidence obtained by illegal methods at criminal trials.

The exclusionary rule is still not adopted in Chinese criminal practice. Regarding the exclusionary rule, the contrast between "law in the books" and "law in practice" is obvious. In the context of the exclusionary rule, China should transform "law in the books" into "law in practice" *immediately*; otherwise, the right to be free from torture is merely lip service paid by the government.

5.2.3 The Political-Legal Committee

The Chinese Communist Party's central Political-Legal Committee is a sub-committee of the Party's Central Committee charged with supervision of China's entire legal system. The Political-Legal Committee usually includes the deputy Party secretary of Political-Legal matters, the president of the court and procuracy, and the heads of various ministries or bureaus including public security, state security, justice and civil affairs.[53]

The function of the Committee is to discuss and decide cases believed to be difficult, important or to have socially significant implications *before* trials. The Committee can make determinations on everything from individual criminal cases, which may result in the phenomenon of "verdict first, trial second." Moreover, in some difficult cases, the Committee may even "recommend" that the Basic Court and Intermediate Court agree a specific verdict before the trial. Courts have to follow Party recommendations. Judges who decide cases contrary to Party dictates may be subject to be discharged or transferred.[54]

52 "人民檢察院刑事訴訟規則" [People's Procuratorate's Criminal Procedure Rule], promulgated on Dec. 16, 1998, effective on Jan. 18, 1999.

53 Shiping Zheng, *Party v. State in Post-1949 China* (Cambridge University Press, Cambridge 1997) 172.

54 M.Y.K. Woo, "Law and Discretion in Contemporary Chinese Courts" in Karen Turner and Others (eds), *The Limits of the Rule of Law in China* (Washington University

The first example is the *Li Huawei* case. In 1986, Li Huawei's pregnant wife Xing Wei was murdered in Liaoning Province. In the horrific crime scene Xing's blood spurted on the floor. As result of trying to rescue his wife and their unborn child, Li had her blood on his clothes. Li protested his innocence, stating repeatedly that finger-print and foot-print found at the scene of the crime were not his. Police challenged Li as to how Xing's blood could have ended up in a spot of blood found on his clothes. Li was questioned and tortured incommunicado for a continuous 72-hour period with very limited food and water.

The police also detained Li's mother Yang for over 10 hours and told her that "your son admitted that he had killed his wife and already told you. Why you did not confess?" Yang said "I don't know." The police said "you are not allowed to say I don't know, otherwise we will put you in jail." Not until Yang had incriminated Li was she allowed to go home. Then the police told Li that "your mother said that you told her you killed your wife." Witnesses were forced to change their statements that Li was not at the scene of the crime. Further, all physical evidence favoring Li was concealed by the police. Li was charged with the murder of his wife.

The Yingkou City Political-Legal Committee decided the sentence before the trial. The torture confessions were admitted and Li was convicted and sentenced to death with a reprieve by the Yingkou City Intermediate Court. Li's defense lawyer Ma visited the Intermediate Court many times and asked them why they had been so "lenient" on Li—that is, why they had decided not to execute Li. The vice president of the court said "Li cannot be executed as this case is not so clear." After Li had served 14 years in prison, the real murderer was caught and admitted the crime.[55]

The second example is a particularly well-publicized case. In 1994, She Xianglin's wife Zhang Zaiyu left their home because of her mental illness. Xianglin was a police officer in Jing Shan County in Hubei Province. Zhang's family suspected that their daughter, Zhang was murdered by Xianglin and they decided to inform the police. Three months later, an unidentified female dead body was found in a pond near Xianglin's home. Xianglin was arrested because Zhang's brother claimed the dead body looked like his sister.

Over a fortnight of police interrogation, Xianglin only ate two meals a day; drank very little and was deprived of sleep. Xianglin was seriously tortured and was forced to confess to the murder. Xianglin made confessions in despair while going through marathon torturing, suggested four ways to "kill" his wife and left the police to pick one among them. His confessions had been entirely fabricated. Xianglin was sentenced to death by the Jing Zhou Intermediate Court. He appealed. The Hubei Province High Court quashed the conviction because of insufficient evidence. After the intervention of the City and County Political-Legal Committees, the case was transferred to the Jing Shan County Basic Court.

Press, Seattle 2000) 171.

55 Kuo Kuosong, "The Truth of a Murder Case" *The China Youth Daily* (Feb. 25, 2001).

The Political-Legal Committee asked the Jing Shan County Basic Court and Jing Zhou Intermediate Court to imprison Xianglin for 15 years. After Xianglin had served almost one decade in prison, surprisingly, Zhang returned home one day in 2005. The Jing Shan County Basic Court retried the case and said Xianglin was completely innocent.[56]

The Chinese court system has four different levels: basic courts, intermediate courts, high courts and the Supreme Court. The Intermediate Court may be the court of first instance over criminal cases punishable by life imprisonment or the death sentence.[57] According to Article 20 of the Code of Criminal Procedure of 1996, the Jing Zhou Intermediate Court should be the court of first instance. The Jing Shan County Basic Court, appointed by the Committee, even did not have jurisdiction to hear this case.

The Chinese criminal justice system should not be operated merely as an instrument of Communist Party control. The Political-Legal Committee should not override the judgments of formal judicial and legal apparatus. I contend that the function of the Political-Legal Committee has to be changed.

5.2.4 The Right to Counsel

In an ideal world, the right to counsel,[58] including the attorney-client privilege, acts to ensure that a defendant receives professional advice exclusively from his attorney. The right to counsel is a fundamental fair trial right.[59] It is of crucial importance for the fairness of the criminal justice system that the defendant be adequately defended. The confrontation between defendant and prosecutors can hardly be called fair if there is no lawyer to assist him. In actual practice this has not been the case. Chinese defense attorneys face at least three difficulties: (1) difficulties in client access;[60] (2) difficulties in reviewing case files; (3) difficulties in obtaining evidence. It seems that the main reason behind these difficulties is because lawyers are in opposition to the law enforcement agents: all these actions of the "trouble makers"—lawyers—will interfere with the investigation, slow down the criminal process and only benefit the guilty.

---

56 Mao Lixin, "佘祥林冤案的偵查錯誤剖析" [The Analysis of Wrongful Conviction of She Xianglin Case] (2006). Available at: http://www.dffy.com/faxuejieti/ss/200601/20060109183013.htm (accessed Oct. 10, 2013).

57 Article 20 of the Code of Criminal Procedure of 1996 provides: The intermediate people's courts shall have jurisdiction as courts of first instance over the following cases: (1) counter-revolutionary cases and cases jeopardizing the State security; (2) ordinary criminal cases punishable by life imprisonment or the death sentence; and (3) criminal cases in which the offenders are foreigners.

58 Article 11 of the Code of Criminal Procedure.

59 *Gideon v. Wainwright*, 372 U.S. 335, 344 (1963).

60 Andrew Worden, "'A Fair Game?' of Law and Politics in China, and the 'Sensitive' Case of Democracy Activist Yang Jianli" (2009) 40 *Georgetown Journal of International Law* 447, 458.

The utilitarian approach dominates the Chinese criminal justice system, where the crime control model prevails. The crime control model represents many of the traditional values of the Chinese criminal justice system.[61] As Trevaskes correctly observed that:

> [i]n the traditional Chinese view, criminal law is used as a sword to be wielded in a fight against crime. Since the law was traditionally conceived as a tool to fight and eliminate crime, other important aspects of the law, such as its function in protecting human rights, did not develop in traditional jurisprudential thinking.[62]

However, when the scales tilt too far in the direction of crime control, due process rights suffer.

One of the tenets of the crime control model is a trust in the fact-finding of police and prosecutors.[63] The criminal justice system practiced the principle of "deciding a case according to facts."[64] In addition, Article 6 of the Code of Criminal Procedure explicitly recognizes that "[i]n criminal proceedings, the People's Courts, the People's Procuratorates, and the public security organs must … base themselves on facts …." However, in the rigorous pursuit of "truth," rules protecting the defendants' rights were often swept aside. Until today, as discussed above in 5.1.1 and as we will see below, China identifies strongly with the crime control model in this regard and the criminal justice policy followed the basic tenets of what Packer called the crime control model.[65]

The criminal process is a linear process, separated into stages that are performed at different times. Each stage calls upon the police, prosecutor and judge to perform specific, compartmentalized tasks. Viewing the criminal process in linear stages suggests that law enforcement agents are composed of an assembly line: investigating, prosecuting, and then convicting. There are three stages of a criminal proceeding in China: investigation, prosecution and the trial. The end product of the assembly line is the conviction. China mainly focuses on efficiency in apprehending, trying, and convicting offenders. I argue that, in *every* single stage, many of the rules which govern the criminal process are based on the principles similar to those which shape Packer's crime control model.

First, right from the first stage of the criminal process—the investigation phase, according to Code of Criminal Procedure, the accused has every disadvantage as soon as the accused is apprehended.

The criminal justice system regards the suppression of crime as the primary function of the criminal process. That is why the Code of Criminal Procedure is

---

61 See 5.1.1.

62 Susan Trevaskes, *Courts and Criminal Justice in Contemporary China* (Lexington Books, Lanham 2007) 185.

63 See 1.3.

64 Article 6 of the Code of Criminal Procedure.

65 See 1.3.

expansive, vague and silent about the limits of police investigative powers. In the investigative phase, the criminal process leans rather heavily toward the crime control model.

(1) There is no general legal requirement of probable cause to arrest, search, seizure, or detain.[66] Prior to an arrest, the police do not need to have probable cause to believe that the defendant engaged in the charged activity. (2) Identity checks need not be based on individualized suspicion, and detention for identification purposes may last for up to 24 hours.[67] (3) Police powers to interrogate are broad. Defendants are not provided with protections against coerced testimony, illegal searches, and presumptions of guilt. Defendants have no right to remain silent and are not immune from questions on their silence; on the contrary, defendants have a duty to answer questions truthfully when asked by investigators.[68] It seems that the entire criminal process was designed to get the suspect to talk. In practice, it becomes the legal duty for suspects to assist the police under Article 118,[69] not to mention the (non)*Miranda* rule. (4) Defendants may be held in investigatory detention for up to 72 hours without probable cause, judicial approval, or mandatory court appearance.[70] (5) There is no general judicial warrant requirement for the use of electronic surveillance, any type of undercover investigations or covert operations.

To ensure that maximum number of criminals are prosecuted, at least to some extent, the criminal process relies on a "presumption of guilt." However, the thought of presumption of guilt in the criminal process is the ideological root of confession by torture. During the investigation phase, China assumes that efficient police investigation and prosecutions could control crime. Therefore, police are given wide investigative powers of arrest, search, seizure[71] and interrogation. The police are so accustomed to exercising their unconstrained discretion arbitrarily that they may honestly believe they are suppressing crime or they are enforcing the "law in action." It seems that for them this is often the quickest means to establish whether the suspect is factually guilty and only the factually guilty have something to hide.

One difficult problem in the Chinese criminal process is generated by dissonance between "law in books" and "law in action." The police are the most powerful of all criminal justice officials in China. The broad power of the police remains unchecked.[72] Meanwhile, police misconduct is widespread. Police torture and coercion, for example, which have a lot to do with ordinary law enforcement,

---

66 See 6.3.

67 Article 84 of the Code of Criminal Procedure.

68 Article 118 of the Code of Criminal Procedure.

69 Wang Haiyan and Hu Changlong, 刑事證據基本問題研究 [The Study of Basic Questions of Criminal Evidence] (Law Press, Beijing 2002) 4.

70 Article 89 of the Code of Criminal Procedure.

71 See 6.3.1.

72 See 5.3.2.

are mostly ignored.[73] The questioning of the accused in the investigation stage is an essential aspect of criminal proceedings. These interrogations were carried out by the police, and the accused was seldom allowed the assistance of a lawyer. It is worth noting that not until 1996 were detained people allowed access to a lawyer in the investigation phase. In practice, lawyers are not appointed until the trial stage. Even in the court phase, defense attorneys have relatively little power and the role of defense attorneys remains highly circumscribed.

What is worse is that some police officers even think the legal rights are in their hands. For instance, according to Article 36 of the Code of Criminal Procedure, during the investigation stage, lawyers may offer legal counseling. Yanfei Ran, an experienced Chinese defense lawyer, recalled his experience when he tried to meet his client at the detention center in Beijing. One police officer refused his request to meet the client. Ran argued that according to the Code of Criminal Procedure, lawyers have the right to meet their clients. The police replied that, "You have a right? Your rights are in my hand."[74]

Secondly, the prosecution phase is a link between the investigation phase and the trial phase in the assembly line.

Gongjianfa (公檢法)[75] carries a kind of "assembly line" meaning because there is such a close relationship between the police, the prosecutor, and the judiciary. Article 7 of the Code of Criminal Procedure provides:

> In conducting criminal proceedings, the People's Courts, the People's Procuratorates and the public security organs shall divide responsibilities, *coordinate* their efforts and check each other so as to ensure the correct and effective enforcement of the law.[76]

From 1975 to 1978, all Chinese Procuratorate[77] offices were abolished. All powers of the Procuratorate were even transferred to the police.[78] Chinese prosecutors work within hierarchical bureaucratic structures. The prosecutors are obliged to obey orders in relation to specific cases. Certainty of "outcomes" is the goal of the criminal justice system, which is supposed to provide certainty of prosecution. Under these circumstances, for the prosecutors the criminal justice system should prevent the "factually guilty" from escaping prosecution and conviction.

Further, as mentioned above, for defense attorneys, it is exceedingly difficult as a practical matter to meet their clients, particularly those defendants in detention centers or in prisons. In general, an accused in detention is unlikely to have much

---

73 See Chapter 5.

74 Yanfei Ran, "When Chinese Criminal Defense Lawyers Become the Criminals" (2009) 32 *Fordham International Law Journal* 988, 1014–15.

75 *Gong* means the police. *Jian* means the procuratorate. *Fa* means the court.

76 Article 7 of the Code of Criminal procedure (emphasis added).

77 Procuratorate means a prosecutor.

78 Article 25 of Chinese Constitution 1975.

opportunity to meet with counsel until the prosecutors have finalized the case. Even when the accused has access to counsel, not only the police but also prosecutors may impose unreasonable conditions on meetings between the accused and counsel.[79]

Because the specific language of the Code of Criminal Procedure is not clear and because courts have interpreted these written provisions narrowly, the criminal justice system provides wide discretion to the investigative authorities. For example, although Article 37 provides that if the case involves state secrets, the lawyer has to obtain the approval of the investigating agency, the investigative authorities, however, distort Article 37 as it is almost impossible for lawyers to meet their clients without getting the approval of investigative authorities in *any* case, not only those limited to state secrets.[80]

Additionally, the meetings with lawyers may be limited to 30 minutes or even interrupted by law enforcement officers or even prosecutors.[81] The true lawyer's personal experience is here. When dealing with a corruption case, Kang Huaiu, a defense lawyer, argues:

> During the meeting, I am very confident. I enquired the facts of the case directly. Suddenly the prosecutor interrupted our conversation and seriously told the suspect that he was not allowed to discuss this issue. I took out the related judicial interpretations from the High Court and High Procuratorate. The prosecutor just ignored these interpretations and argued they know this document but their Procuratorate does not inform the prosecutors to follow the document, thus they cannot enforce it. I said that "can I argue that I do not know the law, and then the law is invalid to me?" The prosecutor did not even want to answer my question and just repeated that "we do this all the time, you are not allowed to ask the facts of the case." I am afraid and asked "may I ask the amount of the bribery? May I ask … ?" He replied: "No, this is the rule." The meeting finished very quickly. Afterwards, the prosecutor patted my shoulder and said: "I hope that you lawyers can cooperate with us." As a lawyer, what did I do in the meeting? All my work, as the law enforcement officers told me, is "letting the suspect feel comfortable." I am here to let the suspect feel comfortable and to bring them some comfort."[82]

---

79 Chen Ruihua, "向誰辯護 ，向誰傾聽？以律師會見權問題為切入的分析" [Defend to Whom? Listen to Whom? The Analysis of the Right to Access Counsel] in Lang Sheng (ed.), 刑事辯護與非法證據排除 [Defence System and the Exclusionary Rule] (Beijing University Press, Beijing 2008) 75.

80 Ibid.

81 Sun Yequan, "做一個刑辯律師究竟有多難—律師參與刑事訴訟活動有關問題的思考" [How Difficult to be a Defense Attorney—Thinking of the Related Questions about Participating Criminal Procedure Activities] (2003) *Chinese Lawyer* 67, 67.

82 Kang Huaiu, "讓我看到法律–刑辯律師的真實處境及其他" [Let Me See the Law—The Real Reality of Defense Attorneys] (2005) *The Lawyer and Law* 1, 2.

Let us return to the context of illegally obtained confessions and the exclusionary rule. If defense attorneys were not allowed to discuss the facts of torture cases with their clients, how could they defend their clients? How could lawyers give opinions about consequences that are likely to result from a client's conduct? How could lawyers assist the client to determine the validity, scope, meaning, or application of the law? Without knowing all the facts, how could lawyers possibly know whether or not their clients were tortured?

Further, the issue of burden of proof and standard of proof offers another example of that the criminal process moves toward the crime control model. There exists no standard of proof in the context of the exclusionary rule. The Code of Criminal Procedure is silent about this important issue. The beyond-a-reasonable-doubt standard does not exist. The silent legislation has again shifted the criminal justice system to a crime control model on the interrogation of suspects to gain evidence of their guilt. As will be discussed in more detail in 6.2, the burden of proof should be on the prosecutor once the defendant has made a police torture case.[83] The Code of Criminal Procedure should impose a higher burden of proof on prosecutors regarding the admissibility of illegally obtained evidence.

In addition, most scholars ignore the question of, "what role should the prosecutor play in excluding illegally obtained evidence?" The prosecutor can evaluate evidence, whether it is admissible or inadmissible, in considering whether it is likely the defendant is guilty. The reality is that Chinese prosecutors keep using illegally obtained evidence to prosecute suspects,[84] as the evidence the prosecutor has against the defendant is instrumental in his decision to pursue a prosecution. A prosecutor's task is to introduce evidence that enables judges to reach the conclusion that the defendant is guilty beyond a reasonable doubt. Even if the evidence is inadmissible,the prosecutor can use it in the indictment and introduce the evidence in the trial stage. The prosecutor, however, shares in the responsibility of ensuring a fair trial. In this context, it is crucial for a prosecutor to increasingly rely on the exclusionary rule prior to arraignment to protect the innocent from conviction pursuant to Article 65 of the People's Procuratorate's Criminal Procedure Rule, which provides that confessions from suspects, victims and witnesses obtained by torture, threat, enticement and deceit cannot be used to incriminate.[85] Prosecutors also play their role in the administration of justice. A prosecutor cannot give evidence obtained by torture of the person in criminal proceedings. Article 16 of United Nations Guidelines on the Role of Prosecutors[86] provides:

> When prosecutors come into possession of evidence against suspects that they know or believe on reasonable grounds was obtained through recourse to

83 See 6.2.1.

84 See 6.1.

85 "人民檢察院刑事訴訟規則" [People's Procuratorate's Criminal Procedure Rule], promulgated on Dec. 16, 1998, effective on Jan. 18, 1999.

86 UN Doc. A/CONF. 144/28/Rev.1 (1990).

> unlawful methods, which constitute a grave violation of the suspect's human rights, especially involving torture or cruel, inhuman or degrading treatment or punishment, or other abuses of human rights, they shall refuse to use such evidence against anyone other than those who used such methods, or inform the Court accordingly, and shall take all necessary steps to ensure that those responsible for using such methods are brought to justice.[87]

In addition, under Article 3 of the Regulations Concerning a Number of Questions of Excluding Illegally Obtained Criminal Evidence,[88] the judicial interpretations regarding the confession exclusionary rule issued by the Supreme Court and the Supreme Procuratorate, a Chinese prosecutor should exclude illegally obtained confessions during the investigative phase.[89]

Another problem is the abuse of power by the prosecutor. Prosecutors exercise their authority with almost no supervision. A striking example of prosecutor abuse of power appears in the *Chen* case. Chen, a Chinese defense attorney and a graduate of Beijing University School of Law, defended a corruption case in 2001. When the prosecutor in charge of this case tried to get information from Chen's client, Chen curtly replied, "I am his lawyer, I cannot reveal my client's information to you because I have the privilege not to do so."[90] The prosecutor angrily told Chen, "Let's wait and see if you can have your privilege."[91] Several days later, Chen was summoned by the prosecutor and was detained for one year.[92]

A license to enforce law is not a license to break law. The attorney–client privilege, the oldest confidential communications privilege in the common law,[93] protects communications, written or oral, between a client and attorney made in confidence for the purpose of obtaining legal advice.[94] This privilege is the main restraint on prosecutors seeking to investigate defense attorneys and helps the proper functioning of the legal system. Unfortunately, the prosecutor's action in this case completely disregarded any concept of the attorney–client privilege.

The suppression of crime cannot justify the use of evidence obtained as a result of illegal investigations by the police. While the rise in crime undoubtedly requires that appropriate measures be taken, the right to a fair administration of justice

---

87 Article 16 of United Nations Guidelines on the Role of Prosecutors.

88 "關於辦理刑事案件排除非法證據問題若干問題的規定" [The Regulations Concerning a Number of Questions of Excluding Illegally Obtained Criminal Evidence], promulgated on July 1, 2010.

89 Article 3 of the Regulations Concerning a Number of Questions of Excluding Illegally Obtained Criminal Evidence.

90 Yanfei Ran, "When Chinese Criminal Defense Lawyers Become the Criminals" (2009) 32 *Fordham International Law Journal* 988, 988.

91 Ibid.

92 Ibid.

93 *Upjohn Co. v. United States*, 449 U.S. 383, 389 (1981).

94 *Klitzman, Klitzman and Gallagher v. Krut*, 744 F.2d 955, 960 (3d Cir. 1984).

nevertheless holds such a prominent place that it cannot be sacrificed for the sake of expedience.

Thirdly, in practice, no exclusionary rule exists in the trial stage.

Courts are the "judicial organs of the state"[95] and carry the responsibility to administer justice, under Article 123 of the Constitution. The judiciary should be the key check on the executive branch. Yet it seems that Chinese courts do not take their responsibility to administer justice seriously. The Code of Criminal Procedure process features no right of confrontation to ensure the quality of the evidence that courts consider. As I will discuss in Chapter 6, the most serious problem in the way courts currently determine facts is their use of illegally obtained evidence.[96]

In practice, illegally or unfairly obtained evidence is not excluded. There is no exclusionary rule that prevent the presentation of illegally obtained evidence at the trial, and almost no opportunity of any kind for the exclusion of evidence. There exists neither the confession exclusionary rule nor the search and seizure exclusionary rule in China. Courts admit almost any type of illegal evidence.

The Chinese presiding judge has full control of the process, asking most of the questions himself and guiding matters with a firm hand. Judges fail to focus on procedural justice, concentrating mainly on the substantive justice. China still adopts the approach that generally allows the admission of almost any evidence, regardless of how obtained. Courts continue to adhere to the crime control model of criminal adjudication when evaluating confessions, interrogations, and searches and seizures. Courts continuously reflect the desire to permit illegally obtained evidence to be admitted in criminal trials, particularly those perceived as "serious," and where the confession and material is central to the prosecution case. Judges prefer crime control model values rather than those of due process model, notwithstanding a police breach of Code of Criminal Procedure.

Despite the frequency and consequences of police torture, current responses to the problem are ineffective. The *Du Peiwu* case and the *Liu Yun* case, for instance, send a clear signal to Chinese courts to admit any evidence in criminal cases.[97] Courts have held that the defendant should prove torture, brutality and similar outrageous conduct. Illegally or unfairly evidence is still admissible because the lack of the exclusionary rule in practice. As a result, exclusion of illegally obtained evidence is still not a remedy in China.

There is no effective remedy for a breach of Article 50 of the Code of Criminal Procedure. In the context of the confession exclusionary rule, the standard and the only court procedure is to do nothing except to claim that the allegation of torture as unsupported by the evidence or unfounded.[98] In a murder case defended by Yanfei Ran in the Beijing High Court, for example, the only evidence was the

95 Article 123 of the Chinese Constitution provides: "The People's Courts in the People's Republic of China are the judicial organs of the state."

96 See Chapter 6.

97 See 6.1.

98 Ibid.

tortured confession. Even within the confession, there were contradictions. The defendant was sentenced to the death penalty with two years' suspension.[99] Until now, I find that no court has held that it is a violation of a suspect's constitutional or legal rights to illegally obtain evidence. Courts still use it against at trial and hesitate to exclude the illegal evidence.

China emphasizes the need for a reliable fact-finding process, repression of criminal conduct and reduction in crime. Courts placed discovering the truth about the factually guilty before the fair treatment of the accused. However, it is crystal clear that the duty of judges is not to continue the work of the police and prosecutors, and then obtain a conviction at all costs but to act as a minister of justice.

All in all, I liken the relationship between the police, prosecutor and judge in the Chinese criminal process as a "relay race." Pursuant to Article 7 of the Code of Criminal Procedure, the police, the prosecutor and the judge work together to go after the predominant goal: the suppression of crime. Applying the physical metaphor, the progress of the Chinese criminal justice system is ideally to be accomplished by passing the physical object from hand to hand, like a baton in a relay race. The handling of criminal cases resembles a relay race. The police, the prosecutor and the judge are the runners in the relay race. The defendant seems like the baton in the race. In the first stage (investigating stage), the baton is in the grasp of the police. Like runners in a relay race, law enforcement officers concentrate on passing the baton to the next runner as soon as possible, leaving the rest of the race to the succeeding runners. When the prosecutor take charge, they take over the baton and retain it until they have made a prosecution. Finally, the prosecutor hands the baton to the court so that the court can make a conviction. During the criminal process, the law enforcement officers avoid dropping the "baton" in the race.[100] At the finishing line, Chinese criminal justice system is devoted to providing certainty of outcomes for criminal offenders.

As one who studies Chinese criminal process, it strikes me that the greatest defect in the criminal process is that most actors in the criminal justice system, including judges, totally identify with the crime control model to the exclusion of fidelity to the due process model, even though law enforcement officers may not even be aware of the content of Packer's crime control model.

I reject the crime control model's over-emphasis on efficiency. It is my belief that the Chinese criminal justice system can prove to be efficient, but not at the expense of human rights. If "efficiency" suggests shortcuts around reliability, these demands must be rejected. The criminal process is more complicated than simply the police finding the "truth" and all crime investigation techniques should be under effective control. Fair trial is more complicated than bad guys getting their

---

99 Yanfei Ran, "When Chinese Criminal Defense Lawyers Become the Criminals" (2009) 32 *Fordham International Law Journal* 988, 1020.

100 In other words, the "factually guilty" were not allowed to escape from prosecution and conviction.

just deserts. We should try to use the due process model as a means to promote human dignity in the criminal process.

It is time to reassess the Chinese criminal justice system. It is time to acknowledge that the insistence on the crime control model of the past 50 years have gradually eroded the right to be free from torture, and the right to be free from illegal searches and seizures imposed upon Chinese citizens.

5.3 Too Much Power and Too Little Supervision

The purpose of this section is to call attention to the scope of powers granted to the Chinese police, and the limited controls established over them. The Chinese police forces seem to have the widest power in the world. As the police are perceived as being effective at crime control, no one even tries to limit their investigatory power. On the whole, China grants the police too much power[101] and there is too little judicial supervision[102] over police investigation. At the same time, law enforcement officers enjoy extremely wide discretion in deciding how to use these far-reaching powers.[103] It creates disequilibrium in the existing Chinese criminal justice system. It is such an imbalance that poses a significant and growing threat for the protection of defendants' rights.

Police wrongdoing has played an important role in most wrongful conviction cases. Police departments, however, lack substantial internal and external mechanisms to regulate and govern the collection of evidence and the conduct of criminal investigations.

5.3.1 Broad Investigatory Powers

On the "too much power" side, the Code of Criminal Procedure confers broad investigatory powers on the police who possess the powers to arrest,[104] detain,[105]

101 See 5.3.1.

102 See 5.3.2.

103 See 6.3.

104 Article 3 of the Code of Criminal Procedure provides: The public security organs shall be responsible for the investigation, detention, execution of arrests and pretrial examination in connection with criminal cases. The people's procuratorates shall be responsible for the procuratorial work, the approving of arrests, and the investigation and initiation of public prosecution in connection with cases accepted directly by them. The people's courts shall be responsible for the trial. No other organ, organization or person shall have the right to exercise such powers, unless the laws otherwise provide.

105 Under Article 80 of the Code of Criminal Procedure, police maydetain a person, if: 1. if he is plotting to commit a crime or is in the process of committing a crime or is discovered immediately after having committed a crime; 2. if he is identified as having committed a crime by the victim or by an eyewitness; 3. if criminal evidence is found on his body or at his residence; 4. if he attempts to commit suicide or escape after committing

interrogate, conduct searches[106] and seizures,[107] and various administratively coercive measures almost without judicial supervision. For example, criminal suspects can be detained for up to 40 days before formal charging.[108] With regard to the individual's privacy, the restrictions and conditions provided by the Code of Criminal Procedure is too lax and full of loopholes.

In order to rule out general warrants, in general, both the United Kingdom and United States have developed a procedure that allows premises to be searched only under authorization by the court. In the United States, for example, the Fourth Amendment of the Constitution provides:

> The right of the people to be secure in their persons, houses, papers, and effects, against unreasonable searches and seizures, shall not be violated, and no warrants shall issue, but upon probable cause, supported by oath or affirmation, and particularly describing the place to be searched, and the persons or things to be seized.

The Fourth Amendment requires the courts to issue warrants.[109] In contrast, the Chinese police can issue arrest warrants[110] and search warrants[111] themselves. It is unclear what degree of suspicion is required. The government is not required to show probable cause to believe that the individual is violating the law before an intrusion is justified prior to execution of the search.

---

the crime, or he is a fugitive; 5. if there is a possibility of destroying evidence or falsifying evidence or colluding to make confession tally; 6. if he refuses to give his real name and address, or his identity is unknown; or 7. if he is strongly suspected of vagrantly committing crimes, frequently committing crimes or committing crimes in gangs.

106 Article 134 of the Code of Criminal Procedure provides: For the purposes of collecting criminal evidence and tracking down a criminal offender, the investigating personnel may search the person, belongings and residence of the crime suspects and persons who might hide the criminal offender or criminal evidence, as well as other relevant places.

107 Article 139 of the Code of Criminal Procedure provides: All articles and documents found in the course of an inquest and search, which may be used to prove the guilt or innocence of the crime suspect, shall be seized; articles and documents irrelevant to the case may not be seized …

108 Article 89 of the Code of Criminal Procedure provides: A public security organ which finds it necessary to arrest a person already detained shall, within three days after the detention, submit a request to the people's procuratorate for approval. Under a special circumstance, the time limit for submitting the request for approval may be extended by one to four days. With regard to major suspects committing crimes from one place to another, repeatedly committing crimes or committing gang crime, the time limit for submitting requests for approval may be extended to 30 days ….

109 *Katz v. United States*, 389 U.S. 347 (1967).

110 Article 91 of the Code of Criminal Procedure.

111 Article 136 of the Code of Criminal Procedure.

At first sight, Articles 84 and 85 of the Code of Criminal Procedure appeared to provide protection for suspects. The Code of Criminal Procedure provides that police may hold a person suspected of committing a crime for up to 24 hours.[112] If police decide to arrest the detained suspect, they should submit a written request for approval of the arrest, together with the case files and evidence, to the procuratorate. The procuratorate then decide whether to approve the request.[113] The procuratorate may issue an arrest warrant on the police officer's application if he or she is satisfied that there are reasonable grounds to believe that a suspect committed a crime within the procuratorate's jurisdiction.[114]

The problem is that these requirements have remained dead letters. In practice, the police bypass the Code of Criminal Procedure[115] and use the much more loosely regulated administrative detention as a substitute for the ordinary criminal procedure. Various forms of incarceration do not provide procedural safeguards for suspects. For instance, according to the Security Administration Punishment Regulation (SAPR), the police can send a suspect who committed minor offenses to labor camp without the participation of lawyers or the approval of the procuracy or courts. The maximum term of *Laodong jiaoyang* (re-education through labor) that can be imposed by the police is detention for four years.[116]

The result of giving sweeping powers to the police with little supervision has been the birth of superpower executive branch in the criminal justice system. Virtually unlimited police power is the very source of police torture. Restrictions on the investigatory power of the police are necessary. The most important rights are the rights to be free from torture, and to be free from illegal searches and seizures. Effective judicial restraints against the huge police power are therefore imperative.

5.3.2 Limited Judicial Supervision

On the "too little supervision" side, there is limited judicial oversight of administrative action, which causes rampant police wrongdoing. There is no check through judicial review with respect to the rights of criminal suspects under the constitution. There are no effective restraints on police wrongdoing.

---

112 Article 84 of the Code of Criminal Procedure.

113 Article 85 of the Code of Criminal Procedure provides: A public security organ intending to arrest a crime suspect shall submit a written request for approval of the arrest, together with the case files and evidence, to the people's procuratorate at the same level for examination and approval. The people's procuratorate may, when necessary, send its personnel to participate in the discussion of major cases at the public security organ.

114 Article 78 of the Code of Criminal Procedure provides: An arrest of a crime suspect or a defendant must be approved by the people's procuratorate or decided by the people's court, and shall be executed by the public security organ.

115 Chen Ruihua, "超期羈押的法律分析" [Legal Analysis of Illegal Detention] (2000) *People's Procuratorial Semimonthly* 4, 8.

116 Article 3 of the State Council Supplementary Regulations about *Laodong jiaoyang* (1979).

Without judicial supervision to speak of and internal constraints, it is no wonder that arbitrary enforcement is high. Chinese criminal courts have almost no control over police work. Article 7 of the Code of Criminal Procedure provides:

> In conducting criminal proceedings, the People's Courts, the People's Procuratorates and the public security organs shall divide responsibilities, *coordinate* their efforts and check each other so as to ensure the correct and effective enforcement of the law.[117]

Article 7 violates the spirit of judicial independence. In performing the checking function of the judiciary, judges must be free from other branches of the government. How could neutral and independent courts coordinate with procurators and the police in criminal proceedings? In practice, courts, procuratorates and the police overly emphasized "coordinate" and completely ignored the "checks."

One of the slogans in China has been that "[p]olice, procuratorate and courts are in a family."[118] The coordination relationship between the three not only seriously affects the proper functioning of the criminal justice system but it also causes the system to appear unfair, especially in anti-crime campaigns.

The 1983 anti-crime campaign provides the most striking example of the improper working relationship. According to Qu Mingsheng, a defense lawyer in Hubei Province, during the campaign, prosecutor, court and defense attorneys were on the team with the police to apprehend criminals. They all were members of a team and shared the same objective. Procurators and judges utilized the same clerical staff. Defense attorneys served as police and procurators. Procurators allowed defense attorneys to ghost-write the interrogation records themselves. Procurators were members of trial panels. They were all on the same side. Instead of a presumption of innocence and of a public trial, all trials were secret and held in detention centers.[119] In addition, some local officials do not view torturing suspects as a serious crime and take no action against it.[120] Local protection been acknowledged as a problem plaguing the judiciary.

117 Article 7 of the Code of Criminal Procedure (emphasis added).

118 Jin Xueren, "公檢法機關之間互相配合——個沉重而陳舊的刑事訴訟法原則" [Public Security Organs, Procuratorial Organs and People's Courts Act in Concert—A Heavy and Obsolete Principle in Code of Criminal Procedure] (2002) 1 *Journal of Huaqiao University (Political and Social Sciences)* 80, 83.

119 Qu Mingsheng, "我也參加了嚴打鬥爭" [I Anticipated the Strike Hard Battles] (2008). Available at: http://www.qfls.com/blog/u/qf-qms/archives/2008/169.shtml (accessed Oct. 10, 2013).

120 See 5.2.3.

5.3.3 The Price of Crime Control

During the second half of the twentieth century the crime rates in China have been spiraling.[121] Its criminal justice system has focused on crime control policies in general. There are some myths in the Chinese criminal justice system, such as the following: the innocent do not confess to crimes they did not commit; defendants receive the effective assistance of counsel; the accused has too many rights; guilt or innocence is resolved through fair and public trials; the presumption of innocence actually guides criminal justice determinations; and the criminal justice system is "soft" on crime. It seems that governments have always found a basis on which to justify harsh criminal justice policies, usually predicated on the perceived desperate consequences, for example the high crime rate, if the affected government is not allowed to resort to these "tough" policies. The combination of these myths fuels government responses to demands for harsher criminal justice policies, for example, coercive interrogation.

To respond to the rising crime rates, the government conducted three much-publicized "Strike Hard" at crime campaigns in 1983–87, 1996 and 2000.[122] During these campaigns, the government ignored procedural rules guaranteed by the Code of Criminal Procedure and imposed frequently brutal methods and tough punishments.[123] Trevaskes identifies four strategies in relation to the implementation of the 1983–86 "strike hard" campaign: announcing crime as a major problem; making criminals the enemy of modernization; changing criminal procedure and sentencing practice.[124] In order to solve the serious problem of crime and punish criminals, the government ignored the legal constraints imposed by the judiciary and did not restrain police arbitrariness, for example large waves of arrests, swift trials and severe punishment (in particular the massive use of the death penalty).[125] Law enforcement officers, detective officers in particular, saw themselves as engaged in a "war" and themselves as "warriors."

First of all, during the 1983 anti-crime campaign, the Standing Committee of the National People's Congress passed "A Decision Concerning Swift Trial Procedure of Criminals Seriously violating Social Safety," which included shortened time periods for the delivery to defendants of bills of prosecution and

121 Craig Smith, "Chinese Fight Crime with Torture and Execution" *New York Times* (New York Sep. 9, 2001) 1.

122 For discussion, see, Murray Tanner, "Campaign-Style Policing in China and Its Critics" in Borge Bakken (ed.), *Crime, Punishment and Policing in China* (Rowman and Littlefield Publishers, Lanham 2005) 171–88.

123 Craig Smith, "Chinese Fight Crime with Torture and Execution", *N.Y. Times* (New York 9 Sep. 2001) 1.

124 Susan Trevaskes, *Courts and Criminal Justice in Contemporary China* (Lexington Books, Lanham 2007) 118–34.

125 Murray Tanner, "Campaign-Style Policing in China and Its Critics" in Borge Bakken (ed.), *Crime, Punishment and Policing in China* (Rowman and Littlefield Publishers, Lanham 2005) 171.

summons and notice, and shortened time periods for appeals in certain cases,[126] from ten days to three days.

Secondly, while Article 11 of the Code of Criminal Procedure provides that the defendants shall have the right to have access to defense, all defendants were not entitled to have counsel. *All* criminal defenses were suspended.[127]

Thirdly, Article 116 of the Code of Criminal Procedure provides that during an interrogation, the number of investigating personnel may not be less than two. Qu Mingsheng, a defense attorney served as a procurator during the 1983 campaign, told his mentor procurator that it was illegal to interrogate a defendant alone. The procurator scolded Qu and told him that "this is the special time. You have to treat it correctly. You do not have to sign in the interrogation records and do not bother to think about which two names will be signed in the records."[128]

From August 1983 to July 1984, the procuratorates prosecuted about 1 million people. The courts passed judgment on 861,000 accused people; 24,000 people were executed.[129] The efficiency of these campaigns is said to be justified by their instrumental contribution to punishing the guilty and reducing crime rates. China's anti-crime policies, however, had limited impacts in curtailing crime and these impacts did not last long. The historical record does not support the claim that harsh police tactics alone can solve the problem of soaring crime rate. The crime rates slightly declined after the 1983 anti-crime campaign. However, crime rates rose gradually again in 1986. Ten years later, China had to again conduct national "Strike Hard" campaigns; crime rates rose again in 1998.[130]

The Chinese criminal justice system resorted to this sacrificing suspects' rights strategy, and the resulting increase in crime rates has shown that such hard-line tactics alone are not the answer. Simply imposing repressive and brutal methods involving torture, cruel, inhuman or degrading treatment or punishment cannot alone solve the problem of the high crime rate in Chinese society.

The cost and potential cost of anti-crime campaigns, achieved at a very high cost of a grave violation of the suspect's human rights, outweighed their relative benefits. The stakes are high, however, and these campaigns would be ineffective. In the long run, these anti-crime campaigns simply do not work. Almost immediately upon the cessation of the 1983–87 campaign, the crime rate quickly resumed its

126 The decisions applied to cases of murder, rape, robbery, bombing, and other seriously violation of public safety.

127 Central Political-Legal Committee, Report Concerning about Strike Hard at Criminal Crime Activities (1984). Available at: http://www.people.com.cn/GB/historic/1031/3642.html (accessed Oct. 10, 2013).

128 Qu Mingsheng, "我也參加了嚴打鬥爭" [I Anticipated the Strike Hard Battles] (2008). Available at: http://www.qfls.com/blog/u/qf-qms/archives/2008/169.shtml (accessed Oct. 10, 2013).

129 Ibid.

130 Ibid.

rapid upward trend.[131] Some legal enforcement agents might think it is better that 100 innocent people be convicted than that one guilty person go free. Under such situations, many of them were convicted with testimony obtained by the police possessed of unrestrained power to seize persons, hold them in secret custody and wring from them confessions by physical and mental torture. Some of them served decades in prison and even lost their valuable lives.[132] As was well described by Vice-Chancellor Knight-Bruce that "[t]ruth, like all good things, may be loved unwisely, may be pursued too keenly—may cost too much."[133]

5.4 Justification for Torture and Torture Evidence?

Is the use of evidence obtained by torture fair or foul? The police investigation scholar Du Jingji purported to justify the use of confessions obtained by torture as an important and necessary anti-crime weapon as "the number of real crimes solved through the illegal criminal practice of tortured confession is far, far greater than the number of false cases it creates."[134] The problem with these arguments is fully cloaked in the formalities of state criminal justice policy. The problem with this argument is threefold.

5.4.1 Ignoring Treaty Obligations

Although the Chinese government had avowed its commitment to international standards prohibiting the use of torture, this commitment had little effect on such conduct. The problem still persists.

First, the Chinese government misconstrues and ignores China's various treaty obligations that prohibit torture in various contexts.

The first problem is that the justification for torture and torture evidence clearly fell foul of the Chinese government's international human rights commitments. The People's Republic of China replaced the Republic of China as a permanent member of the Security Council in 1971. Since World War II, the international community has established numerous treaties and declarations to prohibit torture. The fundamental individual right to be free from torture or inhuman and degrading treatment or punishment is an internationally recognized right, which the court must enforce in all its proceedings. Various international documents obligate

---

131 Murray Tanner, "Campaign-Style Policing in China and Its Critics" in Borge Bakken (ed.), *Crime, Punishment and Policing in China* (Rowman and Littlefield Publishers, Lanham 2005) 181.

132 See 5.1–5.2.

133 *Pearse v. Pearse* (1846) 1 DeG. & Sm. 12; 63 E.R. 950, 957.

134 Du Jingji, "A Superficial Discussion of the Tortured Confession and Policies to Deal with It" in Wang Huaixu (ed.), *Research and Practice of Investigation and Interrogation* (China People's Public Security University Press, Beijing 1998) 374.

China to protect suspects against torture by state, for example, Article 5 of the Universal Declaration of Human Rights (1948) (UDHR).[135] From 1988, China has ratified a number of international human rights conventions which obligated China to refrain from sanctioning or permitting torture or other forms of cruel, inhuman, or degrading treatment. There is an affirmative obligation by China to take all necessary measures to enable individuals to enjoy the rights guaranteed in the international treaties. Two of these conventions expressly prohibit torture, inhuman or degrading treatment. Afterwards, China signed the International Covenant on Civil and Political Rights (1966) (ICCPR) in 1999.[136]

Secondly, adoption of the Convention against Torture and Other Cruel, Inhuman or Degrading Treatment or Punishment (1984) (UNCAT) should be significant move forward in affirming the goal of nations to eradicate torture. UNCAT, ratified in 1988,[137] expressed a revolutionary proposition in Article 15, according to which each state party shall ensure that any statement which is established to have been made as a result of torture shall not be invoked as evidence in any proceedings. Article 15 speaks directly to the inadmissibility of evidence obtained through torture. Governments must make sure that private individuals do not interfere with other individuals' exercise of their rights under the international human rights instruments mentioned above. Accordingly, without exception, China should comply with its international obligations and legal standards.

5.4.2 Prohibition of Torture is Absolute

Torture should never, ever be used. The right to be free from torture is a fundamental human right. Under any circumstances, torture, like cruel, inhuman, or degrading treatment, is absolutely prohibited by international human rights law, for example, the Geneva Conventions, the European Convention on Human Rights (1950) (ECHR) Article 3,[138] the American Convention on Human Rights (1969) Article

---

135 Article 5 of UDHR provides: No one shall be subjected to torture or to cruel, inhuman or degrading treatment or punishment.

136 Article 7 of ICCPR provides: No one shall be subjected to torture or to cruel, inhuman or degrading treatment or punishment. In particular, no one shall be subjected without his free consent to medical or scientific experimentation.

137 Article 2(1) of UNCAT provides: Each State Party shall take effective legislative, administrative, judicial or other measures to prevent acts of torture in any territory under its jurisdiction.

138 Article 3 of ECHR provides: No one shall be subjected to torture or to inhuman or degrading treatment or punishment.

5(2),[139] the African Charter of Human and Peoples' Rights (1981) Article 5,[140] and the Inter-American Convention to Prevent and Punish Torture (1985) Article 1.[141] Prohibitions against torture are a part of international human rights law.

Torture is universally prohibited under all circumstances. Both the Geneva Conventions and the UNCAT absolutely prohibit torture. Specifically, Article 2(2) of the UNCAT recognizes that torture cannot be justified under any circumstances "whether a state of war or a threat of war, internal political instability or any other public emergency." Furthermore, the inadmissibility of evidence obtained by torture is understood without any exceptions whatsoever under international law.

In order to ensure compliance with international law under the UNCAT, Chinese authorities cannot justify police torture by claiming that these apparent abuses are necessary to combat the growing threat of organized crime and other violent elements of Chinese society. If the government could torture suspects to get confessions and then use the confessions to obtain a conviction, there would no mechanism to limit the government's power over the administration of the criminal justice system. Accordingly, police torture must be vigorously denounced under any circumstance even if the accused is suspected of a heinous crime. Since the ban on police torture cannot be derogated from, no claim of fighting crime can ever justify deviating from it. The aim of fighting crime and the high clearance rate may not be invoked as justifications of torture and the use of evidence illegally obtained in investigation to incriminate the accused during the trial proceedings.

5.4.3 Slippery Slopes

Some legal scholars defend torture, arguing that under some circumstances (especially in the name of "war on terror"), it is justified as a proper and necessary means of ensuring efficient law enforcement and crime control.[142] They proclaim that tortured confessions are admissible. Here are two examples: first, in 2002,

---

139 Article 5(2) of the American Convention on Human Rights provides: No one shall be subjected to torture, inhuman, or degrading punishment or treatment. All persons deprived of their liberty shall be treated with respect for the inherent dignity of the human person.

140 Article 5 of the African Charter of Human and Peoples' Rights provides: Every individual shall have the right to the respect of the dignity inherent in a human being and to the recognition of his legal status. All forms of exploitation and degradation of man particularly slavery, slave trade, torture, cruel, inhuman or degrading punishment and treatment shall be prohibited.

141 Article 1 of the Inter-American Convention to Prevent and Punish Torture provides: The State Parties undertake to prevent and punish torture in accordance with the terms of this Convention.

142 A.M. Dershowitz, *Why Terrorism Works: Understanding the Threat Responding to the Challenge* (Yale University Press, New Haven 2002) 142–9; Memorandum from Office of the Assistant Attorney General to Alberto Gonzales, Counsel to the President (Aug. 1, 2002) 33–9.

Alan Dershowitz accepts nonlethal torture, argues that in some scenarios[143] the use of torture is legally justified[144] and suggests that sterilized needles be inserted under fingernails of suspected terrorists to extract information from them when the information may lead to the immediate saving of lives.[145] He claims it might be appropriate for torture to receive explicit authorization in the forms of judicial torture warrants.[146] Second, Jay Bybee, a federal judge and assistant attorney general of the United States, argues that officials can use torture against suspected terrorists without being held liable. According to him, "torture" refers *only* to infliction of the sort of extreme pain associated with death or organ failure.[147]

Those who favor leaving the door open for torture or coercive interrogation tactics usually argue that the more torture, the more crimes will be solved, and more lives will be protected. Yet this chain of proof is not established at all. It has never been shown that there is any correlation between coercive interrogation tactics and a decrease in crime. In contrast, I argue that the more we leave the door open for torture, the more Chinese citizens might be tortured in the future. The fear is that allowing the relevant activity will lead to a practice or outcome that is unequivocally unacceptable; any rationalizations of torture will help the practice thrive. It may "open the floodgates." As Sir William Holdsworth asserted that "[o]nce torture has become acclimatized in a legal system it spreads like an infectious disease."[148]

There are several different aspects of the analysis of slippery slopes in the context of torture. If we give up the no-torture taboo in criminal process, then the criminal justice system will embark on a descent along a slippery slope as enforcement agents will resort to torture in situations that are farther and farther away from the category of "rare" cases, torture methods and the candidate of torture. The contagion effect will definitely emerge. It is my position that if we "legitimize" the use of torture, we won't able to stop; torture will escalate in China.

First, there will be the increasing "rare" cases.

The first serious problem is with a flat exception to torture and the confession exclusionary rule for "rare" cases. We can draw up a short list for "rare" cases, but it is very difficult to keep it short. Torture should be subject to a blanket prohibition. Supposedly, torture of suspects who committed some cases, for example, murderer, career armed robber and rapist, is justified. If the degree of a suspect's guilt is proportional to the permissibility of torturing him, can we torture

143 For instance, "ticking bomb" scenarios.

144 A.M. Dershowitz, *Why Terrorism Works: Understanding the Threat Responding to the Challenge* (Yale University Press, New Haven 2002) 142–9.

145 Ibid.,144.

146 Ibid.,156–63.

147 Memorandum from Office of the Assistant Attorney General to Alberto Gonzales, Counsel to the President (Aug. 1, 2002) 33–9.

148 William Holdsworth, vol. 5 of *A History of English Law* (3rd edn, Methuen, London 1945) 194–5.

the kidnapper who refused to reveal where the innocent children was?[149] Should we torture suspected terrorists to collect information that might be necessary to stop future attacks? Can we use torture as legitimate means of extracting confessions and other information towards suspects who committed the organized crime, human trafficking and international crime? A short list of serious crimes is not likely to stay short.

In terms of efficacy of police torture, does torture produce reliable information? Torture, according to Judge Antonio Cassese, is especially effective with common criminals (for example, theft). Many thieves said that after an hour of torture, they admitted to everything they had done.[150] Under such circumstances, most crimes in the penal code will be subject to torture. Police torture, however, should not be a last resort to solve those cases mentioned above.

Secondly, torture techniques are brutalizing.

The removal of legal and psychological constraints against torture may increase police brutality. Once police torture is authorized, the torturers tend to become more and more expert in using them effectively. When old methods of torment become ineffective, they will be replaced with more subtle and sophisticated ones. Harsh police tactics may become harsher. The torturers will learn to torture their victims without leaving any trace, for example, exposing suspects to extreme cold and heat.

Thirdly, there will be the increasing candidate of torture.

The Roman Republic began using torture to assure that confessions extracted from slaves were true. However, during the late Empire, judicial torture was extended to second-class citizens,[151] and was used against "free citizens charged with high treason, which was known as *crimen majestatis*."[152]

If we legalize police torture, more and more complete innocents, excluding criminal suspects, might be permissible subject to torture. For example, police may threaten that the suspect's mother is going to be tortured if the suspect does not cooperate. Police may torture uncooperative witnesses or informants to secure incriminating information. It may also become a device for punishing prisoners and intimidating political opponents of the regime, potentially disruptive religious-based movements such as Falungong, labor activists, and minority rights activists including Tibetans and Xijiang Muslims claiming self-determination.[153]

---

149 See 1.4 Magnus Gaefgen case.

150 Antonio Cassese, *Inhuman States: Imprisonment, Detention and Torture in Europe Today* (Polity Press, Oxford 1996) 69.

151 Kenneth Roth, "A History of Torture" in Kenneth Roth, Minky Worden and Amy Bernstein (eds), *Torture: Does It Make Us Safer? Is It Ever OK?—A Human Rights Perspective* (Human Rights Watch, New York 2005) 5.

152 Matthew Lippman, "The Development and Drafting of the United Nations against Torture and Other Cruel, Inhuman or Degrading Treatment or Punishment" (1994) 17 *The Boston College International and Comparative Law Review* 275, 276.

153 These are examples of what might happen.

Relaxing the confession exclusionary rule provided in the Chinese judicial interpretations increases the likelihood of police torture and coerced confessions, which may result in its routine use as an instrument of law enforcement.

5.5 Conclusion

This chapter has explored the character and magnitude of the police torture problem in China. China's long history and ongoing police torture coupled with the ghastly conditions of pretrial confinement make imperative the need for a sharper instrument for dealing with this particular police misconduct. Abuses including police torture and threat were not conjectural, but actual and endemic. I am opposed to the use of force, threats, promise of leniency, trickery and deceit in order to secure incriminating information from the suspects as all of which might well induce an innocent person to confess.

The civilization of a society is mirrored in how it treats the suspects and defendants by its law enforcement agents of the nation. In any event, government officials should not view torture as the shortcut to the solving of crime. Physical and psychological violence against defendants to procure confessions and evidence violates fundamental principles of justice. Criminal procedure law should not be used as an instrument of repression to serve the ends of the party in power. The abolition of Article 118 of the Code of Criminal Procedure is necessary.

In fact, there is no greater failure of the Chinese criminal justice system than the conviction and execution of an innocent person. A series of chilling cases, however, ushered in an era of profound concern about police tactics in extracting confessions in China after 1949. There is an understandable impulse to say that these scandals are the result of a few bad apples. Unfortunately, that is not true; there are still many apple trees. Furthermore, the number of unreported cases may be quite large. Have the lessons from the chilling cases mentioned above been learned? It is unlikely without the exclusionary rule. While the Chinese government appears to have taken some measures to strengthen the right to be free from torture, these reforms still cannot solve the problem of torture. Police torture continues to plague China.

Given the failings of the current criminal justice system to protect the right to be free from torture, it is evident that a massive overhaul of the system is in order. An enforceable ban on police torture would be a good start. Obtaining confessions from a defendant by means of torture violates the Code of Criminal Procedure, and the evidence thus obtained should never ever be used at trial. A guarantee of freedom from torture which does not carry with it the exclusionary rule will be reduced to mere words. To comply fully with the Supreme People's Court and Supreme People's Procuratorate interpretations, the Chinese legislature should establish the exclusionary rule to ensure the right to be free from torture, and the right to be free from illegal searches and seizures.

The Chinese authorities should seek to revolutionize the judicial supervision of police interrogation and searches. China should make combating police torture a higher priority and advance this cause through establishing the exclusionary rule. The court should suppress evidence where the investigator has failed to follow the rules.

As we seek a solution to eradicate police torture in China, I propose to resolve the question of torture by using the confession exclusionary rule. In addition, in order to guard against illegal searches, search warrants should be issued by the court. An enforced search and seizure exclusionary rule would be a promising follow-up. We contend that the rule is an indispensable shield against the overzealous police and the most effective way to solve this problem. The judiciary shall not tolerate illegal law enforcement practice and refuse to use such evidence against any suspects. Ban on torture includes a ban on evidence retained through torture.

I conclude that the exclusionary rule places significant restraints on the use of torture and illegal searches that we performed in order to obtain evidence to be used against the suspect in a criminal trial. This is a road of no return. If China leaves the window open a crack, the wind that has chilled to the bone in Imperial China will soon fill the whole room.

Chapter 6
The Operation of the Exclusionary Rule

Although the Chinese government seems intent on solving the problem of police torture,[1] the courts have adopted a purely passive attitude when confronted with illegally obtained evidence. As discussed below, if the police are trying to use illegally obtained evidence, judges almost always find a way to admit it. Judges tried to avoid the torture issue in trial; in the eyes of most of them, the admissibility of evidence seems like an uncomplicated issue.[2]

In civil law systems, including China, criminal judges should render an explanation of the admissibility of evidence at issue in written judgments. Even if the evidence is inadmissible, the court should provide reasons. However, courts often do not address the admissibility of illegally obtained evidence in their judgments.[3]

Additionally, judges are reluctant to suppress testimony as a result of a violation of Article 50 of the Code of Criminal Procedure.[4] Courts also have been reluctant to suppress physical evidence obtained by illegal methods from criminal trials because they are so powerfully probative of guilt.[5] In a empirical study in 2006 on the power to exclude illegally obtained evidence, Wu Danhong concluded that Chinese judges were reluctant to exercise their exclusionary powers following a finding that evidence had been illegally obtained.[6] This reluctance was especially acute in serious criminal cases.[7] Extremely few cases have reported exclusion of crucial evidence due to torture, illegal searches and seizures or other violations of suspects' rights.

China prioritizes the need to maintain law and order over the rights of suspects.[8] This reflects a pragmatic view that a police investigation should not be restricted

---

1 See Chapter 5 Introduction.

2 See 6.1.1–6.1.2.

3 Ibid.

4 Article 50 of the Code of Criminal Procedure provides: Judges, procurators and investigators must, in accordance with the legally prescribed process, collect various kinds of evidence that can prove the criminal suspect's or defendant's guilt or innocence and the gravity of his crime. It shall be strictly forbidden to extort confessions by torture and to collect evidence by threat, enticement, deceit or other unlawful means.

5 See 6.1.1–6.1.2.

6 Wu Danhong, "非法證據排除規則的實證研究—以法院處理刑訊逼供辯護為例" [A Positive Study of Exclusion of Illegally Obtained Evidence—Cases Concerning Using Torture to Coerce a Confession] (2006) 28 *Modern Law Science* 143, 144–5.

7 See 6.1.1–6.1.2.

8 See 6.3.3.

if it produces the "right" outcomes. The practical result of this passive attitude is to undermine the incentive to eliminate police wrongdoing. As a practical matter, having illegally obtained confessions excluded is extremely difficult in China. The difficulty stems from both the passive attitude of judges[9] and the burden of proof.[10]

This chapter ventures into an area of evidence law in which the practical dimension is strong. The chapter will challenge the notion that Chinese courts should maintain a passive attitude toward the illegally obtained evidence by examining the cases of *Du Peiwu* and *Liu Yong*. This chapter is divided into three main parts. First, the major purpose of this section is to canvass the attitude of Chinese criminal judges towards illegally obtained evidence. The Chinese approach to confessions obtained by torture has been mostly consistent from 1949 to today: the chief criterion for admissibility of evidence is its relevance to the charge. Relevant evidence is admissible, however it has been obtained.

The second section then deals with whether, where torture is alleged, the burden of proof should fall on the suspects or prosecution. The main issue here is whether it is for a defendant to prove that statement was obtained by illegal methods, or for the prosecution to prove that it was not obtained illegally. The next question that arises is: what is the relevant standard of proof? The Chinese literature has largely overlooked the subject of the burden and standard of proof. I believe this important subject needs special attention. It explores the reasons why procuratorates should show the nonexistence of police torture.

Lastly, the third section turns to an analysis of evidence obtained by searches and seizures. There were many deficiencies in the Code of Criminal Procedure that led to the lack of a search and seizure exclusionary rule in practice. I will address the deficiencies in the related law. Systematic abuses have accumulated over the past decades and the law's deficiency is the crucial causative factor. A change in the substantive law of search and seizure is necessary.

6.1 Judicial Response to Police Torture

The *Du Peiwu* case and *Liu Yong* case are classic examples of the attitude of the courts when considering the admissibility of confessions obtained through torture. My review of cases shows that Chinese courts are generally reluctant to exclude evidence obtained by torture, especially in the case in which the exclusion would result in releasing a defendant who was clearly guilty of the charged offense. What is most frightening about the court's approach to the admissibility of illegally obtained evidence is its apparent unwillingness to accept the basic principle that the end of efficient crime control does not justify the means used.

9 See 6.1.3.
10 See 6.2.

6.1.1 The Du Peiwu Case

6.1.1.1 If you do not confess, we torture you I will start with two cases, both of which attracted national attention. The first is the *Du Peiwu* case which provides a dramatic illustration of the court's attitude towards a typical wrongful conviction case. In 1998, Du Peiwu, a policeman, was accused of murdering his wife (a policewoman) and her boyfriend (a deputy superintendent) in Kunming of Yunnan Province. Du was illegally arrested, detained and seriously beaten. The Deputy Superintendent of the Kunming Police Station told Du that "if you do not want to confess to others, just tell me the truth. We are all police officers. Once you confess to me, I will try my best to help you."[11] After 10 days of incessant interrogation, incommunicado detention, and torture, he falsely declared that he had murdered two victims.

His hands, legs and knees were covered with bruises. Du had evidence that the charges against him were based on a false confession obtained through torture (sleep deprivation, hanging by the hands and serious beatings). In order to prove the existence of torture, Du asked the procuratorate to take pictures of his injuries.

In trials, Du alleged that he made the statement in order to avoid further torture. His defense lawyer objected to the charge, contending Du's confessions were inadmissible because of they were obtained by torture. Du also asked the procuratorate to show the picture of bruises. The procuratorate at first claimed there was no picture and then argued that the picture was missing. The judge asked Du to prove the existence of torture. To do this, Du had secretly hidden the bloody clothes after he was tortured.[12]

6.1.1.2 If you are not guilty, prove it—The response During his next interrogation by the judge, in order to prove his mistreatment, he took his shirt off to reveal wounds from being beaten, hung by handcuffed wrists, shocked with a cattle prod, and showed the bloody clothes in public. This was plainly visible to all during the trial. However, the judge prevented Du from pursuing this point and said "stop arguing this question. If you are not guilty, prove it."[13] The judges disagreed on whether the evidence obtained through torture should be inadmissible. The court

---

11 Cui Min, "再論遏制刑訊逼供" [Rethinking the Elimination of Torture] (2003) 76 *Journal of Zhejiang Police College* 24, 26.

12 Hu Ming, "刑訊逼供的證明責任之思考—兼談英美法系證明責任分層理論給我們的啟示" [The Thinking of the Burden of Proof for Torture—Lessons on the Burden of Proof in Common Law] (2005) 4 *Journal of Chinese People's Public Security University* 60, 60.

13 Chao Mingwei, "由杜培武案解讀司法程序層面的公正審判權" [Interpreting the Right to a Fair Trial in the Judicial Procedure from the Case of *Du Peiwu*] (2008) 12 *Legal System and Society* 147.

allowed the use of the statements obtained through torture. The trial court had erred in admitting the confessions into evidence.

In spite of a solid alibi and a lack of physical evidence linking him to the murders, Du was convicted and sentenced to death by the Kunming Intermediate Court.[14] Du appealed his death sentence to the Yunnan High Court, apparently arguing that he was entitled to suppression of the illegally obtained confessions. Du was spared immediate execution and given a sentence, peculiar to the Chinese system, namely, the death penalty with a two-year reprieve by the court.[15] After Du had been detained for over two years, the real murderers were caught.[16] Du's convictions rested solely upon confessions shown to have been extorted by the police by brutality and violence.

In the present case, if after examining all the evidence, the judges had a reasonable doubt as to the admissibility of the confession; they should have found Du not guilty. The judges, however, turned a blind eye to torture and took a wholly passive attitude toward the admissibility of confessions obtained by torture in this case. Here, the defendant's "confession" was involuntary and the court should have required the prosecution to prove that the confessions were voluntary. For further analysis of *Du*, see *infra* 6.1.3.

6.1.2 The Liu Yong Case

6.1.2.1 Insufficient evidence to support the claim of torture—The response Another disappointing criminal case is that of Liu Yong. It again illustrates the acceptance of the crime control framework.[17] From 1989 to 2000, Liu Yong, the kingpin of an organized group in Shenyang City of Liaoning Province, was involved in assaults, robbery, possession of firearms and ammunition and bribery of public officials (including the former President and Vice President of the Shenyang City Intermediate Court).

During the trial in the Tieling Intermediate Court (first instance), Liu alleged that he had been beaten and tortured by police officers. Despite this, the court allowed the use of the confession evidence. Referring to the issue of police torture, the court concluded that there was insufficient evidence to support the claim.[18] The confession evidence was admitted at trial despite Liu's objections.

---

14 Kun Xing Chu 394 (The Kunming Intermediate Court, 1998). (1998) 昆刑初字第394號（昆明市中級人民法院).

15 Uan Gao Xing I Chu 68 (The Tieling Intermediate Court, 1999). (1999) 雲高刑一終字第295號（雲南省高級人民法院).

16 Wang Zhao and Zhou Jing, "杜培武案的證據學思考" [The Case of *Du Peiwu* as Viewed from the Science of Evidence] (2003) 19 *Shantou University Journal (Humanities and Social Sciences Bimonthly* 54, 54.

17 See 1.3.

18 Xie Zhong Xing Chu 68 (The Tieling Intermediate Court, 2001). (2001) 鐵中刑初字第68號 （鐵嶺市中級人民法院).

The Intermediate Court emphasized that Liu did not prove that he was tortured by the police. Liu was convicted of all the crimes mentioned above and sentenced to death.

Liu's defense lawyer consulted 14 Chinese scholars, including, Chen Guangzhong (the former President of China University of Political Science and Law) and Chen Xingliang (Vice-Dean of the Beijing University Law School). These scholars concluded that evidence obtained by torture should be excluded.[19]

Liu appealed his case to the Liaoning High Court (second instance). In the trial of second instance, after interrogating the police officers who were in charge of guarding Liu and interrogating Liu, the court concluded that "they cannot exclude the possibility that Liu was tortured by the police during the investigation."[20] It seems that in light of the new information concerning the confessions obtained by torture, Liu was spared immediate execution and sentenced to death with a two-year reprieve.[21] Although the High Court did not explain why the sentence was changed from death to death with a reprieve, the most probable reason is that it accepted Liu's claims of torture.

However, many persons demanded an immediate death penalty.[22] Because of the strident public uproar, in a rare and controversial move, the Supreme People's Court (SPC) held, in 2003, an extraordinary third trial. The Supreme People's Court concluded that there had been no torture by the police at the investigation stage. The Supreme People's Court quashed the verdict and reinstated the original death sentence, which was immediately carried out.[23] After the Supreme People's Court's final ruling in December 2003, Liu was immediately taken from the court to a nearby funeral home to be executed and cremated within four hours.[24]

6.1.2.2 The error of the court Both *Du Peiwu* and *Liu Yun* are very disappointing. The reasoning in the *Liu Yun* case by the Supreme People's Court is extremely vulnerable on several different levels and from several different perspectives. The case *Liu* provided the Supreme People's Court with an opportunity to provide guidance on the issue of the burden of proof of evidence obtained through torture. Unfortunately, the Supreme People's Court missed the chance. I argue that the

19 Chen Xingliang, "中國刑事司法改革的考察：以劉涌和佘祥林案為標本" [The Examination of Chinese Criminal Justice Reform: Taking the Example of *Liu Yun* and *She Xianglin*] (2006) 6 *Zhejiang Social Sciences* 59, 60.

20 Liao Xing I Zhong 152 (The Liaoning High Court, 2003). (2002) 遼刑一終字第152號（遼寧省高級人民法院）.

21 Ibid.

22 Ji Xiangde, "民憤的正讀—杜培武佘祥林等錯案的司法性反思" [An Authentic Interpretation of the People's Wrath—Reflection on Unjust Cases of Du Peiwu and She Xianglin, etc.] (2006) 28 *Modern Law Science* 153, 155.

23 Xing Ti 5 (The Supreme People's Court, 2003). (2003) 刑提字第5號（最高人民法院）.

24 Hong Lu and Terance D. Miethe, *China's Death Penalty: History, Law and Contemporary Practices* (Routledge, London and New York 2007) 113.

Supreme People's Court erred in three respects. To begin with, the SPC claimed that according to the statements of police officers in charge of interrogating and detaining Liu, these officers did not torture Liu,[25] but these officers might be torturers. It seems unrealistic to expect these police torturers would confess to torture if the court takes a passive attitude.

Secondly, the Supreme People's Court argued that between August 2000 and July 2001, the designated Shenyang Police Hospital examined Liu and his co-defendants 39 times; no marks were found in their bodies.[26] Because the marks resulted from torture fade after several days, the fact that no marks were found does not establish the nonexistence of torture. In addition, the designated Police Hospital was under the control of the Shenyang Police Station. The credibility of its reports is very doubtful.

Thirdly, the Supreme People's Court claimed that the way in which the statements (provided by the defense lawyer) obtained from witnesses to prove the existence of torture did not conform to the "related laws" and the witnesses statements contradicted each other[27] but the Court did not explain what the "related laws" are and how the witnesses' statement contradicted. The issue in this case is whether the investigation methods used by police, instead of the defense lawyer, conformed to the Code of Criminal Procedure.

It is worth noting that the Intermediate Court emphasized that Liu did not prove that he was tortured by the police. The High Court stubbornly refused to admit the existence of torture even after interrogating the police officers who were in charge of guarding and interrogating Liu. On the issue of existence or nonexistence of torture the *Du Peiwu* and *Liu Yong* courts were silent. The dicta of both cases are equivocal; they neither affirmed the nonexistence of torture nor admitted its existence.

6.1.3 The Court's Response: Passive Attitude

This section discusses the responses of the court to the defense lawyer's argument that confessions should be inadmissible because they were obtained by torture. The Chinese criminal justice system presented dismal pictures of official lawlessness: the judiciary simply evinced a passive attitude toward confessions obtained through torture. I outline the court's three prevalent responses to this situation.

First, the court completely ignored the issue of torture.

Both the issue of torture and the admissibility of evidence obtained through torture are often not considered by courts.[28] Judges have turned a blind eye to

25 Xing Ti 5 (The Supreme People's Court, 2003). (2003) 刑提字第5號（最高人民法院）.

26 Ibid.

27 Xing Ti 5 (The Supreme People's Court, 2003). (2003) 刑提字第5號（最高人民法院）.

28 See 6.1.1–6.1.2.

cases of police torture. For example, in *Du*, the judges simply ignored the stark evidence that Du had been tortured into confessing. Additionally, in the *Zhong Huazhou* case,[29] the defense lawyer argued that it is very likely the defendant was tortured; therefore the statements obtained during custodial interrogation should be inadmissible. The court said nothing about this important issue at all. The judge did not give his reasons for his decision at this issue. This violates the principle that "the judge must give his reasons for his decision."[30] As Lord Denning put it a half century ago, "in order that a trial should be fair, it is necessary, not only that a correct decision should be reached, but also that it should be seen to be based on reasons."[31]

Furthermore, a number of empirical studies conducted in China in the confession exclusionary rule context provide support for my observation. Using participant observation, Wu Danhong observed a trial of drug case in an Intermediate Court in the south of China. The procuratorate asked whether the first defendant pled guilty. The first defendant pleaded not guilty and argued that the reason he confessed was because the police beat him. The judge did not say anything and asked the procuratorate to keep asking questions. The procuratorate read the first defendant's incriminating confessions and told the first defendant that all other three co-defendants had confessed that he also committed the crime, and that it is useless to attempt to retract the original confessions. The procuratorate also claimed that since the first defendant had overturned his original confessions, he has to provide new evidence; otherwise, he belongs to the category of people who refuse to plead guilty. For this "reason," the procuratorate suggested that the court should impose a severe sentence on the defendant. During the whole trial, the trial judge took a *completely* passive attitude toward the existence of torture. After the trial, the judge made no reference to tortured confessions.[32]

Moreover, in 1984, the General Assembly of the United Nation adopted the Convention against Torture and Other Cruel, Inhuman or Degrading Treatment or Punishment (UNCAT).[33] China became a signatory to the UNCAT in 1988.[34] At that point the UNCAT became binding on China. China is committed to the worldwide elimination of torture. Article 12 of UNCAT requires each state party to investigate any torture allegations when reasonable grounds exist to believe such

29 Xian Xing Chua 0134 (The Hangzhou City Xiaoshan District Court, 2005). (2005) 蕭刑初字第0134號 (杭州市蕭山區人民法院).

30 Alfred Denning, *The Road to Justice* (Stevens and Sons, London 1955), 29.

31 Ibid.

32 Wu Danhong, "非法證據排除規則的實證研究—以法院處理刑訊逼供辯護為例" [A Positive Study of Exclusion of Illegally Obtained Evidence—Cases Concerning Using Torture to Coerce a Confession] (2006) 28 *Modern Law Science* 143, 144.

33 G.A. Res. 39/46, Annex, 39 U.N. GAOR Supp. No. 51 at 197, U.N. Doc. A/39/51 (Dec. 10, 1984).

34 Xue Hongtao, "國際人權公約在中國的實施" [The Practice of International Human Rights Conventions in China] (2008) *Human Rights* 21, 22.

acts have occurred.[35] Article 15 of UNCAT speaks directly to the use of evidence obtained by torture and makes clear that confessions made as a result of torture are inadmissible. It requires states to ensure that "any statement which is established to have been made as result of torture shall not be invoked as evidence in any proceedings."[36] Article 15 provides the court with the right to suppress evidence procured through torture in any proceedings, and an important enforcement and prevention tool in the fight against torture.

As a signatory to UNCAT, China should actively fight the perpetrators of torture and take sufficient steps to investigate and prevent it. Thus, any suspect who alleges that he has been subjected to torture must be assured that allegations of abusive conduct are taken seriously, and that his case will be fully investigated and examined by competent authorities.

I call on China to join with the community of law-abiding nations in prohibiting, investigating, and prosecuting all acts of torture, undertaking to prevent other cruel punishment, and excluding confessions obtained through torture. At the moment, I assert that China should adopt the burden of proof[37] to prove torture used by the international community[38] in UNCAT cases. These decisions[39] decided by the United Nation Committee against Torture may provide some guidance and helpful for Chinese adjudicators. In the future, China should bring its Code of Criminal Procedure into conformity with the UNCAT and enact laws that incorporate the UNCAT's provisions in domestic law. It is important to look to norms of international law for guidance.

Secondly, was there insufficient evidence to prove torture?

In China's inquisitorial system, it is the obligation of the judge to take all steps necessary to decide both questions of fact and law, and then to determine whether the accused has committed the alleged offense. The judge should *ex officio* investigate evidence for the purposes of discovering the truth. The Code of Criminal Procedure explicitly states that "if the collegial panel has doubts about the evidence, it may announce an adjournment, in order to carry out investigations to verify the evidence. When carrying out investigations to verify evidence, the People's Court may conduct inquest, examination, seizure, expert evaluation, as well as inquiry and freeze."[40]

Judges were allowed to investigate evidence on their own initiative. In fact, the court does have broad powers to fully investigate a claim of torture. They can

35 Article 12 of the Torture Convention.

36 Article 15 of UNCAT.

37 Article 3 of UNCAT implicitly lays the burden of proof on the State party.

38 International law and practice in relation to torture place greater emphasis on the role of the States and their duties.

39 Tunisia [2003] UNCAT 13; CAT/C/31/D/189/2001 (Nov. 20, 2003) [9.15]; Sweden [2002] UNCAT 10; CAT/C/28/D/185/2001 (May 25, 2002) [10]; Switzerland [1994] UNCAT 1; CAT/C/12/D/13/1993 (Apr. 27, 1994) [7.3].

40 Article 191 of the Code of Criminal Procedure.

ask the accused (maybe the victim of torture), police, and witnesses before the trial judge, subpoena medical documents and decide admissibility of evidence. Of course when the court refuses to exercise its powers, the only and inevitable result is that there is insufficient evidence to prove torture.

Another study of Hainan province criminal cases from 2000 to 2005 found that in 19 of the 33 cases where lawyers argued that confessions should be suppressed because of torture, the court admitted all confessions and claimed that there was insufficient evidence that defendants could prove the existence of torture.[41]

I assert that the Chinese courts have an obligation to investigate complaints of torture or ill treatment. The obligation to open an investigation arises whenever a suspect has made a credible allegation of torture or ill treatment by the police. The duty to investigate claims of torture is implied under both Article 247 of the Criminal Law[42] and Article 3 of the Code of Criminal Procedure.[43] These two articles establish an obligation for China to investigate claims of torture or ill treatment.

Thirdly, the court asks for "fact sheet"[44] from the police to close the case.

Here the court has not taken all reasonable steps to investigate the abuses. Prompt investigation of violations does not exist, as when defendants file torture claims, the court usually ask the police to provide a "fact sheet" and the investigation of torture will be closed. The "fact sheet" is a simple paper which is supposed to provide the "facts" in the period of interrogation. Some courts asked the police station concerned to provide a paper stating that "after the investigation, there is not any illegal investigation in our police station."[45] The provider of this fact sheet might be the police torturers.[46] In effect, it is virtually impossible to ask these police torturers to confess to the existence of torture in the fact sheet.

---

41 Wu Danhong, "非法證據排除規則的實證研究—以法院處理刑訊逼供辯護為例" [A Positive Study of Exclusion of Illegally Obtained Evidence—Cases Concerning Using Torture to Coerce a Confession] (2006) 28 *Modern Law Science* 143, 144.

42 Article 247 of the Criminal Law provides: A judicial officer who extorts by torture a confession from a suspect of crime or a defendant or extorts, by means of violence, testimony from a witness shall be sentenced to fixed-term imprisonment of not more than three years or criminal detention. A judicial officer who causes another person's deformity or death shall be sentenced heavily in accordance with provisions of Articles 234 or 232 of this law.

43 Article 3 of the Code of Criminal Procedure provides: In conducting criminal proceedings, the People's Courts, the People's Procuratorate's and the public security organs must strictly observe this law and any relevant stipulations of other laws.

44 情況說明書。

45 Wang Jiancheng, "漠視程序的慘痛代價—從杜培武案件引發的思考" [The Price of Ignoring Procedure—Thinking Triggered from Yu Xinglin Case] in Cheng Guangzhong and Jiang Wei (eds), 訴訟法論叢第8卷 [The Procedure Law VIII] (Legal Press, Beijing 2003) 275.

46 Chen Xingliang, "中國刑事司法改革的考察：以劉涌和佘祥林案為標本" [The Examination of Chinese Criminal Justice Reform: Taking the Example of *Liu Yun* and

Furthermore, except under very limited circumstances, the court usually gives police torturers lenient sentences instead of harsh ones. In the *Du Peiwu* case, for instance, two of the police torturers were respectively given 12 and 18 months suspended sentences.[47]

Under Articles 247 and 232 of the Criminal Law, where a police torturer who causes another person's deformity or death, the sentence ranges from three years to death.[48] Some judges even departed from the Criminal Law range, found jail time unnecessary and exempted torturers from punishment. For example, in 1992, three police torturers who tortured suspects to death were exempted from criminal punishment because of their "outstanding work performance" and "good performance."[49] In the *Xingcheng* case,[50] all six defendants are guilty of illegal search and yet free from punishment.[51] However, I do not see why they should be free from punishment by criminal law.

In light of *Du* and *Liu*, the courts, as well as the procuratorates, are unconcerned with the manner in which a confession is procured. It seems that the goals of crime control and "accuracy" are always paramount in China. In these two cases, although the court had opportunities to establish the burden of proof of evidence obtained through torture, they completely ignored the issue. The Supreme People's Court in *Du* and *Liu* are endorsing values that align them with crime control principles.

6.2 Burden and Standard of Proof

The exclusionary rule, broadly speaking, should comprise two major elements. First, the substantive element, which includes the ambit of the illegally obtained evidence and the admissibility of illegally obtained evidence. Second, the procedural element, which includes the procedure to review the admissibility of tortured confessions and the burden of proof of illegally obtained evidence.

Just like two wings of a bird and two wheels of a bicycle, the substantive element and procedural element are two indispensable elements of the rule. On the one hand, without the substantive element, there is no object for the

---

She Xianglin] (2006) 6 *Zhejiang Social Sciences* 59, 62.

47 Wang Zhao and Zhou Jing, "杜培武案的證據學思考" [The Case of *Du Peiwu* as Viewed from the Science of Evidence] (2003) 19 *Shantou University Journal (Humanities and Social Sciences Bimonthly* 54, 54.

48 Article 247 of the Criminal Law.

49 Bi Xiaoqing, "中國犯罪嫌疑人和被告人的權利保護與反酷刑制度" [Protection of the Rights of Suspects and Defendants, and Prohibition of Torture in China] in Liu Hainian, Li Lin and Morten Kjaerum (eds), 人權與司法 [Human Rights and Administration of Justice] (China Legal System Press, Beijing 1998) 59.

50 See 6.3.3.

51 Gu Minkang, "憲法權利的深層保護—從垃圾袋的處理說起" [Further Protections of Constitutional Rights—Cases of Handling Garbage Bags] (2006) 7 *Law Science* 84, 87.

procedural element to review. On the other hand, without the procedural element, the substantive element may become a dead letter and pay lip-service to the exclusionary rule.

According to Article 65 of the People's Procuratorate's Criminal Procedure Rule, confessions from suspects, victims and witnesses obtained by torture, threat, enticement and deceit cannot be used to incriminate.[52] In addition, Article 61 of the Supreme People's Court's Interpretation on Several Questions for Enforcing the Chinese Criminal Procedure Law provides that "[i]t shall be strictly forbidden to collect evidence by illegal methods. Evidence obtained by torture, threat, enticement and deceit or other illegal methods are inadmissible."[53] If any statement obtained from a person under torture *must* be excluded during trial, the next important issue is the burden and standard of proof. The efficacy of the confession exclusionary rule depends on judicial practice in that it is judges who determine whether there is sufficient evidence of police torture. Judges have to decide whether the procuratorates or defendants should prove the existence of torture or other illegal methods, and what the standard for the burden of proof is.

The problem of the burden of proof is significant. Legislatures and courts should be sensitive to burden of proof issues in torture cases and seek to lessen the defendant's burden. So far, however, both the Code of Criminal Procedure and relevant judicial interpretations fail to explicitly stipulate on this matter. In other words, the law has failed definitively to designate the degree of proof necessary, to establish those factors upon which the evidentiary admissibility of a confession depends. I will attempt to defend that we should place the ultimate burden of proof on the prosecution in practice.

6.2.1 Heavy Burden on Defendants

Defendants (i.e., victims of torture) are in strategically more difficult positions. Although no statute places the burden of proof on defendants, most judges have imposed a heavy burden on defendants to prove the existence of torture rather than on the procuratorates to show the nonexistence of the contested declaration.[54] In practice, the defendant's signature on a confession establishes a strong presumption in favor of its validity. For example, in the *Du Xianbing* case,[55] the confession was admissible because he did not provide evidence to prove that the confession

52 "人民檢察院刑事訴訟規則" [People's Procuratorate's Criminal Procedure Rule], promulgated on Dec. 16, 1998, effective on Jan. 18, 1999.

53 "最高人民法院關於執行《中華人民共和國刑事訴訟法》若干問題的解釋" [Supreme People's Court's Interpretation on Several Questions for Enforcing the Chinese Criminal Procedure Law], promulgated on June 29, 1998, effective on Sept. 8, 1998.

54 See 6.1.1–6.1.2.

55 Wu Fa Xing Chu 58 (Ganzhou City Wuxi County Court, 2008). (2008) 巫法刑初字第58號 (重慶市巫溪縣人民法院).

was obtained by torture. In the same year, in the *Zhong Haiming* case,[56] the court argued that there was no evidence to support the existence of torture claimed by the defendant. In order to have an illegally obtained confession excluded, the defendant must overcome the weight of these presumptions first.

Additionally, judges do not explicitly address the issue of on whom the burden would lie to prove the use or non-use of torture in verdicts.[57] I contend that placing the heavy burden of proof on defendants is one of the ways the court has cabined the operation of the exclusionary rule. In one trial, for example, when the defendant argued that "I said so because I was badly beaten up by the police at that time." The judge warned the defendant and said that he should stop talking nonsense without evidence or the defendant would be barred from arguing the issue again.[58] The question is, how could the defendant prove the existence of torture?

It is preposterous to contend that defendants should bear the burden as there exists a significant hurdle for defendants who would bear the almost impossible burden of demonstrating the existence of torture and establishing their innocence. The flaw in placing the burden in defendants is plain. First, the defendant does not even know the identity of the torturer. Secondly, the defendant is in the dark. Obviously, there would be no documentation of torture. Since torture often takes place in private or in places where people are in held in custody, where preservation of physical evidence of the torture by defendants would be extremely difficult if not impossible. Thirdly, the suspects have no access to any corroborating documents from official sources. Logically, it would be completely unrealistic to expect defendants to obtain forensic evidence of torture and then to prove the existence of torture, brutality, and similar outrageous conduct in criminal cases, because defendants are denied access to such evidence. It would be exceedingly rare for defendants to be able to offer any direct evidence to establish that physical abuse occurred. Even assuming that a suspect can demonstrate that beatings occurred, he must further prove that his wounds are caused by the police, he did not hurt himself "accidentally" or by other suspects.

Some police forces in China have learnt to torment defendants in such a way as either not to leave marks or to leave marks that disappear after a couple of days. They have developed new, more sophisticated ways of doing so that are harder to detect. For example, beating the sole of the suspect's feet with a truncheon, beating him over the head with a telephone directory, putting the suspect in front of an air conditioner blowing cold air directly on him, and taking the suspect's

56 Gan Zhong Xing Er Chu 16 (Jiangxi Province Ganzhou City Intermediate Court, 2008). (2008) 贛中刑二初字第16號 (江西省贛州市中級人民法院).

57 See 6.1.1–6.1.2.

58 Wu Danhong, "非法證據排除規則的實證研究—以法院處理刑訊逼供辯護為例" [A Positive Study of Exclusion of Illegally Obtained Evidence—Cases Concerning Using Torture to Coerce a Confession] (2006) 28 *Modern Law Science* 143, 144.

clothes off in a freezing room. The police torturers may illegally prolong detention so as to conceal critical physical evidence of torture.[59]

When defendants argue the existence of torture and produce evidence, for example, showing wounds, providing photographs of bruises or medical reports on those injuries afterwards, in response, the prosecution should show that the preponderance of the evidence favored the nonexistence of torture in the procurement of the evidence; although this is less stringent than the higher standard of proof beyond a reasonable doubt, i.e., proving the nonexistence of torture to a virtual certainty.

There are serious shortcomings in the traditional way of looking at the burden of proof.[60] In both *Du Peiwu* and *Liu Yun*, the court assigned the burden of proof to defendants by requiring them to prove the existence of torture. Given this heavy burden on defendants, it is hardly surprising that illegally obtained evidence is rarely suppressed. As Lord Nicholls has observed:

> [This] approach … place[s] on the detainee a burden of proof which … he can seldom discharge. In practice that would largely nullify the principle … that courts will not admit evidence procured by torture. That would be to pay lip-service to the principle.[61]

The result is that defendants cannot discharge the burden placed on them. Placing the burden of proof on defendants will further discourage allegations of torture as defendants may think it will make no difference to tell judges or procuratorates about the fact of torture.

6.2.2 Limited Burden on the Prosecution

In a criminal case, broadly speaking, the law places the burden of proof on the prosecution. The cardinal principle is that the prosecution bears a burden to prove beyond a reasonable doubt each element of the charged offense; otherwise, the defendant is entitled to an acquittal. The prosecution, not the defendant, bears the burden of showing that the defendant's confession in its case was not obtained illegally. There are six separate reasons for placing the ultimate burden of proof on the prosecution.

The first is that, in criminal proceedings, because an accused must be considered innocent until proven guilty, the burden of proof is on the prosecution to prove guilt beyond a reasonable doubt. The procuratorates bears the burden of proving the guilt of the accused. Defendants do not have to prove their innocence. The

---

59 Cui Min, "再論遏制刑訊逼供" [Rethinking the Elimination of Torture] (2003) 76 *Journal of Zhejiang Police College* 24, 27.

60 See 6.2.1–6.2.3.

61 *A and others v. Secretary of State for the Home Department (No 2)*, [2005] UKHL 71 [80].

procuratorates carries the burden of proving every element of the crime charged against defendants and refuting arguments posed by defendants (this specifically includes the nonexistence of torture). It should be for the state to prove the guilt of a person suspected of having committed an offense as the power and resources of the state are immense in comparison to defendants. It is also for the prosecuting authorities to establish beyond reasonable doubt that the confession was not obtained by torture. If the prosecution fails to adduce sufficient evidence to prove the guilt of the accused then the accused is entitled to an acquittal. It is imperative we abide by this principle.

In the second place, the procuratorate is the party wishing to use the illegally obtained evidence. It is the procuratorate who seek to rely upon evidence which was extracted under torture. Therefore, it is appropriate that the procuratorate prove its veracity.

In the third place, the prosecution has the best access to evidence of nonexistence of torture. Some would say that to always prohibit the state from placing the burden of proof on defendants is too inflexible. However, some matters may be far easier for the prosecution to prove than the defendant, or it is simply be more expedient to require the prosecution to disprove torture than to require the defendant to prove the existence of it. The procuratorate with huge power and abundant judicial resources stands a much better chance than the suspects of obtaining further details on the circumstances of the torture. The procuratorate can obtain access to any place or premises and be able to secure the setting where torture allegedly took place. The videotaping of interrogation in custody and physical examination reports in detention centers are more readily obtained by the prosecution than the defendant. On the contrary, the defendants have no means or resources to investigate.

In addition, referring to Article 2 of ECHR, the ECtHR held that where the events in issue lie wholly within the exclusive knowledge of the state, as in the case of persons within their control in detention, strong presumption of fact will arise in respect of injuries and death occurring during the detention. In such a situation the burden of proof should be regarded as resting on the state to provide a satisfactory and convincing explanation.[62]

In the fourth place, on one hand, the imposition of burden of proof not only will force the procuratorate and police to collect evidence in a more thorough manner, for example, mandatory videotaping or audiotaping of interrogation in custody, medical testimony, mandatory physical examination in detention centers and prisons. On the other hand, the police can use these mandatory measures, such as videotape confessions, to protect themselves regarding the claim of torture. That is why I insist that interrogations need to be entirely recorded.

Fifthly, we must never forget the bedrock Anglo-American principle of the presumption of innocence. The Chinese law also recognizes the right of the accused

62 *Salman v. Turkey* (App no 21986/93) (2002) 34 EHRR 425 [100] .

to the presumption of innocence.[63] The existence of a legal burden imposed on the accused may violate the presumption of innocence.[64] The prosecution bears the burden of proof, which is inextricably linked to that basic premise fundamental to all criminal trials: the presumption of innocence.

Sixthly, and finally, but not least, it may deter police misconduct. Given the terrible danger that the innocent will be convicted on the basis of false confessions obtained through torture, imposing the burden of proof on the prosecution is an indirect means of regulating police wrongdoing. The allocation of the burden to the prosecution is particularly important because it may help deter police misconduct. This imposition provides the Ministry of Public Security with greater incentives to educate and monitor its police officers. Placing the burden on the prosecution also gives additional protection to the citizen's right to be free from torture.

From the aforementioned analysis, one must conclude that, the statutory prohibition on police torture in the criminal law cannot succeed in eliminating the practice without substantial changes in the Code of Criminal Procedure about the burden of proof. When a suspect falls into the hands of the police and, later shows wounds, bruises, fractures or other traces of trauma, ill treatment by the police is presumed as long as no other cause has been proven by the government. This is crucial because by placing the burden of proof on the procuratorate, courts can eliminate the prior insurmountable hurdle that had required defendants to prove the existence of police torture. A failure on the prosecutor's part to submit related information without a satisfactory explanation may give rise to the drawing of inferences as to the well-foundedness of the defendant's allegations of torture.

6.2.3 A Party That Asserts It Must Prove It?

Chinese procuratorates, including procuratorates in *Du Peiwu* and *Liu Yun*, insisted that the burden of proof of torture falls on the defendant. The following argument by a Senior Procuratorate of the Supreme People's Procuratorate is representative of this position:

> If the defendant argued that he was tortured by the police, then he should prove that. As the procuratorate is not the party wishing to accuse the torture by law enforcement agents, it is impossible for them to bear the burden of proof. According to the rule that a party that asserts an issue must prove it, the defendant should bear the burden.[65]

---

63 Article 12 of the Code of Criminal Procedure.

64 Fan Chongi and Xa Hong, "聯合國刑事司法準則與中國刑事訴訟法的再修改" [United Nations Criminal Justice Regulations and Revision of Chinese Code of Criminal Procedure] (2007) 11 *People's Procuratorial Semimonthly* 24, 27.

65 Zhang Jun, Jiang Wei and Tian Wenchang (eds), 刑事訴訟：控辯審三人談 [Criminal Procedure: Talks between the Procuratorate, Lawyer and Judge] (Law Press, Beijing 2001) 169.

Chinese courts, including the Supreme People's Court, also took the same view that the burden of proof of torture falls on the defendant. For example, in the *Liu Yong* case, the Liaoning High Court (second first instance), took this position. The High Court declared that:

> Referring to Liu Yong … and their defense lawyers argued that defendants were tortured, after the investigation, this issue had arisen during the first-instance proceeding and the defense lawyers had submitted relevant evidence. The opinion of the prosecution was the torture issue should not affect the trial and adjudication. During the second-instance proceeding defense lawyers again submitted relevant evidence, after interrogating the police officers who were in charge of guarding Liu and interrogating Liu, this Court cannot exclude the possibility that Liu was tortured by the police during the investigation.[66]

In the famous case of *Liu Yong*, the Supreme People's Court took the same view and stated that: "The way in which witness statements gathered and submitted by defense lawyers of Liu Yong did not conform to related law. There were sometimes contradictory confessions."[67] According to the opinions of the court, it seems that the prosecution bears no burden of proof at all.

These opinions held by the Supreme People's Procuratorate and Supreme People's Court are plainly wrong. In urging that the burden of proof of torture should fall on the defendant, the Senior Procuratorate mentioned above places considerable reliance on the rule that "a party that asserts an issue must prove it."[68] I have great difficulty seeing why.

We need to distinguish between the burden and standard of proof in civil cases and that in criminal cases, especially in an inquisitorial system. In the context of the burden of proof, there is a sharp line between civil and criminal cases. It is here that there exists a fundamental difference between civil and criminal law cases with regard to the burden and standard of proof, evidence gathering, and protection of defendants' rights.

The trial of a civil action involves a dispute between persons in their private dealings. The chief role of the judge is to adjudge rights between two persons. The judge must give equal consideration to the interests of each of the parties. Thus, it is reasonable to require the party asserting a claim to bear the burden of proof. The general rule is that he who asserts must prove, meaning that anyone who is seeking to convince the legal system to take action on behalf of a party, bears the

---

66 Liao Xing I Zhong 152 (The Liaoning High Court, 2003). (2002) 遼刑一終字第152號（遼寧省高級人民法院）.

67 Xing Ti 5 (The Supreme People's Court, 2003). (2003) 刑提字第5號（最高人民法院）.

68 Zhang Jun, Jiang Wei and Tian Wenchang (eds), 刑事訴訟：控辯審三人談 [Criminal Procedure: Talks between the Procuratorate, Lawyer and Judge] (Law Press, Beijing 2001) 169.

burden of establishing whatever propositions are necessary to justify that action. Thus, it appears logical to place that burden on the plaintiffs. Additionally, the standard of proof in civil cases is lighter and only requires the plaintiff to prove against the defendant by the preponderance of the evidence standard. Furthermore, in *Khudoyov v. Russia*,[69] the ECtHR reiterates that ECHR proceedings "do not in all cases lend themselves to a rigorous application of the principle *affirmanti incumbit probatio* (the person who alleges something must prove that allegation)" because in certain instances the state alone has access to information capable of corroborating or refuting torture allegations.[70]

By contrast, at a criminal trial, unlike the position in civil trials, the primary task of the criminal judge is to *protect the accused from a wrong conviction.*[71] This protective attitude is squarely aligned with the principle of the presumption of innocence, which also protects the accused from wrongful conviction. This is the reason why the prosecution bears the burden of proof when criminal conduct is alleged.

The principle in criminal trials is that the prosecution bears the burden of proof when criminal conduct is alleged. The burden of proof always remains with the prosecution. Because, at a criminal trial, society would deprive the defendant of his life, liberty, or property, the burden and standard of proof was designed to exclude the likelihood of an erroneous conviction. That is why the standard of proof here requires a high degree of certainty; during trial, the prosecution must prove beyond all reasonable doubt that there is no reasonable question that the defendant has committed the offense, otherwise, the court must rule in favor of the defendant and set him free due to lack of evidence. In other words, the defendant is not guilty unless guilt is proven beyond a reasonable doubt.

Furthermore, there is a significant difference between the Anglo-American adversarial criminal justice system and the Chinese inquisitorial system with regard to the burden and standard of proof. I contend that in an inquisitorial system of China, where the court itself is inquiring into the facts, there exists no "a party that asserts an issue must prove" rule in criminal law cases.

If the accused argued that "I was not at the crime scene on the night of victim's killing" or "John Doe committed the crime," he has no burden to prove an alibi or the third party guilt. The only thing he needs to do is point to some evidence on the issue, and then the court will verify his claim and find out whether he is telling the truth. By the same token, if the accused is charged with murder, he asserted that he did not kill the victim; does he need to prove he is not guilty? The answer is undoubtedly no.

We are currently dealing with the burden and standard of proof in *criminal* cases instead of that in civil cases. It is a serious mistake to argue that because "a

69 *Khudoyorov v. Russia* (App no 6847/02) (2006) .

70 *Khudoyorov v. Russia* (App no 6847/02) (2006) 113.

71 H.L. Ho, *A Philosophy of Evidence Law—Justice in the Search for Truth* (Oxford University Press, Oxford 2008) 227.

party that asserts an issue must prove it," therefore we should place the burden of proof on criminal defendant in China. The prosecution should carry the burden of showing that the defendant was not tortured.

6.2.4 Anglo-American Approach

The burden of proof includes the evidential burden of proof (evidential burden, the burden of producing of evidence or the burden of production) and the persuasive burden of proof (persuasive burden, the burden of persuading the trier[72] as to his guilt or innocence or legal burden of proof).[73]

The *evidential burden of proof* means that the responsibility of one party to show that there is sufficient evidence to raise an issue as to the existence (or nonexistence) of a fact in issue. This burden determines "whether an issue should be left to the trier of fact."[74] By contrast, the *persuasive burden of proof* means that the obligation of one party to meet the requirement that a fact in issue be proved (or disproved). This is the burden of persuading the trier of fact that the alleged fact is true. This burden determines "how the issue should be decided."[75]

The difference between these burdens was explained by the House of Lords in *R v. DPP, ex parte Kebeline*,[76] the Court of Criminal Appeal in *R v. Gill*[77] (a case concerning duress) and Supreme Court of Canada in *R v. Fontaine*[78](a case concerning mental disorder automatism). This essential difference was never better expressed than it was by Lord Hope:

> It is necessary in the first place to distinguish between the shifting from the prosecution to the accused … the "evidential burden," or the burden of introducing evidence in support of his case, on the one hand and the "persuasive burden," or the burden of persuading the jury as to his guilt or innocence, on the other. A "persuasive" burden of proof requires the accused to prove, on a balance of probabilities, a fact which is essential to the determination of his guilt or innocence. It reverses the burden of proof by removing it from the prosecution and transferring it to the accused. An "evidential" burden requires only that the accused must adduce sufficient to raise an issue before it has to be determined as

---

72 The jury or magistrates.

73 Peter Murphy, *Murphy on Evidence* (10th edn, Oxford University Press, Oxford 2008) 72–3; Fiona Raitt, *Evidence* (3rd edn, W. Green/ Sweet and Maxwell, Edinburgh 2001) 11–22; Margaret Ross and James Chalmers, *Walker and Walker: The Law of Evidence in Scotland* (Tottel, Edinburgh 2006) 11. Colin Tapper, *Cross and Tapper on Evidence* (11th edn, Oxford University Press, Oxford 2007) 139–48.

74 *R v. Fontaine*, [2004] 1 SCR 702 [11].

75 Ibid.

76 *R v. Director of Public Prosecutions Ex Parte Kebeline and Others*, [2000] 2 AC 326.

77 *R v. Gill*, [1963] 2 All ER 688.

78 *R v. Fontaine*, [2004] 1 SCR 702.

> one of the facts in the case. The prosecution does not need to lead any evidence about it, so the accused needs to do this if he wishes to put the point in issue. But if it is put in issue, the burden of proof remains with the prosecution. The accused need only raise a reasonable doubt about his guilt.[79]

The burden of proof lies on the prosecution on every issue except that of insanity. The principle that the burden of proof in criminal cases falls to the accuser and not on the accused had long been established in English common law in 1935. The classic exposition of this principle is to be found in the leading case of *Woolmington v. The Director of the Public Prosecutions*.[80] Lord Sankey best articulated this principle and stated that "throughout the web of the English Criminal Law one golden thread is always to be seen, that it is the duty of the prosecution to prove the prisoner's guilt."[81]

Before the court determines that a statement obtained through torture is inadmissible, it has to determine whether the prosecution or the suspects should prove the existence or nonexistence of torture, and what should be the standard for this burden of proof. At common law the judge decides on how the relevant confession has been obtained, whereas the jury decides whether the confession was true. In England, the admissibility of confession evidence is governed by Section 76 (2) of PACE. Following the common law, Section 76 (2) of PACE stipulates that if the prosecution wish to adduce the accused's confession in evidence they must prove that it was not secured in the prohibited ways.[82] Otherwise, a confession by the accused is inadmissible in proof of his guilt. The standard imposed on the prosecution is to prove beyond a reasonable doubt that the confession was voluntary. Lord Bingham describes the view of placing the burden of proof on the individual to show that the disputed evidence has not been obtained by torture[83] as "a test which, in the real world, can never be satisfied."[84]

---

79 *R v. Director of Public Prosecutions Ex Parte Kebeline and Others*, [2000] 2 AC 326, 378–80.

80 [1935] AC 462.

81 [1935] AC 462, 481.

82 Section 76(2) of the Police and Criminal Evidence Act provides: If, in any proceedings where the prosecution proposes to give in evidence a confession made by an accused person, it is represented to the court that the confession was or may have been obtained—(a) by oppression of the person who made it; or (b) in consequence of anything said or done which was likely, in the circumstances existing at the time, to render unreliable any confession which might be made by him in consequence thereof, the court shall not allow the confession to be given in evidence against him except in so far as the prosecution proves to the court beyond reasonable doubt that the confession (notwithstanding that it may be true) was not obtained as aforesaid.

83 *A and others v. Secretary of State for the Home Department* [2005] UKHL 71 [121].

84 Ibid. [59].

In the United States, the use of a confession obtained by torture is prohibited. When a confession challenged as involuntary is sought to be used against a criminal defendant at his trial, the Supreme Court has held that the Fifth Amendment requires that the prosecution must prove at least by a preponderance of the evidence that the confession was voluntary.[85]

When the defendant files a motion to exclude the confession as being the result of torture, a voluntariness hearing must be conducted in the absence of the jury before a confession can be admitted.[86] Courts are very strict in keeping from the jury evidence of confessions when there is any reasonable doubt of their being voluntary. The procedure is known as the *voir dire*, or trial within trial. At this hearing, it is for the prosecution to prove the confession was voluntary by a preponderance of the evidence.[87] The "truth" and accuracy of these confessions will not be considered at the voluntariness hearings.[88] The judge must determine an issue as to the voluntariness of a confession before it can be submitted to the jury in a criminal trial.

Furthermore, the states are free to adopt a higher standard. Some states, for example, the State of Maine, have adopted a stricter standard of proof. In *State of Maine v. Collins*,[89] the Supreme Judicial Court of Maine held that the Maine Constitution requires the prosecution to prove beyond a reasonable doubt that the confession was voluntary.[90] Overall, in the United States, the government has the burden of persuasion that its evidence is not tainted by illegal searches.[91]

For those reasons mentioned from 6.2.1 to 6.2.3, therefore, I think that it would be completely wrong to place burden of providing involuntariness on the defendant.[92] In my opinion, this position, taken by Anglo-American law, is very desirable. Moreover, there is a growing European Union dimension to criminal justice. The ECHR is an additional human rights instrument that implements the customary international law prohibition on torture. Decisions of the ECtHR may also be useful for guidance to Chinese adjudicators in implementing in dealing with torture claims.

In regards to Article 3 of ECHR, for example, say X was ill treated by the police, if the victim was not detained, he can see the doctor. The doctor reports several injuries on the body of X, corresponding the allegations of X. In this situation, of course X can provide the related medical report to prove his claim.

---

85 *Lego v. Twomey*, 404 U.S. 477, 489 (1972).

86 *Jackson v. Denno*, 378 U.S. 368, 376–7 (1964); *Sims v. Georgia*, 385 U.S. 538, 543–44 (1967).

87 *Lego v. Twomey*, 404 U.S. 477, 489 (1972); *Colorado v. Connelly*, 479 U.S. 157, 168 (1986).

88 *Lego v. Twomey*, 404 U.S. 477, 483–5 (1972).

89 297 A.2d 620 (Me. 1972).

90 *State of Maine v. Collins*, 297 A.2d 620, 627 (Me. 1972).

91 *Alderman v. United States*, 394 U.S. 165, 183 (1969).

92 *United States v. Burger*, 739 F. 2d 805, 809 (2d Cir. 1984).

Plainly, it is natural for victims to provide relevant evidence to prove their claim. However, it is impossible for most detained defendants to access this evidence.

The reversal of the burden of proof means that once the applicant has an arguable claim[93] that he has been tortured by agents of the state,[94] the burden of proof then moves to the state to disprove the existence of torture. The state is responsible for proving that the state is not liable, instead of applicants proving the existence of torture. The burden of proof of torture should fall on the state, not the applicant. In short, the ECtHR places the burden of proof on the government.[95]

There are two situations in which the reversal of the burden of proof occurs. First, the state alone has access to sources of information. Second, the events in issue lie wholly within the exclusive knowledge of the state, for instance, in the case of persons within their control in custody.[96] Referring to the standard of proof, the ECtHR has generally applied the standard of proof "beyond reasonable doubt."[97]

To summarize, I argue that China should place the burden on the prosecution to prove the non-use of torture, as long as the defendant can establish an arguable claim that authorities obtained the evidence through violence. In other words, the defendant must first satisfy the evidential issue—i.e., to make torture an issue which the judge has to consider and then places the legal burden upon the prosecution to prove beyond reasonable doubt that there was no torture.[98]

6.3 Evidence Obtained by Illegal Search and Seizure

According to my observation, China has not historically seen it as part of its function to exclude items of evidence on the grounds of illegality. It is apparent, for China, that the exclusion of physical evidence for breaches of constitutional rights is a relatively new and uncommon practice. The basic assumption is that all relevant evidence, especially physical evidence, should be available to the court, and that the police should deal internally with questions of misconduct,[99] apart from examples of extreme wrongdoing. In other words, all relevant evidence is admissible, however obtained. Chinese courts thus apply an inclusionary rule of

93 A claim that contains grounds for believing there exist torture. For example, the defendant argued that he was tortured by police officers or prison guards in custody into making false confessions.

94 For example, the defendant argued that he was tortured by police officers or prison guards in custody into making false confessions.

95 *Ribitsch v. Austria* (App no 18896/91) (1995) 21 EHRR 573.

96 *Salman v. Turkey* (App no 21986/93) (2002) 34 EHRR 425.

97 *Khudoyorov v. Russia* (App no 6847/02) (2006) 112.

98 The prosecution has to disprove the existence of torture.

99 "公安部：命案必破不會引發刑訊逼供" [The Ministry of Public Security: Death Cases Must Be Solved Will not Trigger Torture]. Available at: http://news.sina.com.cn/c/l/2006-05-16/12419876496.shtml (accessed Oct. 10, 2013).

evidence. However, it would be ironic if the government did not allow the police to torture and commit illegal searches, but permits prosecutors and judges to use evidence obtained by the methods mentioned above.

The focus of this section is mainly on the law of search and seizure, and real evidence discovered in breach of the law. Because of the generally wide scope of search and seizure powers and the lack of close judicial supervision in this area, the police enjoy almost complete discretion in deciding against whom to use their vast array of search and seizure powers. I contend that the search and seizure law in China imposes almost no limits on the means the government may use to pursue its crime control objectives. Under the circumstances it is not surprising that no physical evidence has been suppressed based on an illegal search and seizure. The Code of Criminal Procedure provides no safeguards for the accused at all against the admission of evidence obtained by illegal searches and seizures.

6.3.1 Deficiency of Search and Seizure Law

A search is a governmental invasion of a person's privacy and we try to minimize the intrusion of the search to what is necessary to complete the search for the items listed with particularity in the warrant.

At the constitutional level, while Article 39 of the Constitution provides that "[t]he home of citizens of the People's Republic of China is inviolable. Unlawful search of, or intrusion into, a citizen's home is prohibited,"[100] once the government violates Article 39, there is no remedy of excluding evidence from the criminal process. At the statutory level, the search and seizure law in China is impossibly simplistic. All searches and seizures by government agents are controlled by merely 10 articles, 5 articles related to search[101] and seizure[102] respectively, in the Code of Criminal Procedure. The general provisions of the Code of Criminal Procedure could not be used to satisfy the fundamental rights standards on the right to be free from illegal searches and seizures.

In effect, I will contend that the Chinese government leaves the power to search and seize solely in executive hands.[103] Unless the search and seizure exclusionary rule is explicitly established and applied, the current "warrant requirement" in the Code of Criminal Procedure is unlikely to fully eliminate police wrongdoing problems.

The requirement of warrants was designed to protect suspects from investigatorily overreaching. Whilst Article 136 of the Code of Criminal Procedure provides that "[w]hen a search is to be conducted, a search warrant must be shown to the person to be searched,"[104] the Code of Criminal Procedure has failed to

100 Articles 39 of the Chinese Constitution.
101 Articles 134–8 of the Code of Criminal Procedure.
102 Articles 139–43 of the Code of Criminal Procedure.
103 See 6.3.1–6.3.2.
104 Article 136 of the Code of Criminal Procedure.

unravel four important questions in need of resolution: (1) Under what condition searches and seizures can be carried out? (2) Who has the authority to issue search and seizure warrants? (3) What is the scope of searches and seizures? and (4) How should evidence obtained by illegal searches and seizures be dealt with?

First and foremost, the Code of Criminal Procedure lacks the "probable cause" requirement.

The Code of Criminal Procedure's shortcomings are apparent. One striking deficiency of the search and seizure law is what it omits: probable cause. On the one hand, probable cause is an important validating element of a search. On the other hand, it is a restraint on the government's search power. It serves to protect the public by limiting the government.

With regard to the condition to carry out searches and seizures, with all criminal investigations, the threshold question as to under what condition law enforcement investigators can conduct searches and seizures initially, it seems that the answer is, whenever investigators would like to "collect evidence and track down an offender."[105]

Currently, probable cause for a search or seizure is not required in China. Law enforcement officials are not required to believe that the items sought are related to the criminal activity under investigation, and that the items reasonably may be expected to the located in the place to be searched at the time the search warrant issues.[106] Thus, the police always have the legal right to search and seize incriminating evidence even when they lack probable cause to search.

The probable cause requirement in criminal investigation has been applied for good reason: to protect citizens from unauthorized and unreasonable government intrusion. The lack of this requirement widely opens the door to abuses by government agencies.[107] Therefore, I contend that the Code of Criminal Procedure should require that search warrant will be issued only upon a showing of "probable cause." I would emphasize, above all things, that no warrants should be issued except upon probable cause.

Second, there is the issue of who is authorized to grant warrants.

The second question is who has the authority to issue search and seizure warrant. Ironically, the Code of Criminal Procedure, the bedrock source of law pertaining to search and seizure issues, provides nothing to govern this issue. As noted before,[108] a central proposition in warrant procedure in the Anglo-American legal system is that the determination of issuing the warrant (or the determination of probable cause) is to be made by the judge or prosecutor, not the police officer

105 Ibid.

106 Articles 134 and 139 of the Code of Criminal Procedure.

107 The Editor, "延安黃碟案引發的法學思考" [Legal Thoughts Triggered from the Blue Videodisc Case in Yanan] (2003) *Jurist Review* 10, 10–11.

108 See 4.1.2.

who seeks the warrant. However, Article 217 of the Public Security Criminal Case Procedure Provisions[109] provides:

> In order to collect criminal evidence and track down an offender, under the authorization of the superintendent of public security bureau at county level or above, investigators may conduct searches of the person, belongings, residences and other relevant places of criminal suspects.[110]

In addition, Article 221 of the People's Procuratorate's Criminal Procedure Rules,[111] adopted by the Supreme People's Procuratorate, provides that "[w]hen a search is to be conducted, a search warrant must be shown to the person or his family members to be searched. The Chief Procuratorate issues search warrants."[112]

In the Anglo-American criminal justice system, search and seizure warrants are usually obtained from a judge. Information should be presented to a neutral judge, who will make the determination whether a search warrant will be issued.[113] In contrast, in the Chinese criminal justice system, only the judge *cannot* issue search and seizure warrants. A judge cannot review an application for search warrant and determine that there is probable cause to believe that evidence of a crime exists in a particular place before issuing the warrant. Yet, the police and procuratorate can issue search and seizure warrants. The judge's power in this context was totally superseded by the power of the police and procuratorate.

Additionally, the Public Security Criminal Case Procedure Provisions and People's Procuratorate's Criminal Procedure Rules are merely "quasi-judicial interpretations," not even "judicial interpretations." They are internal regulations respectively for public security organs and procuratorate. In practice, these "quasi-judicial interpretations" have superseded the Code of Criminal Procedure. The Public Security Bureau and Supreme People's Procuratorate authorized themselves to issue warrants.[114] Under these circumstances, it is impractical to expect "neutral" police and procuratorate to issue the search warrant. It is extremely easy for the police to get a search warrant anytime they want to.

Thirdly, the scope of searches and seizures is an important issue.

Referring to the particularity of warrants, a search warrant should describe with particularity of (1) the criminal activity under investigation; (2) the items to be seized; and (3) the place or person to be searched. If a warrant lacks particularity,

---

109 "公安機關辦理刑事案件程序規定" [Public Security Criminal Case Procedure Provisions], effective on May 14, 1998. Degree No.35 of the Ministry of Public Security.

110 Article 217 of the Public Security Criminal Case Procedure Provisions.

111 "人民檢察院刑事訴訟規則" [People's Procuratorate's Criminal Procedure Rule], promulgated on Dec. 16, 1998, effective on Jan. 18, 1999.

112 Article 221 of the People's Procuratorate's Criminal Procedure Rules.

113 See 4.1.2.

114 Article 217 of the Public Security Criminal Case Procedure Provisions and Article 221 of the People's Procuratorate's Criminal Procedure Rules.

there is no limitation to safeguard the individual's privacy interest against the wide-ranging exploratory searches. A search warrant is intended for purposes of searching physical evidence. Such limitation prevents the seizure of one thing under a warrant describing another.

The actual content of the search warrant is much too simplistic in this difficult area. Chinese executing officers can examine any evidence bearing a relationship to the offense and may "conduct searches of the person, belongings, residences and other relevant places of criminal suspects and persons who might conceal criminals or criminal evidence."[115] It is completely unclear how far the "other relevant places" may eventually reach. The court has also refused to define the concept of the overbroad term within a warrant. During an examination or search, any belongings or document "that may be used to prove the guilt or innocence of a defendant shall be seized."[116] We need to limit government authority to search and seize only particularly described items. Without checks and balances on the initiation of searches, decisions about whom to search, for what reasons, and how, were largely entrusted to the police.

Fourthly, there is the question of the admissibility of evidence obtained by illegal searches and seizures.

The admissibility of confessional and physical evidence is an issue that the Code of Criminal Procedure and the Supreme People's Court have never explicitly addressed. This issue is ignored in practice. There was no provision for this issue in Code of Criminal Procedure before 2012. In practice, a general rule for the admissibility of physical evidence is without regard for how the evidence was obtained.[117]

6.3.2 General Warrants

General warrants, issued without sufficient basis and capable of being used as instruments for intrusive official searches, were an evil because they constituted a license to law enforcement officers to abuse their powers in a manner that was *ultra vires*. I consider general warrants to be the most serious concern with regard to searches and seizures, because the power of Chinese law enforcement officers is almost unlimited in this context and warrantless searches are common.[118]

It appears, at least on the surface, that the Code of Criminal Procedure provides for a warrant requirement.[119] In fact, the equivalent of blank search warrants is permitted in China. The warrant is nothing more than a fishing license and leads to an exploratory rummaging in a person's belongings. The scope of warrants

115 Article 134 of the Code of Criminal Procedure.

116 Article 139 of the Code of Criminal Procedure.

117 Zhou Fuming, "我國確立非法證據排除規則的必要性和可行性" [The Necessity of Establishing the Exclusionary Rule in China] (2007) 1 *Law Science* 142, 142.

118 See 6.3.1.

119 Article 136 of Code of Criminal Procedure.

covers only the contents of an investigator's name, suspect's name and address of premises which it is intended to search. The content of the search warrant used by the police is that "[a]ccording to Article [134] of the Code of Criminal Procedure, we send investigator ______ [*insert name of person who is to execute warrant*] to search the premises of suspect ______ in _________ [*insert address of premises which it is intended to search*]."[120]

By the same token, the content of the search warrant used by the procuratorate is that "[a]ccording to Articles [134, 136 and 162] of the Code of Criminal Procedure, we send investigator ______ [*insert name of person who is to execute warrant*] to search the premises of suspect ______ in _________ [*insert address of premises which it is intended to search*]."[121]

Law enforcement does not have to go to the judge in China and obtain a warrant specifying the particularity. All they have to do is complete the three blanks in the overreaching warrants. Without specifying the reason and item to be searched and seized, the chief procurator is unable to truly verify that the law enforcement officer is conducting a search for legitimate reasons. The inevitable consequence is that the searching officer has complete and unsupervised authority to search the entire premises from the attic to the basement at any time for the sole purpose of collecting evidence. The Chinese search and seizure powers are too broad, potentially interfering with the everyday lives of innocent citizens. If a premises can be searched anywhere at any time without a search warrant, there is no limit to the search power of a police officer.

Take the Blue Videodisc Case as one example. The facts in the Blue Videodisc Case were these: on 18 August, 2002 at 2300, Mr. and Mrs. Chang lived in Yanan City of Shaanxi province. Four police officers arrived in their residence pursuant to information that people were watching a blue movie. The police entered the house without a search warrant and tried to seize the TV, videodisc player and the blue videodisc. As Mr. Chang tried to stop the seizure, he was detained for the crime of disrupting public service. Afterwards, medical reports indicated that Mr. Chang were suffering from varying degrees of acute stress reaction (ASR), which symptoms continued to persist in 2003 (for example, intense bursts of anger and laughter, sleep disturbance, anxiety and depression, extreme mood swings, and eating cigarette butts).[122]

In fact, however, the behavior of Mr. and Mrs. Chang was neither illegal nor immoral. The Criminal Law does not forbid watching a blue movie. They were merely watching a movie in their own private space. The police still can conduct

120 Wang Bin, 刑事搜查制度研究 [The Research of Search] (Chinese People's Public Security University Press, Beijing 2008) 282. Available at: http://doc.laweach.com/doc_31490_1.html (accessed Oct. 10, 2013).

121 Ibid. Available at: http://doc.lawtime.cn/info/wenshu/qitaws/2007012944988.html (accessed Oct. 10, 2013).

122 The Editor, "延安黃碟案引發的法學思考" [Legal Thoughts Triggered from the Blue Videodisc Case in Yanan] (2003) *Jurist Review* 10, 10–11.

an illegal search without approval from anybody for any reason. This unapproved search was unconstitutional and illegal.

In China, there is no question of botching the timing of the execution of the warrant, because there is no time limit. It seems that the Code of Criminal Procedure permits the execution of search warrants at any time of the day or night. Moreover, there is no question of seizing unauthorized items, as no item is unauthorized. It is frivolous to argue that officers are prohibited from seizing items that are not described in the warrant, because the warrant does not particularly describe what things will be seized. Removing the judge's determination from what items should be seized could transform a legal warrant into a general warrant. It may lead to the unbridled intrusion into a person's life and property. What, then, is the extent of searches and seizures? The short answer is: the sky is the limit. There are no limitations on what can or will be searched.

Therefore, a warrant requirement in the Code of Criminal Procedure applied to the current searches and seizures is a mere paper tiger which provides suspects with very limited actual protection. It makes the general warrant such a dangerous weapon.

6.3.3 The End Justifies the Means?

Over the past six decades in China, priority is given to the end (convicting offenders) above the means (compliance with exclusionary rule). The judiciary dotes on the discovery of the "truth."[123] No matter which method is chosen for investigating, if the evidence proved the defendant's guilt; they would rather know exactly how the crime occurred.[124] Furthermore, Chinese courts cannot provide the external check on the investigation method of the executive branch in the matter. In many cases, the attitude that the ends justify the means seems to be gaining ground.[125]

For some of the police and procuratorates—and by extension some of the judges—they are naturally prone to view their role as striking hard against crime and seeking "the truth."[126] Using illegally obtained evidence may encourage efficiency and expediency in the criminal justice system, a central goal of the crime control model.[127] Therefore, the need to get a conviction is far more important than preserving suspects' constitutional rights. For example, one procuratorate publicly claimed that "to those criminals, we should give these defendants hell. It

123 Allison Conner, "True Confessions? Chinese Confessions Then and Now' in K.G. Turner, J.V. Feinerman, and R.K. Guy (eds), *The Limits of the Rule of Law in China* (Washington University Press, Seattle and London 2000) 151–2.

124 Han Yang, 被訴人的憲法權利 [Constitutional Rights of the Accused] (Chinese People's Public Security University Press, Beijing 2007) 195.

125 See 6.1.1 and 6.2.2.

126 Ibid.

127 See 1.3.

is impossible for me to talk about equality with them, and tell them they can decide to say or not to say; I cannot touch him anyway."[128]

This is also the argument some of the police use when they trample on suspects' rights. For instance, Article 39 of the Constitution forbids illegal searches. Article 247 of the Criminal Law prohibits the use of torture to obtain confessions. In *Liu Yun*,[129] the police acted as if they were above the law and regarded their "search for truth" as an end that justifying any means including torture. They undermined one of the central tenets of criminal justice: No one is above the law.

One crucial question must be asked: does the end justify the means? I do not believe that the end justifies the means. This argument is never acceptable. I believe in the rule of law. The means we use must always be in keeping with the law. It is fairly clear for me that the answer definitely would be "no" for three reasons.

First, the nature and characteristic of illegal means does not change.

The end will never justify the illegal means. The illegal investigatory method, for example torture, is an evil that can never be justified or excused, no matter what the result it may produce. It is the violence and the killing of human beings that make torture wrong. Torture is torture. An illegal search is an illegal search. The nature of this police wrongdoing will not change by what result they can produce. The means to achieve the crime control goal have been horrific. Without a fair judicial process, there is no justice.

Secondly, the horrific means will bring terrible retribution.

Eight decades ago, Justice Brandeis correctly made the following observations in a famous dissent in *Olmstead v. United States*[130] and said the following:

> In a government of laws, existence of the government will be imperiled if it fails to observe the law scrupulously … Crime is contagious. If the government becomes a lawbreaker, it breeds contempt for law; it invites every man to become a law unto himself; it invites anarchy. To declare that in the administration of the criminal law the end justifies the means—to declare that the government may commit crimes in order to secure the conviction of a private criminal—would bring terrible retribution. Against that pernicious doctrine this court should resolutely set its face.[131]

How can the government guarantee a bad means may lead to a good end? A bad means may lead to a bad end, instead of a good one. The terrible retribution is the evil to punish the innocent and let the real guilt free.

---

128 Huang Qiang and Wang Lily, "非法證據排除規則中國化過程中的矛盾分析" [Analyzing the Contradiction of the Exclusionary Rule with Chinese Characteristics] (2005) 10 *Chongqing Social Science* 84, 87.

129 Xie Zhong Xing Chu 68 (The Tieling Intermediate Court, 2001). (2001) 鐵中刑初字第68號 （鐵嶺市中級人民法院）.

130 277 U.S. 438 (1928).

131 277 U.S. 438, 485 (1928).

Thirdly, a good means does not necessary lead to a bad end.

The result should not be more important than the process. We should consider both the means and ends of our actions. A bad means should not justify a good end. "Due process" may lead to "due result." When we deserve "due process," it does not necessary mean that we cannot deserve "due result" at the same time. They are not necessarily incompatible.

One misunderstanding of the exclusionary rule is that once the court excludes a piece of illegally obtained evidence, the criminal defendant who did in fact commit the act as charged will definitely go free. As a matter of fact, even if particular evidence were excluded, it is likely that overwhelming other evidence will exist to support a conviction. For example, in the *Liu Yong* case,[132] it was impossible for Liu Yong to be set free because of the exclusion of a piece of confession obtained by torture.

What better evidence is there of the ineffectiveness of the existing search and seizure law than the reaction of the Chinese police to illegal search and seizure? The reaction of the police chief in the *Xingcheng* case also expressed the view of the ends justify the means. In 2004, one informant and five police officers, who had neither a search warrant nor any evidence to constitute probable cause, committed an illegal search in Xingcheng City of Liaoning Province. Four of them climbed into the victim's home with a ladder through window. Medical reports indicated that the female victim in her twenties was suffering from acute stress reaction (ASR) as a result.[133]

It is unlawful for any policeman to enter and search any private dwelling house or place of residence without the authority of a search warrant. Article 245 of the Criminal Law provides that:

> A person who unlawfully subjects another person to a bodily search or a search of his residence or unlawfully intrudes into another person's residence shall be sentenced to fixed-term imprisonment of not more than three years or criminal detention. A judicial officer who abuses his power and commits a crime under the preceding paragraph shall be sentenced heavily.[134]

Again, the police conducted an illegal search in this case.

It is clearly apparent from the police officers' testimony that they casually regard illegal searches as trivialities. In trial, all the police officers admitted that they not only did not get a search warrant in this case but also that they had *never* applied for a search warrant before. The police officers all testified to using the

---

132 Xie Zhong Xing Chu 68 (The Tieling Intermediate Court, 2001). (2001) 鐵中刑初字第68號 （鐵嶺市中級人民法院).

133 Gu Minkang, "憲法權利的深層保護—從垃圾袋的處理說起" [Further Protections of Constitutional Rights—Cases of Handling Garbage Bags] (2006) 7 *Law Science* 84, 87.

134 Article 245 of the Criminal Law.

method noted above, but said they believed that they did not commit a crime. "Before we never took out search warrants," said two officers. They argued that they were not "searching" but "taking a look at" the house. They also testified that "we are not guilty because we just followed superior orders."[135] However, the Criminal Law does not grant a defense to the police who follow superior orders if those orders are manifestly illegal.

Surprisingly, according to the police chief's testimony, he did not consider that an illegal search is a big deal. He argued that "is it a big deal? The only problem is that we did not catch the criminal. If we catch the criminal, everything will be fine."[136] Again the police chief firmly believes that the end (catching the criminal) justifies the means (illegal searches and seizures).

6.4 Conclusion

The Chinese judiciary has been a bystander to some reforms of the criminal justice system. They are hostile to the scrutiny of confessions obtained by torture. In this chapter, I have argued that the courts have tended to take an extremely conservative approach to arguments related to the exclusionary rule. In my judgment, that both the *Du Peiwu* and *Liu Yong* cases were decided wrongly. In the *Liu* case the Supreme People's Court wasted an opportunity to establish the confession exclusionary rule. Given the passive attitude of the court, it should be no surprise that there are extremely limited opportunities for exclusion of evidence obtained by torture and no exclusion of physical evidence obtained by illegal searches in China.

In my view, misconduct should not be condoned or redefined as proper conduct. The Chinese Supreme Court should not work in an intellectual vacuum. The court's current passive attitude in this area is inadequate and should be replaced with positive duties.[137] In practice, the exclusionary rule has been administered in a perfunctory fashion; it made no impact on police.

If we cannot actualize the judicial checks, Article 61 of the Supreme People's Court's Interpretation on Several Questions for Enforcing the Chinese Criminal Procedure Law[138] and Article 65 of the Chinese People's Procuratorate's Criminal

135 Gu Minkang, "憲法權利的深層保護—從垃圾袋的處理說起" [Further Protections of Constitutional Rights—Cases of Handling Garbage Bags] (2006) 7 *Law Science* 84, 87.

136 Ibid.

137 For a more detailed discussion, see 8.1.2.

138 Article 61 of the Supreme People's Court's Interpretation on Several Questions for Enforcing the Chinese Criminal Procedure Law provides that "[i]t shall be strictly forbidden to collect evidence by illegal methods. Evidence obtained by torture, threat, enticement and deceit or other illegal methods are inadmissible."

Procedure Rule[139] are merely dead letters and hypocrisies. The authority is obligated to investigate and dispel an arguable claim of torture when a defendant claims torture by the police.

The issue of the standard of proof in police torture cases is closely linked to the confession exclusionary rule. In China the confession exclusionary rule may apply if the defendant could prove torture, brutality, and similar outrageous conduct; the point is that almost no one can prove that. In practice, the court places on the accused person the burden of proof that the confession has been obtained by torture. The accused faces the almost impossible task of proving the existence of torture to a virtual certainty. It is not right to contemplate a requirement on the defendant to prove that he or she was not tortured by the police. In order to properly balance vulnerable suspects and powerful procuratorates, the court should place the burden of proof on the prosecution whenever the accused pleads inadmissibility of a confession obtained by torture.

The prosecution has the burden of proving every essential fact beyond a reasonable doubt and the defendant has no burden to produce any evidence at all. It is important to determine whether the burden of proof of torture should fall on the prosecutor or the defendant. Our commitment to ending torture and police wrongdoing in China is questioned when we construe our own laws in ways that make it overly burdensome for suspects to maintain torture claims. Accordingly, I argue that the current approach in China for burden of proof (a heavy burden on defendants) is unclear, unprincipled, unfair and ought to be abolished in practice. The defendant need not prove the existence of torture. It cannot be presumed that he has not been tortured by the police simply because he fails to prove the existence of torture.

Courts should adopt a better burden and standard that is better equipped to administer justice. Thus, I contend the prosecution should bear the burden of proving nonexistence of torture in practice. The burden should on the prosecutor to establish lack of torture, i.e., the prosecutor have the burden to disprove torture. The prosecutor must discharge the burden of proof. I argue that the main reason why the burden of proof should be on the procuratorates who want to use the illegally obtained evidence, not the defendants. If torture is probably or likely, a confession should be excluded.

As to the issues regarding the argument about the search and seizure warrants, legislatures and courts are granting law enforcement officers not only broad powers but also discretion over under what condition searches and seizures can be carried out and whom has the authority to issue search and seizure warrants.

---

139 Article 65 of the Chinese People's Procuratorate's Criminal Procedure Rule provides that "[i]t shall be strictly forbidden to collect evidence by illegal methods. Confessions from suspects, victims and witnesses obtained by torture, threat, enticement and deceit cannot be used to incriminate."

Chapter 7
Shaping the Exclusionary Rule in Practice

Both global and domestic forces share the goal of helping to cement good governance, including proper administration of the criminal justice system and the rule of law, throughout China. At the same time, the Chinese legal system is experiencing a substantial process of reform and transformation.[1] This reform process responds to global and domestic actors and pressures. In recent years, to some extent, it seems that China has started to acknowledge that human rights have a universal nature and show some interest in the right to be free from torture. This movement is to be applauded. In 2009, for example, China published its first action plan on human rights—the National Human Rights Action Plan of China (2009–10)[2]—vowing to solve the problem of torture. It argued that:

> Effective measures shall be taken to prohibit such acts as corporal punishment, abuse, and insult of detainees or the extraction of confessions by torture. All interrogation rooms must impose a physical separation between detainees and interrogators. The state establishes and promotes the system of conducting a physical examination of detainees before and after an interrogation.[3]

In 2010, the Supreme Court, the Supreme Procuratorate, the Ministry of Public Security, the Ministry of State Security and the Ministry of Justice issued the Regulations Concerning a Number of Questions of Excluding Illegally Obtained Criminal Evidence.[4] However, the power of justice lies in actions, not just pronouncements.

Criminal procedure reform is an important issue in the development of the rule of law in China. The interaction of Chinese and foreign criminal procedure laws is an irreversible trend. Throughout China, criminal procedure reform is in the air. The administration of justice is inefficient, however, unable or unwilling

---

1 Neil Diamant, Stanley Lubman and Kevin O'Brien, "Law and Society in the People's Republic of China" in Neil Diamant, Stanley Lubman and Kevin O'Brien (eds), *Engaging the Law in China* (Stanford University Press, Stanford 2005) 3.

2 Gau Quanxi, "國家人權行動計劃值得期待" [The National Human Rights Action Plan of China Deserves Expectation] *Legal Daily* (Beijing Nov. 9, 2008).

3 Ibid.

4 "關於辦理刑事案件排除非法證據問題若干問題的規定" [The Regulations Concerning a Number of Questions of Excluding Illegally Obtained Criminal Evidence], promulgated on July 1, 2010.

to respond to human rights abuses.[5] Chinese police wrongdoing is still like the weather; everybody talks about it but nobody does anything. Police wrongdoing has played an important role in most wrongful conviction cases throughout China.[6] The risk of miscarriages of justice that police torture creates could be reduced if certain procedural changes were made. The ultimate question for criminal process related to interrogation, and search and seizure is what happens when the Code of Criminal Procedure is violated.

Historically, there is no exclusionary rule to disqualify illegally obtained evidence from Chinese criminal trials. It should be noted that the Chinese government itself vacillated on this important topic. Practically speaking, the exclusionary rule in judicial interpretations[7] and the Code of Criminal Procedure[8] does not applied in Chinese criminal practice. Chinese courts have consistently declined to articulate the exclusionary rule.[9] Moreover, law and practice are also unclear about the exclusionary rule issues, for example, the purpose, scope, and application of the rule, whether to exclude illegally obtained evidence and what are the criteria for excluding. The lack of legislative and judicial guidance might contribute to various illegal practices by the police. Accordingly, such assurances in judicial interpretations are nonbinding, unenforceable, and therefore inadequate to protect the right to be free from torture. One of the goals of establishing the exclusionary rule in practice is to provide Chinese police with a clear standard as to the legality of their actions.

The establishment of the exclusionary rule in Chinese criminal practice is especially important because criminal investigations appear to revolve around obtaining torture statements from suspects.[10] For this reason there is increasing interest in reform; then we will need to reform interrogation techniques. In this chapter, the topic is the future—not only whether we should establish the exclusionary rule, but how the persistence of the exclusionary rule should shape our thinking about the criminal justice system.

The overarching objective of this chapter is to explore the appropriate approach of the exclusionary rule for China. This chapter proceeds in three parts. It begins with the threshold question: what is the appropriate approach for China to establish the exclusionary rule? In the first place, I will examine why we need to establish the exclusionary rule in Chinese criminal practice. As will be shown later, I contend and hope to demonstrate that it is time to establish the exclusionary rule in Chinese criminal practice. In this part, it analyzes the admissibility of illegally

5 See Chapters 5 and 6.

6 See Chapter 5.

7 Article 61 of the Supreme People's Court's Interpretation on Several Questions for Enforcing the Chinese Criminal Procedure Law. Article 65 of the Chinese People's Procuratorate's Criminal Procedure Rule.

8 Article 54 of the Code Criminal Procedure.

9 See 6.1.

10 See 5.1–5.3.

obtained confessions. I recommend that the evidence obtained from torture must be excluded completely from criminal proceedings. Then, two different approaches of the exclusionary rule are discussed: first, mandatory exclusion; and second, the discretionary exclusion. I recommend the adoption of the mandatory confession exclusionary rule in China. This part then analyzes the problems with discretionary exclusion.

The second part then turns to address the admissibility of illegally obtained physical evidence. In China, there exists no deterrent mechanism in this area to this day. The exclusion of illegally obtained physical evidence, in my opinion, is the most efficient remedy in China for such violations. I contend that China should adopt a prima facie exclusionary rule requiring the exclusion of physical evidence discovered in violation of search and seizure rules. Next, I turn to the issue of which procedural safeguards should be in place when establishing the exclusionary rule.

Finally, the last part depicts several regional rules of criminal evidence and analyzes the possible effects of each regional rule that can occur when the court dealing with the admissibility of illegally obtained evidence. I show how some exceptions are dangerous because they will replace the exclusionary rule per se.

7.1 The Exclusion of Illegally Obtained Confessions

In the light of the problems associated with the exclusionary rule examined in the preceding chapters, it is clear that the reality is that powers to exclude illegally obtained evidence have rarely existed[11] and the establishment of the exclusionary rule to prohibit illegally obtained evidence from being introduced at trial in China is urgently necessary.

The Criminal Law and the Code of Criminal Procedure are the laws for law enforcement agents to follow when they are enforcing the law in the criminal process. These laws must be observed. Their enforcement must be strict and lawbreakers must be dealt with. The Code of Criminal Procedure differed greatly from the constitutional criminal procedure model. Specifically, the "law" of criminal investigation in China, however, is in a totally unsatisfactory state.[12] A written Code of Criminal Procedure as the primary source of law thus serves as the hallmark of the civil law tradition country like China. Neither the Constitution nor the Code of Criminal Procedure requires the explicit suppression of illegally acquired physical evidence.

Under these circumstances, what is the likelihood that a closed, powerful police system with very limited checks and balances would have protected the suspects' human dignity, or, if it somehow did, that Chinese criminal judges would invent the explicit exclusionary rule by case law, especially if the crime is brutal, the female

11 See 6.1.

12 See Chapter 6.

victim is young, or public sentiment is otherwise particularly aroused? In my view, the answer to the first of these questions is "impossible at all," and to the second it is, "not likely." Currently, courts play a relatively minor role in the criminal process regarding the exclusionary rule. For one thing, strictly speaking, judges are not allowed to make law, only to interpret and apply it. There are no binding precedents, nor judicial reviews of the constitutionality of statutes. Additionally, given the political system within which most Chinese judges operate, a judge will be disinclined to exercise his discretion to exclude evidence.

The current practice results in almost no exclusion. Chinese courts have so far shown an unwillingness to even consider suppressing illegally obtained evidence. In other words, courts appear unwilling or unable to adopt the confession exclusionary rule, not to mention the search and seizure exclusionary rule. Furthermore, we cannot tell how the court decides the admissibility of illegally obtained evidence because the court gives very limited or even no explanation of the treatment of the evidence. Under these situations, we should establish the Chinese exclusionary rule in practice immediately for four reasons.

First, the exclusionary rule shields the citizenry from unbridled police power. The rule has the effect of deterring (or at least tending to deter) the police misconduct.[13] Secondly, the core protection of the confession exclusionary rule involves protection against compelled testimony at trial. Regarding the confession exclusionary rule, the rule prevents convicting the innocent.[14] Thirdly, establishing the exclusionary rule in practice will educate the police and the public about the sanctity of the fundamental individual right to be free from torture, and will encourage the right to be free from illegal searches and seizures. The search and seizure exclusionary rule is the primary tool for enforcing search and seizure law. Fourthly, the failure to exclude evidence may encourage reliance on illegally obtained evidence. The exclusionary rule is the most appropriate method the court has to show its respect for the rule of law in China. Otherwise, it is difficult for the citizenry to believe that the Chinese government sincerely meant to forbid police torture.

Furthermore, if it is necessary to establish the exclusionary rule in China, it begins with the next logical question: what is the most appropriate approach for China to establish the exclusionary rule?

7.1.1 The Mandatory Confession Exclusionary Rule

Broadly speaking, there are two general approaches to the exclusionary rule. First, a mandatory exclusionary rule refers to that courts must exclude illegally obtained evidence. Second, a discretionary exclusionary rule refers to that the exclusion of illegally obtained evidence is primarily decided upon a case-by-case determination. A comparison of the two approaches will be made.

---

13 See 3.1.4.

14 See Chapter 5.

The exclusion of illegally obtained confessions is especially important in China. The current practice results in very little exclusion and that the failure to exclude confessions may encourage reliance on illegally obtained confessions. Regarding the confession exclusionary rule, I recommend the adoption of the most rigid approach—Anglo-American-style automatic or mandatory confession exclusionary rule[15]—confessions obtained by torture, violent, coercive, threat, oppressive, inhuman or degrading conduct *must* be excluded and these confessions are inadmissible in judicial proceedings.

The beauty of this mandatory approach lies in its simplicity. It is not necessary for courts to decide whether to admit the illegally obtained confession evidence. Such a mandatory approach would lead to a considerable uniform application. Under the confession exclusionary rule, where a judge concludes that confessions were obtained by torture, he *has the duty, not the discretion*, to exclude these "confessions." The judge should exclude all confessions directly obtained by torture, regardless of its probative value or the seriousness of the case. There is no need and no room for balancing. We should permit absolutely no exception to the prohibition on illegally obtained confessions, even those suspected of perpetrating heinous crimes. The Code of Criminal Procedure should impose an absolute duty upon courts to exclude this evidence.

7.1.2 The Inadequacy of the Discretionary Exclusion

In China, a much-advocated way of establishing the exclusionary rule is the discretionary approach. Critics of the proposed use of the American exclusionary rule in China point out such rule conflict with the national psychology and culture.[16] But as this part will show, this widespread assumption is simply wrong. According to this approach, the exclusion of illegally obtained confessions must be determined upon a balancing of competing interests on a case-by-case basis. The judge would consider that in all the particular circumstances of this acquisition whether the interest of justice are advanced more by admission or exclusion. Is the discretionary exclusionary rule the answer in China? The answer is no.

I will criticize the discretionary confession exclusionary rule. I contend that mandatory confession exclusionary rule is preferable to a discretionary one. The discretionary approach is inadequate to protect the fundamental individual right to be free from torture or inhuman and degrading treatment or punishment; it can hardly be considered an adequate safeguard for civil liberties.

Accurately predicting the development of the law is always a challenge, but I predict that the discretionary confession exclusionary rule will become lip

15 In the United States, the mandatory exclusionary rule had been developed to address Fourth and Fifth Amendment issues.

16 Fan Peigen, "我國不宜移植美式非法證據排除規則" [It is Improper to Transplant American Exclusionary Rule in China] (2002) 2 *Journal of Henan Public Security Academy* 35, 37–8.

service paid by the government and will not be seriously enforced. Why should a discretionary confession exclusionary rule be rejected? It is worthless for defending against governmental invasion of liberty, and hence has no substantial impact on police behavior. A discretionary confession exclusionary rule in China will be *no* exclusionary rule at all for four reasons.

First, the discretionary nature may lead to judicial uncertainty.

The first weakness of the discretionary approach is its legal uncertainty and it results in unpredictable decision-making. The discretionary nature may lead to inconsistent case law and lack of certainty, and thereby impair judicial integrity by decreasing the predictability of cases involving police torture. At first sight, the discretionary approach seems attractive. This approach seems gives courts much flexibility. Although this approach might meet the current policy temporarily,[17] it may face serious challenges in the immediate future. The benefit of flexibility can also be the cost of unchecked discretion, hence having no substantial impact on police illegal behavior. Once the police get the incriminating confessions from the suspects, the subsequent procedure, including the trial, is often barely a formality. The suspects would face the almost impossible task of countering their confessions.

In criminal practice, if the courts are going to establish vague discretionary exclusion, it may simply make for unpredictability. This approach may foster uncertainty among police officers and lawyers as to which confessions will be excluded by court. This "case-by-case" discretionary approach may not only lead to inconsistency but also make for unpredictability.

Secondly, it makes for a lack of judicial accountability.

Accountability is important to ensure that the judiciary branch is competent and honest. In the absence of clear principles and guidelines to govern judicial discretion, it is very difficult for judges to justify their decisions on rational grounds. The discretionary approach would signal to the police that in those situations in which courts will not exercise its discretion to exclude evidence, the confession exclusionary rule no longer applies.

With regard to the search and seizure exclusionary rule, similarly in England, although the discretion existed in PACE, it was only to be used rare and exceptional cases. How can we expect Chinese judges to exercise their discretion granted by the Code of Criminal Procedure?[18] Furthermore, if, in each case, the judge must ask herself, "Are the interests of justice advanced more by admission or exclusion of the physical evidence at issue?" one may posit that Chinese jurists would be strongly tempted toward admission.

Thirdly, the misuse of vague discretion by law enforcement officers could be a problem.

---

17 Susan Trevaskes, *Courts and Criminal Justice in Contemporary China* (Lexington Books, Lanham 2007) 114–15.

18 Article 54 of the Code Criminal Procedure.

The Chinese dictum that "[i]n times of chaos, harsh punishment must be used"[19] remains a prominent part of the law and order psyche. In the future, if Chinese legislators include ambiguity when drafting the exclusionary rule in the Constitution or the Code of Criminal Procedure, the trouble with this approach is that the undefined broad terms may be free to be used by authorities to include all evidence they deem relevant and necessary. Judges may admit illegally obtained evidence.

Fourthly, there would be no deterrent effect in "serious crime."

"Wherever there is discretion," as Dicey points out, "there is room for arbitrariness."[20] If the standard is the seriousness of the case, this means the judge has to take into account the reprehensibility of a particular defendant's crime (or the gravity of crime generally) and then decide whether the confession obtained by torture are admissible. In other words, once the defendant is charged with a "serious" crime, the judge is not allowed to exclude the confession in issue. For example, say the defendant was charged with a serious drugs offence, and the only evidence against him was his confession by torture. The relevant and probative confession may be held to be admissible, as the alleged offence is serious and there is a public interest in the detection of serious crime.

For one thing, the short list of "serious crimes" is not likely to stay short. Furthermore, courts may tend to create more exceptions to the exclusionary rule to allow evidence in cases dealing with serious crimes into the courts. Also, the police may learn them and adjust their conduct accordingly. The consequence is that there will be little or even no deterrent effect for unconditional police conduct in investigations of "serious crime" cases because the police will know that almost anything they do will not lead to exclusion of evidence. More significantly, an exception to exclusion for evidence of murder, kidnapping, rape or drug cases would in essence change the confession exclusionary rule. It is sensible that fairness and equality of process should be adjusted to apply to every criminal defendant.

For these reasons and, subject to what I have said, the combination of judicial uncertainty and the misuse of vague discretion in the hands of law enforcement officers may forebode potentially destructive consequences to a suspect's constitutional right (for instance, the right to be free from torture, and the right to be free from illegal searches and seizures). As a result, adopting a discretionary confession exclusionary rule would be ill-advised because it is not only very unlikely to deter police wrongdoing but also would further reduce already low constitutional safeguards.

As alluded to above, the problem with the discretionary exclusion is fourfold. For these four disadvantages which affect fundamentally the way in which justice is administered and this is why I suggest that China should adopt mandatory confession exclusionary rule.

---

19 治亂世用重典。

20 A.V. Dicey, *Introduction to the Study of the Law of the Constitution* (10th edn, Oxford University Press, Oxford 1964) 188.

7.1.3 Opinions of the Supreme Court and Supreme Procuratorate

Both the Supreme People's Court and the Supreme People's Procuratorate call for exclusion of confessions obtained from torture and ask judges to exclude these confessions. According to Article 61 of the Supreme People's Court's Interpretation on Several Questions for Enforcing the Chinese Criminal Procedure Law, it provides that "[i]t shall be strictly forbidden to collect evidence by illegal methods. Evidence obtained by torture, threat, enticement and deceit or other illegal methods are inadmissible."[21]

Regarding the opinion of the Supreme People's Procuratorate, the Procuratorate has explicitly recognized the confession exclusionary rule and declared that all evidence obtained by torture should not be used. In 2001, the Supreme People's Procuratorate promulgated the Notice of the Supreme People's Procuratorate Concerning the Prohibition of Using the Confessions Obtained from Torture as Evidence.[22] This Notice is the strong support for the mandatory confession exclusionary rule in China.

There are five paragraphs of this Notice. The first paragraph argues that we should "*never* allow condoning torture."[23] The second paragraph argues that we should "*never* miss out any link that might cause problems."[24] The crucial third paragraph explicitly argues that "[a]ll procuratorate ***must*** strictly enforce the [confession exclusionary] rule. When the procuratorate find that confessions from suspects, victims and witnesses were obtained by illegal methods, they should firmly exclude that. *Never* leave any leeway to torture."[25] The fourth paragraph argues that "once the procuratorate find a torture case, investigate it. *Never* condoning [torture]."[26] The fifth paragraph argues that we should "find out the existing problems, work out practical solutions and report to the Supreme People's Procuratorate."[27] From the tone of this Notice, the attitude of the Supreme People's Procuratorate is very firm. The Supreme People's Procuratorate hopes to impose a mandatory confession exclusionary rule on the procuratorate in order to ban the introduction of confessions obtained by torture.

In addition, according to Article 65 of the People's Procuratorate's Criminal Procedure Rule, confessions from suspects, victims and witnesses obtained by

---

21 "最高人民法院關於執行《中華人民共和國刑事訴訟法》若干問題的解釋" [Supreme People's Court's Interpretation on Several Questions for Enforcing the Chinese Criminal Procedure Law], promulgated on June 29, 1998, effective on Sep. 8, 1998.

22 "最高人民檢察院關於嚴禁將刑訊逼供獲取的犯罪嫌疑人供述作為定案依據的通知" [The Notice of the Supreme People's Procuratorate Concerning the Prohibition of Using the Confessions Obtained from Torture as Evidence], promulgated on Jan. 2, 2001, Gao Jian Fa Su [2001] No. 2.

23 Ibid. [1] (emphasis added).

24 Ibid. [2] (emphasis added).

25 Ibid. [3] (emphasis added).

26 Ibid. [4] (emphasis added).

27 Ibid. [5] (emphasis added).

torture, threat, enticement and deceit cannot be used to incriminate.[28] Although it remains to be seen how Article 61 of the Supreme People's Court's Interpretation on Several Questions for Enforcing the Chinese Criminal Procedure Law and Article 65 of the People's Procuratorate's Criminal Procedure Rule will be applied by judges and procuratorates, from the tone of the Notice of the Supreme People's Procuratorate Concerning the Prohibition of Using the Confessions Obtained from Torture as Evidence it is crystal clear that whether to impose exclusion under the Notice is mandatory instead of discretionary.

In sum, the Code of Criminal Procedure should impose a mandatory exclusionary rule on courts in order to ban the introduction of evidence obtained in violation of its provisions. Establishing the exclusionary rule would have a profound effect on judicial behavior. If the exclusionary rule is mandatory, the Chinese judge will be able to say he had no choice: the Code of Criminal Procedure required him to exclude the evidence obtained by torture. However, if the exclusionary rule is discretionary, the judge cannot make this statement.

7.2 The Exclusion of Illegally Obtained Physical Evidence

I now turn to the exclusion of illegally obtained physical evidence. Illegally obtained physical evidence remained "prima facie admissible" in Chinese criminal practice. People should be free from illegal searches and seizures. To protect this right, as I explain below, the establishment of the search and seizure exclusionary rule in Chinese criminal practice is necessary to preclude the use at trial of evidence obtained by an illegal search and seizure. Physical evidence has always been treated differently. Partly because there is no concept of search and seizure exclusionary rule in China, and partly because there is no doubt about the reliability of physical evidence, courts refuse to exclude such evidence where there are concerns about police behavior.

On the one hand, with regard to search and seizure, the Code of Criminal Procedure grants broad power to the police.[29] On the other hand, with regard to the search and seizure exclusionary rule, in order to protect the right to be free from illegal searches and seizures, I contend judicial discretion should be minimized. I hope that the admissible illegally obtained physical evidence becomes a rarity, exceptions rather than the common practice. China should adopt a strict exclusionary rule—in other words, a new Chinese Code of Criminal Procedure should utilize the "mandatory exclusion with exception" approach to control police wrongdoing for two primary reasons.

First, it will provide clear guidance to police and courts, avoiding the slippery slope of an unprincipled discretion. The Code of Criminal Procedure does not

---

28 "人民検察院刑事訴訟規則" [People's Procuratorate's Criminal Procedure Rule], promulgated on Dec. 16, 1998, effective on Jan. 18, 1999.

29 See 6.3.1–6.3.2.

provide adequate guidance to police how to conduct search and seizure. The current practice in China results in almost no exclusion and that the failure to exclude evidence may encourage reliance on illegally obtained physical evidence. The second reason is that the search and seizure exclusionary rule is the only effective weapon that the citizen has to enforce his right against illegal searches and seizures. If we adopt the lax search and seizure exclusionary rule, we might remove this weapon.

7.2.1 The Strict Search and Seizure Exclusionary Rule

China has constitutional provisions that explicitly prohibit illegal searches and seizures. The use of unconstitutionally searched and seized evidence against a citizen may violate his constitutional rights. China should be forbidden from using evidence searched and seized in violation of the constitutional rights granted to a criminal defendant. The court should impose the search and seizure exclusionary rule in cases of constitutional rights violations.

The triple constitutional principles that "unlawful search of the person of citizens is prohibited" (Article 37 of the Chinese Constitution),[30] "[t]he home of citizens of the People's Republic of China is inviolable. Unlawful search of, or intrusion into, a citizen's home is prohibited." (Article 39 of the Chinese Constitution),[31] and "[t]he State respects and preserves human rights" (Article 33 of the Chinese Constitution),[32] set the tone and provide the constitutional basis of the Chinese search and seizure exclusionary rule.

Article 39 provides that all persons should be free from illegal searches. Although Article 39 contains no explicit provision precluding the use of evidence in its violation, in order to enforce protections granted by the Article 37, the court should rule that unconstitutionally obtained evidence cannot be used against a defendant. The primary purpose of the Chinese search and seizure exclusionary rule is to protect the vitality of Articles 37, 39 and 33 of the Constitution.

---

30 Article 37 of the Chinese Constitution provides: The freedom of person of citizens of the People's Republic of China is inviolable. No citizen may be arrested except with the approval or by decision of a people's procuratorate or by decision of a people's court, and arrests must be made by a public security organ. Unlawful deprivation or restriction of citizen's freedom of person by detention or other means is prohibited; and unlawful search of the person of citizens is prohibited.

31 Article 39 of the Chinese Constitution provides: The home of citizens of the People"s Republic of China is inviolable. Unlawful search of, or intrusion into, a citizen's home is prohibited.

32 Article 33 of the Chinese Constitution provides: All persons holding the nationality of the People's Republic of China are citizens of the People's Republic of China. All citizens of the People's Republic of China are equal before the law. The State respects and preserves human rights. Every citizen enjoys the rights and at the same time must perform the duties prescribed by the Constitution and law.

Furthermore, as noted before,[33] the separation of powers is the basis of the exclusionary rule. The Chinese Constitution, to some extent, also recognizes the separation of powers principle requiring each branch to respect the constitutional responsibilities that have been assigned to the rival branches. Article 126 of the Constitution provides: "The People's Courts shall, in accordance with the law, exercise judicial power independently, and are not subject to interference by any administrative organs, public organizations or individuals."

Chinese courts, however, are not concerned with the admissibility of evidence obtained by illegal searches and seizures. As adopting lax exclusionary rule increases the likelihood of illegal searches and seizures, I propose the establishment of a strict search and seizure exclusionary rule in China. In other words, if real evidence is obtained by illegal searches and seizures, it should be generally excluded. This book suggests that the Chinese legislature is in a better position than the court to adopt the exclusionary rule. It might be naive to think that Chinese courts will establish the exclusionary rule on a case-by-case basis under the current political climate. We might establish exceptions as there may be some cases where the officer exceeds by only a little the limits of the law and has no intention of neglecting the law. The legislature, however, must be extremely careful about the exceptions. We must be very careful about establishing the exception; otherwise the exception may replace the principle (i.e., the exclusionary rule). This important issue will be discussed in more detail in 7.3.1. In the context of the search and seizure exclusionary rule, it is imperative that the court formulate principles which provide sufficient guidance as to how the discretion should be exercised in individual cases.

7.2.2 Adopting the British Approach?

Britain, Canada and Australia have employed only a discretionary search and seizure exclusionary rule. In England, under Section 78 of PACE, it is the duty of the judge to have regard to the circumstances in which the evidence was obtained and then apply the statutory criterion whether "the admission of the evidence would have such effect on the fairness of the proceedings that the court ought not to admit it."[34] Some people might ask, "If a discretionary search and seizure exclusionary rule has worked in Great Britain, why not try it in China? Maybe this approach could also be effective." There is, however, some danger in assuming that discretionary exclusionary rule effective in the United Kingdom will also work in China. The situation is different in China from that in the United Kingdom. Before we decide whether to follow other countries in adopting a discretionary exclusionary rule, some of the differences between China and the United Kingdom must be examined. I argue that the British model may not suitable for China for two reasons.

---

33 See Chapter 4.

34 Section 78 of PACE.

First, it is doubtful whether those Chinese judges with no formal legal training have the competence to exercise a discretionary search and seizure exclusionary rule.

I am concerned with the quality of the Chinese judge. The search and seizure exclusionary rule revolves around the question as to whether to exclude illegally obtained physical evidence by judges. Accordingly, judges have a vital role to play here. Incompetent judges may make the criminal justice system unfair regarding the exclusionary rule.

One obvious difference is that the overall legal ability, which encompasses a sound knowledge of the law and experience of its application, of British judges is much higher than their counterparts in China. In general, recruitment to the bench in England is limited to barristers. Only barristers are eligible for appointment to Crown and County courts, appellate courts, the High Court, Court of Appeal, and the Judicial Committee in the House of Lords. The concentration of educational backgrounds is intensive. In the twentieth century, for example, three-quarters of the judges in England and Wales received their education from private schools, their law training from either Oxford or Cambridge, the two elite universities in Britain,[35] and thereafter obtained pupilage at prominent chambers of barristers.[36] Furthermore, it is nevertheless impressive that more than half of the Lord Justices of Appeal (53 percent) attended either New College or Corpus Christi College at Oxford, or Trinity College or Magdalene College at Cambridge.[37]

By contrast, in the last several decades, while the judiciary in China is increasing in education, it is doubtful whether those Chinese judges with no formal legal training and sometimes little or no formal education have the competence and courage to serve as the guardians of the Constitution.

I cannot think of any reason to believe that Chinese courts' administration of a discretionary exclusionary rule would be similar to the administration of such a rule in England. I think legal training and qualification of a judge is the answer. Many Chinese judges either lacked formal legal training, or the training they did receive was very abstract, as in the late 1970s, China emerged from the disasters of the Cultural Revolution (1966–76). In 1967, Mao Tse-tung asked the Red Guards

---

35 A.H. Manchester, *A Modern Legal History of England and Walse 1750–1950* (Butterworths, London 1980) 81.

36 Maimon Schwarzschild, "Class, National Character, and the Bar Reforms in Britain: Will There Always Be an England?" (1994) 9 *Conn Journal of International Law* 185, 195–208.

37 Burton Atkins, "Judicial Selection in Context: The American and English Experience" (1989) 77 *Kentucky Law Journal* 577, 596. On one side of the spectrum, the problems were caused by the lack of education and qualification of Chinese judges. On the other hand, the homogeneity and elite status of the (mostly white male middle class) judiciary in the United Kingdom has long been critiqued by feminists and others.

to "smash *Gongjiafa*[38] (police, procuracy and courts)."[39] Judicial organs (procuracy and courts) were suspended. Finally, law schools were closed. Not until 1979 were law schools reopened to offer law training programs. As a consequence, during the 1980s judges were appointed from the ranks of the Chinese Communist Party and the military.[40] Only rarely did these judges have a college education. Merely 10 percent of the judges and procurators at all levels in the entire country had an education above college level in 1989, and only 65 percent of all court personnel were college-educated in 1991.[41] In the 1990s, there were about 140,000 judges, but merely 10,000 had degrees in law. In 1993 only two-thirds of judges had post-secondary training in any subject, including non-legal subjects. About 30 percent of chief judges of High Courts in China lacked a university background.[42] One senior procuratorate pointed out that in a South China municipal procuratorate, 15.6 percent of procuratorates were college-educated and only 8 percent of procuratorates had earned a law degree. In some county courts and procuratorates, there was no college graduate.[43] Even today, more than 200,000 Chinese judges have not earned a law degree.[44]

Secondly, it is more difficult to keep qualified judges.

It has been more difficult to keep qualified judges in the west and southwest of China because of the difficult working environment. It is important to note that the problem of a lack of qualified judges is especially serious in the west and southwest of the country,[45] and rural China. After 2002, when the first National Judicial Examination was held in China, these young law school students who passed the exam preferred staying in high level courts and procuratorates or

38 打爛公檢法。

39 Leng Shao-Chuan, "The Role of Law in the People's Republic of China as Reflecting Mao Tse-Tung's Influence" (1977) 68 *The Journal of Criminal Law and Criminology* 356, 356.

40 S.B. Lubman, *Bird in a Cage: Legal Reform in China after Mao* (Stanford University Press, California 2002) 253.

41 Li Maoguan, "Why Laws go Unenforced?" (1989) *Beijing Review* 18–24.

42 He Weifang, "透過司法實現社會正義：對中國法官現狀的一個透視"[The Realization of Social Justice through Judicature: A Look at the Current Situation of Chinese Judges], in Xia Yong (ed.), 走向權利的時代：中國公民權利發展研究 [*Toward an Era of Rights: Research on the Civil Rights Development in China*], (China University of Political Science and Law Press, Beijing 1995) 328.

43 Liu Yousheng, "司法官的素質與職業培訓研究" [The Study of Competence and Career Training of Judges](2008) 12 *People's Procuratorial Monthly* 24, 27.

44 He Weifang, "透過司法實現社會正義：對中國法官現狀的一個透視" [The Realization of Social Justice through Judicature: A Look at the Current Situation of Chinese Judges], in Xia Yong (ed.), 走向權利的時代：中國公民權利發展研究 [Toward an Era of Rights: Research on the Civil Rights Development in China], (China University of Political Science and Law Press, Beijing 1995) 328.

45 For example, the Xinjiang, Sichuan, Yunnan Province.

wealthy areas instead of staying in remote and poor areas.[46] The difficult working environment and the low wage are two significant reasons why most law students decide not to work in these areas.

In short, in order to rectify the situation mentioned above, the Chinese Judges Law sets forth qualifications for judges after 1995. All judges must have an associate bachelor's, bachelor's or graduate degree in law, or if not in law, then the judge must have professional legal knowledge and two years' work experience.[47] The general lack of legal education of judges, however, leaves many of them without ability to make rulings in this context. As a result, it is completely unrealistic to expect judges without a proper educational background, professional knowledge and experience to exercise a search and seizure exclusionary rule.

The Chinese exclusionary rule, of course, has its limits, as the Chinese criminal justice system differs from the common law model—continental courts decide both questions of law and of fact. The exclusionary rule in China is not aimed at insulating the trier of fact (the Chinese judge himself) from the impact of the inadmissible evidence. The momentous difference between the Chinese model and the Anglo-American model concerning the exclusionary rule is that in the Chinese criminal justice system, the judge decides both the question of admissibility and determines the defendant's guilt or innocence. Therefore, the bifurcated trial common to the Anglo-American setting in which the judge handles questions of law—including the admissibility of evidence—and the lay jury handles questions of fact, does not exist in the Chinese model. It is of course far from certain that excluding evidence is the same thing as forgetting evidence.

7.2.3 Complementary Measures

It is undoubtedly the case that I am a great supporter of establishing the exclusionary rule in Chinese criminal practice. We may consider transplanting Anglo-American notions of the exclusionary rule into Chinese law. This is not to say that adoption and adaptation of the exclusionary rule to China would provide a panacea for its interrogation woes and cure all ills with China. There are no easy answers to the problems posed by wrongful convictions in China.[48] There are no quick fixes and the exclusionary rule is not an overnight solution to the current problem of police wrongdoing. In order to ensure the smooth development of the establishment of the exclusionary rule in China, there are a number of complementary measures

46 Liu Yousheng, "司法官的素質與職業培訓研究" [The Study of Competence and Career Training of Judges] (2008) 12 *People's Procuratorial Monthly* 24, 27.

47 Article 9 of the Chinese Judges Law.

48 Other factors, for example, widespread use of administrative detention, inadequate monitoring mechanisms in the criminal justice system, denying defendants' communications with lawyers before trial, and political control of the judiciary, may contribute to wrongful convictions.

that should be accomplished. These measures are explicitly and implicitly linked to the exclusionary rule.

First of all, and most significantly, China should consider the establishment of the right to silence.

Until today, Chinese defendants have enjoyed no right to silence.[49] On the contrary, under Article 118 of the Code of Criminal Procedure suspects were obligated to tell the "truth." The accused has no right to refuse to answer questions.[50] These circumstances convey the message: that the government has the power to interrogate suspects, and the suspects have a duty to talk, and to help to convict themselves. Critics of the right to silence have argued that China should not adopt the right to silence as the economic, cultural and legal environment is not mature.[51] Moreover, some may argue that the guilty do not need the right, and that it will hinder the investigation, thus increasing the incidence of erroneous acquittals.

Absent the right to silence, however, in my opinion, any real right to be free from torture will not occur. Specifically, Article 118 provides guilty suspects and defendants an attractive alternative to lying. Absent the right to silence and under Article 118, innocents were obliged to tell the "truth," whereas guilty suspects and criminals have no option but to tell lies instead of confessing. If guilty (as well as innocent) suspects and defendants were compelled to submit to interrogation, the result would be innocent suspects offer true exculpatory evidence and the guilty would tell lies to avoid conviction. Consequently, guilty and innocent defendants become more indistinguishable as all of them offer exculpatory statements.

Secondly, there is the issue of allocating the burden of proof to the prosecution.

The problems regarding the burden of proof are very significant when dealing with the exclusionary rule issues. Under the current approach in China, how will an individual be able to demonstrate the existence of torture? As I have argued in

---

49 Chinese defendants enjoy neither privilege against self-incrimination nor the presumption of innocence.

50 Article 118 of the Code of Criminal Procedure provides: When interrogating a criminal suspect, the investigators shall first ask the criminal suspect whether or not he has committed any criminal act, and let him state the circumstances of his guilt or explain his innocence; then may ask him questions. The criminal suspect shall answer the investigators' questions truthfully …

51 Yang Yuan, "淺談我國沉默權應當緩行" [The Right to Silence in China Should Not be Established Currently] (2009) *Legal System and Society* 32, 32–3; See also Zhang Songmei, "中國尚不具備確立沉默權的社會條件" [China Does Not Have the Social Condition to Establish the Right to Silence] (2001) *Law Science* 26, 26–9; Zhang Songmei, "沉默權生長的社會條件" [The Social Condition for the Right to Silence] (2001) *Public Administration and Law* 45, 45–6; Cui Min, "關於沉默權問題的理性思考" [The Rationale Knowledge about "the Right to Silence"] (2001) 89 *Journal of Chinese People's University of Public Security* 55, 55–63; Cui Min, "關於沉默權問題的理性思考" [The Rationale Knowledge about "the Right to Silence"] (2001) 66 *Journal of Hubei Public Security College* 23, 23–9.

the previous chapter,[52] China should reject the traditional practice of allocating the burden of proof to the defendant when the defendant argued that they were subjected to torture. Otherwise, an exclusionary rule established in the books will be useless unless the burden of proof was allocated to the prosecution.

Thirdly, mandatory videotaping is required.

A suggestion would be the mandatory videotaping of entire interrogations. Mandatory videotaping (or even audiotaping) of interrogations would be helpful to judges deciding whether the defendant in fact made a confession and, if so, under what circumstances. Mandatory videotaping of interrogation is one of the solutions to Chinese problem of false confessions. It will limit police coercion. Video recordings are devastating to a defendant's contention that he was tortured or did not in fact make the statements the police claim. Judicial police and the Ministry of Public Security may oppose mandatory taping and argue that additional requirement requires additional funding, but the cost of the equipment is small.

Furthermore, mandatory videotaping of interrogation benefits not only defendants but also the police. On the one hand, it creates conditions that protect suspects from suffering torture. It deters law enforcement officers from using torture or other illegal tactics that put innocents at risk. On the other hand, it deters the suspects from claiming they were tortured when they were not. It is apparently very rare for suspects to fake torture on videotape or allege that videotape have been tampered with. If guilty confessors intentionally fabricate torture by the police, the videotaping of interrogation can prove the innocence of the police. For example, in *Chen Zhiming* case,[53] the videotaping of interrogation was used to prove that the police did not torture the suspect. Relying on the video evidence, the judge found the innocence of the police proven.

In the United Kingdom, violence is rare in police interrogations since they are tape recorded.[54] As John Baldwin rightly observes, "[t]here is reason to believe that the introduction of an effective system of tape recording is proving to be the single most important reform of the criminal justice system in this country in the 1980s."[55] Of course, there are other safeguards including the keeping of accurate and corroborated custody records, and access on demand to legal and medical assistance.

---

52 See 6.2.

53 Kun Xing San Chu 73 (The Kunming Intermediate Court, 2005). (2005) 昆刑三初字第73號 （雲南省昆明市中級人民法院）.

54 Andrew Sanders and Richard Young, "From Suspect to Trial" in Mike Maguire, Rod Morgan and Robert Reiner (eds), *The Oxford Handbook of Criminology* (4th edn, Oxford University Press, Oxford 2007) 966.

55 John Baldwin, "Police Interviews on Tape" (1990) 11 *New Law Journal* 662, 663.

7.3 Problems with Regional Rules of Criminal Evidence

In China, provincial high courts have provided lowers courts with their own regulations of criminal evidence and powers to supervise conditions in their own areas.[56] In recent years, regional high courts have enacted regulations that endow the criminal defendant with procedural rights, including the exclusionary rule, not otherwise fully guaranteed by the Code of Criminal Procedure. For example, the Beijing city,[57] the Jiangsu Province,[58] the Jiangxi Province,[59] the Hubei Province,[60] and the Sichuan Province[61]—all issued regulations governing police torture.

Referring to the confession exclusionary rule, for instance, Article 76 of the Regulations Concerning Evidence Issues in Beijing High People's Court (Provisional) provides that "a confession obtained by torture, duress, incitement, deceit and psychological torment should be inadmissible."[62] In addition, Article 23 of A Number of Opinions Concerning Criminal Trial Evidence in Sichuan Province stipulates that "a confession obtained by torture, incitement and deceit should be inadmissible."[63] Moreover, it appears that effective mechanisms to enforce these regional rules of criminal evidence may not exist.

In this section, I explore the existing problems of regional rules of criminal evidence and contend that the new Chinese Code of Criminal Procedure in relation to the exclusionary rule must put the principle (the exclusion of the illegally

---

56 Fang Baoguo, "現實已經發生—論我國地方性刑事證據規則" [The Fact is There—On Rules of Criminal Evidence in China] (2007) 25 *Tribune of Political Science and Law (Journal of China University of Political Science and Law)* 41, 41.

57 "北京市高級人民法院關於辦理各類案件有關證據問題的規定(試行)" [Regulations Concerning Evidence Issues in Beijing High People's Court (Provisional)], promulgated on Apr. 2, 2003.

58 "江蘇省關於刑事案件證據若干問題的意見" [The Opinions Concerning a Number of Questions of Criminal Evidence in Jiangsu Province], promulgated on Apr. 3, 2008; "江蘇省關於刑事審判證據和定案的若干意見(試行)" [A Number of Opinions Concerning Criminal Trial Evidence and Conviction in Jiangsu Province (Provisional)], promulgated on Aug. 28, 2003.

59 "江西省關於死刑案件言詞證據的若干意見(試行)" [A Number of Opinions Concerning Confessions in Death Cases in Jiangxi Province (Provisional)], promulgated on Aug. 10, 2006.

60 "湖北省關於刑事證據若干問題的規定(試行)" [A Number of Regulations Concerning Criminal Evidence in Hubei Province (Provisional)], promulgated on Jan. 1, 2006.

61 "四川省關於規範刑事證據工作的若干意見(試行)" [A Number of Opinions Concerning Criminal Trial Evidence in Sichuan Province (Provisional)], promulgated on May 1, 2005.

62 Article 76 of the Regulations Concerning Evidence Issues in Beijing High People's Court (Provisional).

63 Article 23 of the A Number of Opinions Concerning Criminal Trial Evidence in Sichuan Province.

obtained evidence) and its exception in the right place. The Court never should forget that its primary obligation is to prevent tyranny.

7.3.1 Future Dangerousness: Exceptions Replace the Exclusionary Rule

The search and seizure exclusionary rule is designed to protect a suspect's right to be free from illegal searches and seizures by prohibiting the admission of physical evidence obtained from illegal searches and seizures. As analyzed in detail above,[64] we might adopt some statutory exceptions to the search and seizure exclusionary rule. However, we must be very careful about exceptions. Some exceptions might replace the exclusionary rule per se. Once the exception replaces the principle, then, the hollow "exclusionary rule" provides little or no guidance to lower courts and law enforcement agencies. As a practical matter, there are two examples that the exception replaces the principle.

First, let us take a look at the regional version of the exclusionary rule in China—The Opinions Concerning a Number of Questions of Criminal Evidence in Jiangsu Province,[65] which was promulgated in 2008. Article 61 provides that "[a] confession obtained by illegal methods should be inadmissible." Article 61 defines the term "illegally obtained confession" as "[c]onfessions of defendants, witnesses, and victims obtained by any of the following means are illegally obtained confessions: (1) interference by beating and rope; (2) the use of duress, seduction and deceitful means."[66] This is the confession exclusionary rule. Article 62, however, stipulates: "A confession obtained by illegal methods would be admissible if matched with another confession obtained by legal methods, as long as these confessions were collected by different investigators in the same force."

It is very easy to replace Article 61 (the principle) with Article 62 (the exception). The Opinions Concerning a Number of Questions of Criminal Evidence in Jiangsu Province allowed a second bite of the apple for the government. If officers' actions did not meet the specific requirements of the right to be free from torture, they could have another chance for admission of evidence under Article 62. For example, if police officer A first tortured the suspect to get the confession, the suspect admitted that he committed the crime. Then police officer B interrogated the suspect; the suspect admitted again. The second confession, according to Article 62, is admissible. Unfortunately, the exception replaces the principle.

64 See 7.2.1.

65 "江蘇省關於刑事案件證據若干問題的意見" [The Opinions Concerning a Number of Questions of Criminal Evidence in Jiangsu Province], promulgated on Apr. 3, 2008.

66 Article 61 of the Opinions Concerning a Number of Questions of Criminal Evidence in Jiangsu Province.

Second, Article 63 of A Number of Opinions Concerning Criminal Trial Evidence and Conviction in Jiangsu Province (Provisional)[67] argues that "physical evidence obtained by illegal methods is inadmissible."[68] This is the search and seizure exclusionary rule. However, Article 63 then argues that "if combined with other evidence obtained by legal methods, it can prove facts, it is admissible."[69] Once again, the exception replaces the principle. Under these circumstances, the exclusionary rule is unlikely to achieve its objective, primarily because the exceptions to the rule make exclusion uncertain or even replace the rule per se.

7.3.2 Once the Evidence Can Prove Facts, Is It Admissible?

First, Article 63 of A Number of Opinions Concerning Criminal Trial Evidence and Conviction in Jiangsu Province (Provisional) governs the admission of illegally obtained physical evidence; it stipulates "physical evidence obtained by illegal methods cannot be used as evidence directly. However, combined with other evidence obtained by legal methods, if it can *prove facts*, *it is admissible*."[70] Second, similarly Article 64 involved the admissibility of derivative evidence of illegally obtained confessions; once again, it argues that:

> If derivative evidence obtained from illegally obtained confessions can *prove facts*, *it is admissible*. The derivative evidence obtained from illegally obtained confessions are inadmissible, if it cannot directly prove the fact; however, combined with other evidence obtained by legal methods, if it can *prove facts, it is admissible*.[71]

These articles suggest, I assume, that if the evidence can prove facts, it is admissible. The evidence will help courts to ascertain the truth. A central reason behind this, as I have explained,[72] is that China identifies strongly with the crime control model. Of course, this is not to imply that seeking the truth is not a goal of the criminal process. I add merely that when due process is subordinated to truth-seeking, Articles 63 and 64 distort the exclusionary rule; Articles 63 and 64 articulated a new rule: once the evidence can prove facts, it is admissible.

---

67 "江蘇省關於刑事案件證據若干問題的意見" [The Opinions Concerning a Number of Questions of Criminal Evidence in Jiangsu Province], promulgated on Apr. 3, 2008.

68 Article 63 of The Opinions Concerning a Number of Questions of Criminal Evidence in Jiangsu Province.

69 Ibid.

70 Article 63 of The Opinions Concerning a Number of Questions of Criminal Evidence in Jiangsu Province.

71 Article 64 of The Opinions Concerning a Number of Questions of Criminal Evidence in Jiangsu Province.

72 See 5.2.4.

This is problematic in that the drafter of Article 63 mistakenly mixed up the concepts of the "admissibility of evidence" and the "weight of evidence." These are two quite distinct issues. It is worth pointing out that there is a distinction between admissibility and weight. In my judgment the most significant cost of this mistake is an overemphasis on factual guilt.

In the United Kingdom and the United States, the distinction between a concept of admissibility and one of weight is critical. In common law systems, admissibility is decided by the judge, whereas weight is determined by juries. The exclusionary rule is not based on concerns about the value of the evidence. That is the reason why the reliability rationale is no longer the principal and only test of admissibility in this context after the 1940s in the United States and 1980 in the United Kingdom.[73]

7.3.3 The Absence of the Search and Seizure Exclusionary Rule

This book draws a distinction between two kinds of exclusionary rule: the confession exclusionary rule, and the search and seizure exclusionary rule. The latter seeks to prevent constitutional violations that deny individuals their freedom from illegal search and seizure; the rule serves as another check against an overzealous police officer. Whilst there exist substantial differences between two kinds of exclusionary rule, most regional rules of criminal evidence merely ignore the search and seizure exclusionary rule. For instance, A Number of Regulations Concerning Criminal Evidence in Hubei Province (Provisional), A Number of Opinions Concerning Confessions in Death Cases in Jiangxi Province (Provisional), A Number of Opinions Concerning Criminal Trial Evidence in Sichuan Province (Provisional) and the Regulations Concerning a Number of Questions of Excluding Illegally Obtained Criminal Evidence,[74] are all silent about the search and seizure exclusionary rule.

With regards to the issue of the burden of proof, it seems that the burden of proof was on defendant to show the existence of torture. For instance, under Article 32 of A Number of Regulations Concerning Criminal Evidence in Hubei Province (Provisional), it is for a victim, witness, suspect, defendant or, their lawyers, where torture is alleged, to enumerate related facts.[75] Likewise, Article 7 of A Number of Opinions Concerning Confessions in Death Cases in Jiangxi Province (Provisional) requires a defendant or witness, where torture is alleged,

---

73 See 2.2.1.

74 "關於辦理刑事案件排除非法證據問題若干問題的規定" [The Regulations Concerning a Number of Questions of Excluding Illegally Obtained Criminal Evidence], promulgated on July 1, 2010.

75 Article 32 of A Number of Regulations Concerning Criminal Evidence in Hubei Province (Provisional) .

to provide the name of police officer committing torture, the time, and location.[76] I find it inherently unfair to expect defendants to provide this information, if it is possible. How could the defendant know the name of police officer committing torture? The detainees are allowed no watches. How could they know the time of torture?

At first sight, although confession exclusionary norms were addressed by a few judicial interpretations,[77] it should be emphasized that these judicial interpretations were not a legislative product, nor were they promulgated with formal legal consultation. These judicial interpretations are not rules of law but merely administrative directives which police officers were encouraged to follow. That is to say, judicial interpretations do *not* have any legal binding status.

Most of these judicial interpretations are provisional only.[78] They are "experimental" and the place to experiment is their own areas. In the regions with confession exclusionary norms in judicial interpretations,[79] police officers were expected to follow them. Take the example of the Opinions Concerning a Number of Questions of Criminal Evidence in Jiangsu Province. While this is what the police in Jiangsu Province are supposed to follow, this judicial interpretation may be regarded in a general way as prescribing a standard of propriety rather than a rigid requirement. It does not carry the force of law, and the violation of it does not necessarily lead to any negative consequences. Therefore, evidence was not inadmissible per se for lack of conformity with judicial interpretations. Recognition of the very limited status of judicial interpretations regarding the exclusionary rule, courts and the police do not pay attention to these interpretations. These judicial interpretations are routinely ignored or flouted. Because of this, the right to be free from torture is still illusory. And for this reason these judicial interpretations do not bind the courts as well as the police.

It is also noteworthy that, strictly speaking, the authority to undertake judicial interpretation belongs to the Supreme People's Court and Supreme People's Procuratorate.[80] Other courts should not provide lower courts with their own

---

76 Article 7 of A Number of Opinions Concerning Confessions in Death Cases in Jiangxi Province (Provisional).

77 For example, Article 61 of the Opinions Concerning a Number of Questions of Criminal Evidence in Jiangsu Province (Provisional) and Article 32 of A Number of Regulations Concerning Criminal Evidence in Hubei Province (Provisional).

78 For example, Regulations Concerning Evidence Issues in Beijing High People's Court (Provisional); A Number of Opinions Concerning Criminal Trial Evidence and Conviction in Jiangsu Province (Provisional); A Number of Opinions Concerning Confessions in Death Cases in Jiangxi Province (Provisional); A Number of Regulations Concerning Criminal Evidence in Hubei Province (Provisional) and A Number of Opinions Concerning Criminal Trial Evidence in Sichuan Province (Provisional).

79 For example, Jiangsu Province, Jiangxi Province, Hubei Province and Sichuan Province.

80 Li Wei, "Judicial Interpretation in China" (1997) 5 *Willamette Journal of International Law and Dispute Resolution* 87, 93.

interpretations of the law. Therefore, the legal status of "judicial interpretations" issued by provincial higher courts is questionable per se.

7.4 Conclusion

Lying at the heart of this book is a wish to establish a suitable exclusionary rule in Chinese criminal practice. I am a proponent of the exclusionary rule. I have no doubt that we should establish the exclusionary rule in China. The right to be free from torture and the confession exclusionary rule in China are necessities, not luxuries. I can think of no substantial argument against the establishment of the exclusionary rule. I also firmly believe that the exclusionary rule has the effect of deterring or at least tending to deter the police misconduct. The exclusionary rule is an idea whose time has come. In China, the time is ripe for a change in the context of exclusionary rule. The judicial response to the illegally obtained evidence should be based on the need to uphold the rule of law. The evidence obtained by illegal methods should be excluded, not because it has no weight, but because the police have behaved illegally. The admission of the evidence would bring the administration of justice into disrepute. It has been noted that the current scheme affords little practical protection to the accused as Chinese judges often condone procedural violations by the police which would trigger the exclusionary rule as long as evidence indicates the defendant's guilt.

In addition, the establishment of the exclusionary rule in practice is urgently needed. To improve human rights conditions, I recommend that the Chinese government explicitly establish the exclusionary rule in criminal practice. Although the confession exclusionary rule existed in the judicial interpretations, it was only to be used in rare and exceptional cases. The exclusionary rule should not continue to hang in China on the slender thread of judicial interpretations. The judicial interpretation of the exclusionary rule is far from enough. It should be written into the Chinese Constitution. The right to be free from torture is one of the highest values protected by the Chinese Constitution. My basic notion is that breaches of the rights can and should lead to the exclusion of evidence. We require the closest scrutiny of the fairness of a process designed to find whether an individual is at a substantial risk of torture. I advocate the major reforms would require reconceptualizing a considerable amount of constitutional criminal procedure. The exclusionary rule will become a bulwark of constitutional protection for criminal suspects in China.

Referring to the illegally obtained confessions, I am unalterably opposed to the use of any evidence obtained by police torture. Confessions obtained illegally would be subject to mandatory exclusion, rather than discretionary exclusion. Referring to the confession exclusionary rule, my essential thesis is that prevailing discretionary exclusion is insufficient and should be replaced by compulsory exclusion. I argue that the constitutionally and legally mandated exclusion from the trial of illegally obtained evidence will have dramatic effects on law enforcement procedure in China. Under the confession exclusionary rule, where a judge concludes that confessions were obtained by torture, he has the duty, not the discretion, to exclude these confessions.

Referring to the illegally obtained physical evidence, I cannot recall any decisions by judges to exclude evidence on the ground that the evidence had been obtained by an illegal search and seizure in China. Ostensibly, there are some alternatives to the exclusionary rule in China—including criminal prosecution of the offending officer[81] payment of monetary damages by the officer after a civil lawsuit, internal discipline and termination of employment. In 2007, He Xing, Chief of Criminal Investigation Department, Ministry of Public Security, claimed that there is a mechanism in the police force to oversee the quality of cases. Each level of the police force, from officer to captain to inspector to superintendent to commander, will oversee the cases. The difficulty, however, is that, no effective alternative to the exclusionary rule has yet been discovered in China. At present, criminal prosecutions of the police are rare. Internal police discipline is also ineffective. Obviously, these sanctions are not strong enough to motivate police officers to avoid inappropriate forms of search and seizure. Accordingly, in the Chinese criminal justice system, police illegality in obtaining evidence of guilt becomes immaterial.

Although the confession exclusionary rule is an attempt to curb police torture in China, we should then ask the next question: why do you think the exclusionary rule would prevent the police behaving lawlessly? I argue that the mandatory exclusionary rule will make a difference in China for the following two reasons.[82]

First, the exclusionary rule will extract the "firewood" (i.e., incentive) from under the cauldron (i.e., police torture).

One of the deterrent functions of the exclusionary rule is its tendency to promote institutional compliance with Article 50 of the Code of Criminal Procedure requirements on the part of law enforcement agencies. Now we understand the reasons why an interrogator might resort to torture;[83] one important reason is that the police desire to obtain confessions. The drive behind police torture is rooted in a police desire to extract confessions. Hence, police officers who wish to secure confessions for trial will not waste their time in activities made unproductive, once they find that they cannot use evidence obtained through torture anymore. Under

---

81 Article 245 of the Criminal Law provides: A person who unlawfully subjects another person to a bodily search or a search of his residence or unlawfully intrudes into another person's residence shall be sentenced to fixed-term imprisonment of not more than three years or criminal detention. A judicial officer who abuses his power and commits a crime under the preceding paragraph shall be sentenced heavily.

82 In 7.1.2, I have analyzed why a discretionary confession exclusionary rule in China will be no exclusionary rule at all. We are not dealing here with any question of whether China will enforce the law. Of course, the exclusionary rule is worthless if no one can enforce it.

83 See 5.1.

this situation, it is fairly clear that they have less incentive to seek confessions by torture. Then there will be no practical necessity for evasion of Article 50 of the Code of Criminal Procedure by the police.

Secondly, from a historical perspective, the exclusionary rule solved the same problem of police torture in the United Kingdom and the United States.

History is an important part of the story here. As described above,[84] one thing is clear; the exclusionary rule deters police misconduct. Historically, torture was a contagious disease in Northern Ireland,[85] the United States,[86] and around the world;[87] the solution of exclusionary rule seems sensible and workable in the jurisdictions mentioned above.[88] And, as Agustin Parise has noted, "[i]deals tend to spread quickly when they are successfully implemented. Legal ideas are no exceptions."[89] The Chinese have become aware of the seriousness of the problem of police torture gradually. If they find the exclusionary rule workable, it would be natural for them to adopt it in practice. Hence, the Chinese legal system might well benefit from adopting by way of reform certain evidence rules that operate sensibly in common law systems. It is a practical problem not a theoretical one for the Chinese criminal justice system and that practically it does not matter that the original ideals are Western.

Opponents of the exclusionary rule say that China should not adopt the exclusionary rule as the social and economic condition is not mature; the crime rate is high. It seems they suggested that we should wait until conditions change.[90] But we might be waiting a long time. Of course, crime and the public interest are of grave concern to society. Regarding the right to be free from torture, the public interest cannot justify the use of evidence obtained as a result of police torture. Regarding the right to be free from illegal searches and seizures, whether this right should reasonably yield to another right is to be decided by the court, not by the police. In addition, the crime rate fear does not appear to have been borne out in other countries which have adopted the exclusionary rule: the United Kingdom and the United States.

Furthermore, to argue for the balanced approach is one thing, but knowing how to do so is quite another. Some judges often turned a blind eye to defendants

---

84 See 3.1.4.

85 Michael O'Connor and Celia Rumann, "Into the Fire: How to Avoid Getting Burned by the Same Mistakes Made Fighting Terrorism in Northern Ireland" (2003) 24 *Cardozo Law Review* 1657, 1682.

86 See 2.1.2.

87 Amnesty International, *Torture Worldwide: An Affront to Human Dignity* (Amnesty International, New York 2000) 10.

88 See Chapter 3.

89 Agustin Parise, "Legal Transplants and Codification: Exploring the North American Sources of the Civil Code of Argentina (1871)" (2010) 21 *Jindal Global Law Review* 40, 40.

90 Wang Zhjian and Yang Yamin, "我國非法證據排除規則的模式選擇" [The Choosing of the Model for Chinese Exclusionary Rule] (2009) *Law Science* 145, 148.

charged with specific crimes in the name of balancing and just ignored the illegality and admitted the illegally secured evidence. I found this reluctance was especially acute in guns and drugs-related criminal cases in the context of the search and seizure exclusionary rule. Hence, I propose that the current metaphor of a balancing approach in the exclusionary rule jurisprudence in Taiwan actually may encourage the police to violate the standards of conduct imposed upon them by the Constitution doctrine. Before 2003, Taiwan had no legislated rule of evidence concerning illegally obtained physical evidence. In 2003, the Taiwanese Code of Criminal Procedure amended Article 158(4) provides that "[u]nless otherwise provided by law, evidence obtained in violation of statutory procedure by officials having the responsibility of carrying out criminal procedure shall be decided as to its capacity of proof taking into account the maintenance of the balance between the protection of human rights and public interests." For the first time in the history of Taiwanese criminal justice, the judiciary was given statutory power to exclude improperly obtained non-confessional evidence. After scrutinizing the cases of the Taiwan Supreme Court from 2003 to 2014, however, I found that the Court was almost unwilling to exercise their discretion to exclude illegally obtained evidence when the cases were related to guns and drugs.

Certainly, the exclusionary rule *alone* is no panacea for preventing police torture.[91] However, with no effective alternatives to exclusion seemingly in sight,[92] and with the prospect of a worsening of the problem of police torture, the exclusionary rule is essential and a desideratum for the Chinese criminal justice system and without which it is impossible to eliminate police torture. Establishing the exclusionary rule at the level of criminal procedure law is merely the necessary first step in protecting the right to be free from torture. After all, the exclusionary rule is worthless if no one can access it from the Code of Criminal Procedure and enforce it. Change is hard. However, inertia begets inertia. We still have a long way to go, but it is time to move.

91 See 7.2.3. In addition, we are not dealing here with any question of whether China will enforce the law. This is the question of implementation of the law.

92 See 3.2 and 8.3.1.

Chapter 8
Conclusion

The study of foreign law can lead to new concepts, notions, ideas, and even solutions infiltrating national law and may also help dispel myths[1] about imagined consequences in the event of establishing a new rule or a change in the local criminal procedure law. As Thomas Mann remarked: "it is only by making comparisons that we can distinguish who we are, in order to become all that we are meant to be."[2]

In assessing the exclusionary rule from a comparative perspective, this book is divided into two major parts. The first part of this book explored lessons from the past; it dealt in depth with the development of the exclusionary rule both in the United Kingdom[3] and United States, covering rationales, debates and theoretical foundation of the exclusionary rule in the constitutional context. The purposes of this research were to (1) assess the exclusionary rule in the United Kingdom and United States;[4] and (2) explore the theoretical constitutional foundation of the rule.[5] The second part then looked to the future, to (3) establish a Chinese exclusionary rule in criminal practice. Part II focused on the exclusionary rule in China, including the effect of police torture, the passive attitude of judges and the necessity of establishing the rule. It explored the reasons why we value both the right to be free from torture and the right to be free from illegal searches and seizures primarily for its capacity to protect citizens' rights in the future.

The topic of the exclusionary rule is wonderfully perplexing. This book combines diagnosis and prescription—the problem of police torture in China[6] and the solution of the exclusionary rule.[7] This research also illustrates many of the problems with past and present patterns in this context, and shows that existing Chinese laws do not adequately address these problems. The ultimate goal of the research is to find a suitable exclusionary rule for China to solve the serious problem of police torture and wrongdoing.

---

1 See 3.4.

2 Thomas Mann, *Joseph in Egypt* (Alfred A. Knopf, New York 1933), translated in D.P. Currie, *The Constitution of the Federal Republic of Germany* (Chicago University Press, Chicago 1994) v.

3 More specifically, England and Wales.

4 See Chapters 1–3.

5 See Chapter 4.

6 See Chapter 5.

7 See Chapters 6 and 7.

8.1 The Constitutional Foundation of the Exclusionary Rule

In this book, my concern is a fundamental one—the constitutional foundation. The rejection of torture and illegal search is characterized as a constitutional principle and *not* merely a criminal procedure or evidence rule. The exclusionary rule is essential to the enforcement of fundamental rights and appropriate to safeguard a criminal's constitutional rights. As suggested in Chapter 4, the exclusionary rule is more aptly categorized as a constitutional principle than as a rule of evidence. The exclusionary rule is constitutionally required and has constitutional roots. At the level of theory, my exclusionary rule framework is grounded in the separation of powers. We should proceed with the exclusionary rule on the constitutional level. Constitutional law, however, is not an empty promise. If the Constitution or the Code of Criminal Procedure is to have any meaning, it necessarily must provide a remedy whenever its terms are violated. Accordingly, the courts should provide some means of enforcing the constitutional prohibitions, otherwise, the constitutional provision will be reduced to a form of words only.

That constitutional level of concern for preventing official lawlessness, unfortunately, has never been present in China. On the one hand, from an intrinsic perspective, the exclusionary rule is designed to improve truth-finding.[8] On the other hand, from an extrinsic perspective, the exclusionary rule is governed by considerations extraneous to fact-finding accuracy. I argue that an explicit exclusionary rule should be written into the Chinese constitution. My study addressed two aspects of this constitutional foundation in the context of the exclusionary rule: (1) separation of powers and (2) the positive duties.

8.1.1 Separation of Powers

The concept of the separation of powers is not merely limited to constitutional law and political theory. What has been completely overlooked in the scholarly literature is what the separation of powers requires when the government proceeds in the criminal justice system. The separation of powers captures core exclusionary rule values. I propose that the separation of powers doctrine should stand as a primary animating principle of the exclusionary rule. While separation of powers as a concept has always been the structural safeguard centered on the constitution, in the context of the exclusionary rule, it has been severely underdeveloped both in the case law and in the academic literature. I seek to bring separation of powers to the fore as a usable interpretive device that supports a truly protective exclusionary rule.

The separation of powers doctrine perfectly fits into the primary animating principle of the exclusionary rule in at least two ways. First, the separation of powers is a core component of the constitution's system of checks and balances, a system in which each branch of the government is endowed with a constitutional

8 See 2.2.1.

control over the others. As I have indicated throughout the book, our purpose with the exclusionary rule is to prevent, and to protect people from, torture and illegal searches. Under the scheme of separation of powers, the various branches of government have exclusive, and limited, spheres of operation. The executive does not have the authority to apply any means of interrogation that are illegal. The judiciary is a necessary check on the executive exuberance, and it must safeguard constitutional limits on policing. The search warrant is the intrinsic and preventive measure. The search and seizure exclusionary rule is the extrinsic and deterrent measure.

Second, the primary responsibility for enforcing the constitution's limits on government is vested in the judiciary. Thus, as Ashworth has convincingly argued, "it seems contradictory for one organ of the State, the courts, to take advantage of a breach of the law by another organ of the State, a law enforcement officer."[9]

The United States Supreme Court's decisions in cases like *Boyd* also emphasized the judicial duty to enforce constitutional rights against even the mildest forms of overreaching by the executive and legislative.[10] Without the exclusionary rule and the power of judicial review, what check—what constitutional control—would the judiciary have on the executive in the context of the right to be free from torture, and the right to be free from illegal searches and seizures? The answer is none. As a consequence, the exclusionary rule is an essential and inevitable component of constitutional judicial review of police wrongdoing in the criminal process. The constitution is absolutely not a set of unenforceable guiding principles or a code of ethics under an honor system. The related principle is *ubi ius, ibi remedium*: where there is a right, there should be a remedy to fit the right. The right without remedy is nonsense. Historical experience and a review of the violations of the right to be free from torture[11] and the right to be free from illegal searches and seizures[12] in today's China suggests that defendants' rights are better protected in the criminal justice system and with checks and balances that prevent excessive concentration of the executive power.

Above all, my approach depends crucially on the construction of a judicial system of checks and balances. The exclusionary rule has three essential characteristics: the first, for the court, is the protection of constitutional rights; the second, for the rule per se, is preventing arbitrary governmental invasion and the third, for the police, is adherence to the constitution law and criminal procedure law. The police would usually seek search warrants before searching, magistrates or judges would screen search warrants requests, and courts would exercise the exclusionary rule to exclude the illegally obtained evidence.

9 Andrew Ashworth, *Human Rights, Serious Crime and Criminal Procedure* (Sweet and Maxwell, London 2002) 35.

10 *Boyd v. United States*, 116 U.S. 616, 625–7 (1886).

11 See Chapter 5.

12 See 6.3.

8.1.2 The Positive Duties

As I have indicated above,[13] the right to fair trial is connected to the exclusionary rule at the constitutional level. Further, in this section, I intend to highlight the absence of attention to the positive duties of states—not negative duties to restrain from acting (such as a duty not to infringe upon the right to be free from torture), but positive, affirmative duties to protect people[14]—from our criminal procedural and constitutional dialogue about the exclusionary rule. Traditionally, in the field of constitutional criminal procedure, most of the constitution is aimed at prohibiting the government from acting in various ways, such as the Fourth Amendment and the Fifth Amendment in the Bill of Rights, which protects a variety of activities from government interference. The international bodies, however, established under human rights treaties have interpreted states' obligation as giving rise to take positive actions to protect people from arbitrary state interference. States were obligated not only to refrain from the intentional and unlawful police torture, but also to take concrete and appropriate steps to safeguard the right to be free from torture of their nationals within its jurisdiction. These obligations are often known as positive obligations, or obligations to protect.

Governments have not only negative duties but also have positive duties. The right to be free from torture, and the right to be free from illegal searches and seizures entails first, the obvious correlative negative duty not to use illegal methods, for example using torture to obtain evidence; second, positive duties such as a duty to educate people about the wrongfulness of illegal methods, a duty to investigate complaints of illegal methods, and a duty to prevent illegal methods. From a human rights law perspective, I argue that the exclusionary rule imposes two distinct but complementary duties on the state: negative duty and positive duty. At first, there is a negative duty not intentionally to use illegal methods in investigation. This undertaking compels governments to abstain from arbitrary public authorities' interference. In addition, governments should do more than eschew illegal practice of torture and illegal search. The second duty is that states are obligated to take substantive positive actions to protect individuals from arbitrary intrusion. In relation to substance of the exclusionary rule, governments should establish a threefold obligation in relation to illegally secured evidence cases.

First, governments should develop clear judicial guidance to the police about what is expected of them. The legislature has positive, affirmative duties to enact and pass laws to punish torture and illegal investigation practices. If there is a set of clear rules of permissible police conduct, the police should be expected to follow them. The lack of detailed guidance will result in police transgressions of constitutional rights. In order to decide which evidence should be excluded, courts should establish a set of criteria to replace the vague ones. The court needs to

13 See 4.1.4.

14 It is connected to the protective rationale. See 2.2.4.

formulate a clearly identifiable standard of review for police misconduct claims and apply it consistently.

Secondly, governments should take reasonable preventive measures to protect defendants whose constitutional rights are at risk, whether from illegal acts of the police or other agents of the state. There should be effective official investigations when defendants have been tortured or illegally searched by the police. Complaints about torture or ill treatment must be investigated immediately and effectively by impartial prosecutors. In addition, Article 2(3) of the ICCPR imposes an obligation to investigate allegations of torture. The duty to investigate is implicit in the notion of an "effective remedy."[15] As the ECtHR stated in *Aksoy v. Turkey*:[16]

> Accordingly, as regards Article 13, where an individual has an arguable claim that he has been tortured by agents of the State, the notion of an "effective remedy" entails, in addition to the payment of compensation where appropriate, a thorough and effective investigation capable of leading to the identification and punishment of those responsible and including effective access for the complainant to the investigatory procedure.[17]

Thirdly, it is the duty of governments to establish a substantive mechanism to protect their people by excluding evidence adduced by torture or other unfair techniques. Past history also demonstrates that the very idea of protecting the defendant's right is completely empty unless it is linked to an efficient mechanism.[18] The capricious exclusionary rule cannot provide substantial protection for people.

Further, the ECHR also imposes positive duties. Positive duties exist under Articles 2, 3, 8[19] ("everyone has the right to respect for his private and family life and his home), and 13. The ECtHR found that Article 2 imposes positive duties on the member states to take steps to prevent police or other activities which may endanger life.[20] The ECtHR has interpreted the ECHR and the duty of the Court much differently from the traditional passive approach. A member state has positive duties under the ECHR. The duty to investigate claims of torture is implied under both Articles 3 and 13 of the ECHR.[21] States have an obligation to ensure that there are adequate prevention measures. Under Article 13, states have an obligation to investigate complaints of torture or ill treatment. The obligation arises whenever an individual raises an "arguable claim" of torture or ill treatment by state authorities.[22] The jurisprudence in the ECtHR emerging from the human rights law suggests that

15 *Aksoy v. Turkey* (App no 21987/93) (1997) 23 EHRR 553.
16 Ibid.
17 Ibid. [98].
18 See 4.3.
19 *Lopez Ostra v. Spain* (App no 16798/90) (1993) 20 EHRR 277.
20 *McCann v. United Kingdom* (App no 18984/91) (1995) 21 EHRR 97.
21 *Aydin v. Turkey* (App no 23178/94) (1997) 5 EHRR 1866.
22 *Silver and Others v. United Kingdom* (App no 6205/73) (1983) 6 EHRR 62.

there are principles that can be developed to help police-malpractice victims in the criminal justice system. States must recognize their accountability in ensuring an adequate legal framework as a supportive legitimating safety net. A member state has a positive duty to undertake actions that will enforce the protections to people granted by the ECHR.[23]

The ECtHR held that the positive obligation to launch an official investigation into accusations of torturous conduct "cannot be considered in principle to be limited solely to cases of ill-treatment by state agents."[24] These measures should provide effective protection of the accused and include reasonable steps to prevent ill treatment of which the authorities had or ought to have had knowledge.

8.2 Lessons from Anglo-American Exclusionary Rule History

The United Kingdom and the United States have created and expanded many related defendants' rights and formulated civilizing structures in the context of the exclusionary rule. The Anglo-American exclusionary rule history has offered valuable lessons to the rest of the world.[25] If introduced against a defendant at trial, false confessions are highly likely to lead to the mistaken convictions of the innocent. In a 1998 study of 60 false confessions, Leo and Ofshe found that 73 percent of the false confessors who took their cases to trial were erroneously convicted.[26] In a 2004 study of 125 false confessions, Drizin and Leo found that the number went up to 81 percent of the false confessors whose cases went to trial were erroneously convicted.[27] Furthermore, wrongful convictions "may inflict unnecessary and unpleasant treatment on someone who is in fact harmless; deprive her, needlessly, of the ability to predict and control her own life; and injure her reputation and her prospects, if it leads others to believe mistakenly that she is a law-breaker."[28]

The exclusionary rule is no longer "unique to American jurisprudence."[29] In English law, a confession that is obtained by oppression must be excluded.[30] For the last century, in the United States, the confession exclusionary rule stems from the rights granted defendants in the Fifth, Sixth, and Fourteenth Amendments to the

23 *Z v. United Kingdom* (App no 29392/95) (2002) 34 EHRR 3.

24 *MC v. Bulgaria* (App no 39272/98) (2003) 15 EHRR 627 [151].

25 See 3.1.5.

26 Richard Leo and Richard Ofshe, "The Consequences of False Confessions: Deprivations of Liberty and Miscarriages of Justice in the Age of Psychological Interrogation" (1998) 88 *Journal of Law and Criminology* 429, 481–2.

27 Steven Drizin and Richard Leo, "The Problem of False Confessions in Post-DNA World" (2004) 82 *North Carolina Law Review* 891, 891.

28 R.A. Duff, *Trials and Punishment* (Cambridge University Press, Cambridge 1986) 105.

29 403 U.S. 388 (1971) (Burger, C.J., dissenting).

30 Police and Criminal Evidence Act 1984, Section 78(1).

Constitution. The United States Supreme Court has banned torture, cruel, inhuman or any degrading conduct whatsoever. In addition, from 1914, evidence seized in violation of one's Fourth Amendment rights cannot be used against that person in a criminal prosecution.[31] There are a number of lessons about the exclusionary rule to be learned from the United Kingdom and the United States.

8.2.1 No Shortcut Methods

> We must emphasize the fact that the short-cut of an involuntary confession becomes a boomerang which flies back and hits not only the officer himself but his entire department and the community as a whole.
>
> *Quinn Tamm*[32]

The purpose of this book is to demonstrate how comparative research into the Anglo-American criminal justice systems can offer a variety of choices for the reform of Chinese criminal procedure. At first sight, in the short run, police wrongdoing might seem to get the "results" and "convictions" faster. These misconducts by the law enforcement authorities, however, are by no means the shortcut methods. In the long run, the criminal justice as a whole and even society has to pay the price someday. The price may be much higher. Police wrongdoing is unfair, dangerous, and even illegal. The history of the Anglo-American exclusionary rule proves that tolerance of shortcut methods in law enforcement not only impair its enduring effectiveness, but also encourages law enforcement officers to engage in them.[33] History has shown that torture, illegal searches and entrapment are not the shortcuts. In order to rule out general warrants, in general, both the United Kingdom and United States have developed a procedure that allows premises to be searched under authorization by the court.[34]

Referring to the rationales of the exclusionary rule, I identity four justifications for the exclusionary rule: (1) the reliability rationale (ensuring the reliability of confessions), (2) the self-incrimination rationale (protecting the right of suspects to make autonomous decisions), (3) the deterrence rationale (preventing future police wrongdoing) and (4) the protective rationale (protecting suspects' rights from disadvantages).[35] Some rationales are complementary. There are two primary considerations: the *internal rationale*, i.e., the reliability rationale which is more relevant to the confession exclusionary rule; the *external rationale*, the dominant consideration, which is relevant to both the confession exclusionary rule, and search and seizure exclusionary rule. The exclusionary rule can be justified by

31 *Weeks v. United States*, 232 U.S. 383 (1914).

32 Quinn Tamm, reported in 8 *Civil Liberties in New York*, No. 2, p. 4, col. 5 (Nov. 1959).

33 See 2.1.

34 See 4.1.2.

35 See 2.2.

reference to considerations of internal and external rationale. I argue that no specific rationale is perfect, absolutely better than the others; furthermore there is a trend to combine both internal and external rationale.

8.2.2 The Right to be Free from Torture

If the wrongful conviction of the innocent is a pressing issue in China today, police torture is the flashpoint. The right to be free from torture, one of the most fundamental values of democratic society, is considered a fundamental right at the international, European[36] and national levels. It is the most fundamental human right already apparent from its long history and widespread codification, and has been repeatedly recognized by British, United States, and international courts. In the United Kingdom, for example, the Police and Criminal Evidence Act (PACE), along with its attached codes of practice, was enacted in 1984. PACE was, among other things, intended to produce a series of safeguards against torture during police questioning.

From the perspective of international human rights law, the international prohibition of torture or cruel, inhuman, or degrading treatment enjoys the highest normative force recognized by international law. The question of whether a government's decision to commit torture could ever be invoked as a justification of torture when states of war or a threat of war, internal political instability, or states in a state of emergency receives the answer, no, because an exception in this case would undermine the right to be free from torture. The right to be free from torture is an absolute right and must not be derogated from any exceptional circumstances, whatsoever. This right was included in the list of non-derogable rights under Article 4 of the International Covenant on Civil and Political Rights. However, the right was not seriously enforced in China. Official statements, government documents, newspaper articles, writing of Chinese intellectuals, and other materials indicate that torture gradually became a controversial issue that could not be ignored or minimized.[37]

The right to be free from torture is a basic principle, and it should not give way in the face of complex or unusually serious types of cases. Once these exceptions of the right to be free from torture were introduced it will be interpreted with greater and greater elasticity, meaning that far more suspects and defendants will be affected than originally intended. Given the general unreliability of confessions extracted under torture and our fears about the "slippery slope,"[38] Chinese society is more secure with an absolute prohibition on torture.

In this book, regarding the power to exclude illegally obtained evidence, I conclude that Chinese judges were generally reluctant to exercise their confession exclusionary powers following a finding that evidence had been illegally obtained.

---

36 Article 3 of the ECHR.

37 See Chapter 5.

38 See 5.4.3.

However, the judiciary should act as an impartial, independent arbiter, rather than merely a tool of policy. It would be appropriate that judges be given a free hand to shoulder their responsibilities in this respect. Chinese judges may play crucial backstopping roles within the criminal justice system. On the macro-level, they help enforce the mechanism of checks and balances. On the micro-level, they protect the defendant's core right to fair trial. In addition, this is the right understood to apply to every critical step of the proceedings, not only the trial stage but also pretrial proceedings. I argue not only that the absolute prohibition on torture should remain in force, but also that any attempt to use evidence obtained by torture would affect our ability to sustain the constitution's commitment to human dignity and non-brutality.

In my opinion, the evidence obtained from torture must be excluded completely from proceedings. I hold to views about torture and evidence obtained from torture that are rather simple and straightforward. First, I denounce torture, threat, enticement, deceit or other unlawful means under any circumstances. There is no exception to it and there is no room for balancing. Second, as also pointed out in 7.1, we should permit absolutely no exception to the prohibition on illegally obtained confessions. False confessions lead to miscarriages of justice when the procedural safeguards built into the criminal justice system fail. The fear of opening the floodgates would lead China down the slippery slope to torture. There is no going back. If China leaves the window open a crack, the wind that has chilled to the bone in imperial China will soon fill the whole room.

8.2.3 The Right to be Free from Illegal Searches and Seizures

The right is sacrosanct; it protects the sanctity of our homes. When the sanctity is violated by the lawless actions of the police, the exclusionary rule remedies the violation by the status quo *ante*. Furthermore, the search and seizure exclusionary rule is a bulwark of the right to be free from illegal searches and seizures. The rule is the most appropriate and effective route to ensure the protection of the right to be free from illegal searches and seizures. It is also the only remedy that provides sufficient incentives to prevent future violations of the right to be free from illegal searches and seizures. That is the reason why the United States Supreme Court has relied on the search and seizure exclusionary rule for the last 100 years.

One of the important lessons is that the exclusionary rule of history in the United Kingdom and United States had a huge impact on the police. While tracing the evolution of the exclusionary rule,[39] history tells us that the exclusionary rule had a huge impact on the police.[40] In contrast, the lack of the exclusionary rule would result in little or no protection for privacy rights.[41] The exclusionary rule deters, both specifically (by deterring those whose searches result in exclusion)

39 See 2.1.
40 See 4.2.2.
41 See 4.3.

and generally (by deterring other officers). Accordingly, the deterrence of the exclusionary rule generally comprises specific deterrence and general deterrence.

8.3 Shaping the Chinese Exclusionary Rule

The common law forbids the admission of evidence obtained by torture. The confession exclusionary rule is perhaps the most fundamental rule of English criminal law.[42] There is no reason to believe that the position should be any different in the jurisprudence of Chinese courts. In contrast, in China, evidence extracted by torture has been routinely used to secure guilty verdicts.[43] Throughout the history of the People's Republic of China, no enforcement mechanism protected both the right to be free from torture and the right to be free from illegal searches and seizures. Protection, if any exists, against illegal and unreliable evidence is relaxed. The court is not concerned with how evidence is obtained and considers only the probative value of the evidence gathered by the police. Judges close their eyes to the exclusionary rule.[44] The sole issue is whether the confession is true; whether the confession was obtained by torture or coerced is irrelevant. The reliability principle always outweighs the other principles. The current Chinese approach in the context of the exclusionary rule is inappropriate, unfair, and immoral by punishing innocent suspects.

8.3.1 No Feasible Alternative to the Exclusionary Rule

Again we are forced to confront the fundamental and nagging question of whether adequate alternative remedies exist in China to safeguard the protections of the exclusionary rule. At least in theory, there are three alternatives to the exclusionary rule: criminal prosecution of the offending officer; payment of a fine by the officer; and internal discipline (including termination of employment). Under current practice, however, existing criminal, civil and administrative remedies are unfortunately ineffectual and sadly inadequate. The remedies which China has neither deter nor compensate. Again, I emphasize that other methods of enforcing the right to be free from torture have proven to be a failure in curbing the brazen, illegal practices of Chinese police. These "alternatives" are *not* working in China. The current approach leaves many individuals with no remedy when the government violates their rights to be free from torture. I conclude that there exists no viable and effective alternative to the exclusionary rule in China. The exclusionary rule is the only efficient weapon in the Chinese court's armory as reliance on other remedies is worthless and futile.

---

42 *R v. Mushtaq* [2005] UKHL 25, [2005] WLR 1513, [7], [45]–[46], [71].

43 See Chapter 5.

44 See 6.1.

Civil and criminal penalties without force cannot constitute a disincentive to torture. First, in theory, police are significantly less likely use torture if they know that that punishment is likely to be severe. As regards the criminal prosecution of the officials responsible for the conduct, however, prosecutors are reluctant to indict police. Successful prosecutions do happen, but they are relatively rare and the number of prosecution is small. In addition, Chinese judges are reluctant to convict police officers. For example, in the *Cheng Jinhao* case, the suspect was tortured to death by three police officers, including Wang Jiti. The defendant was exempted from criminal punishment.[45] In the *Sh Ming* case, the suspect was tortured to death by five police officers. Three police torturers and murderers were sentenced to three years with three to five years' probation.[46] Moreover, two other police torturers and murderers were exempted from criminal punishment. In the *Zhung Hanzhong* case, the police torturer was sentenced to one year and six months with two years' probation.[47] The failure of the Chinese government to investigate torture claims and the courts to hold police torturers accountable for their acts of torture indirectly encourages the continuing use of torture by the police. The most obvious cost of the passive attitude from the court is the general public's loss of confidence in the criminal justice system, both in policing and in adjudication.

Next, there is no effective measure to provide civil compensation to victims of torture in all cases. In China, innocent victims of illegal searches and seizures generally recover nothing. Few Chinese plaintiffs filed civil suits against police officers for their wrongdoing. In the context of illegal searches and seizures, reported cases involving civil actions against law enforcement officers are rare, and those involving successful criminal prosecutions against police officers are nonexistent.

Police know and count on the fact that the exclusionary rule in the judicial interpretations is rarely applied, and believe that the wrongdoing will not result in prosecution. It creates an incentive for law enforcement officers to disregard constitutional guarantees. Thus, considering the "benefits" of using illegal investigative methods, police have much to gain and almost nothing to lose if the statements obtained by torture are trustworthy or the illegally seized physical evidence can prove the defendant guilty. Currently, there exists no deterrence in China at all.

45 Jin Xing Er Zhong 72 (The Shanxi High Court, 2002). (2002) 晉刑二終字第72號 (山西省高級人民法院).

46 Dong Xing Chua 11 (The Qinghai High Court, 2007). (2007) 東刑初字第11號 (青海省海東地區高級人民法院).

47 Hai Nan Xing Chua 15 (The Hainan Intermediate Court, 2003). (2003) 海南刑終字第15號 (海口市海南中級法院).

8.3.2 The Confession Exclusionary Rule

Today, abusing suspects to obtain confessions has resulted in scandal and miscarriages of justice in China.[48] The confession exclusionary rule is an essential ingredient of the right to be free from torture. However, when faced with the possibility of excluding reliable confessions, courts often strain logic to find that no violation of Article 50 of the Code of Criminal Procedure has occurred, thereby leaving the confessions admissible. If there is no action by the courts to ensure adequate protection by a suitable route for an individual's right to be free from torture under Article 50 of Code of Criminal Procedure, then China's Code of Criminal Procedure requirements will remain unfulfilled.

The exclusion of illegally obtained confessions is especially important in China since confessions were considered admissible no matter how they were obtained. Regarding the confession exclusionary rule, I recommend the adoption of the most rigid approach—a mandatory confession exclusionary rule—as confessions obtained by torture, violent, coercive, threat, oppressive, inhuman or degrading conduct *must* be excluded and these confessions are inadmissible in judicial proceedings.

Of course, China could adopt a case-by-case approach in the context of confession exclusionary rule. But this makes for such uncertainty and unpredictability that it would be impossible to foretell. This approach will make the exclusion of evidence the exception rather than the rule when police violate the right to be free from torture. By contrast, a benefit of the mandatory confession exclusionary rule is its consistency. Furthermore, from a practical perspective, the discretionary confession exclusionary rule in judicial interpretations has not worked in China and merely tinkering with it by arguing that China's social and economic conditions are not mature will be unlikely to solve the torture problems, especially since the judges have shown little inclination toward deterring police misconduct through the exclusionary rule. The high frequency of Article 50 of Code of Criminal Procedure violations, despite substantial efforts to restrain illegal police conduct, is cause for deep concern. There can be little doubt that the level of Article 50 of Code of Criminal Procedure violations is high. In China, the operation of the confession exclusionary rule should *not* involve the exercise of discretion.

The next question is about who must prove an incident of torture. The current approach in China requires that, before evidence can be excluded, the defendant must establish two separate propositions. First, the defendant must demonstrate that beatings occurred. Second, the defendant must further prove that his wounds are caused by the police, and he did not hurt himself "accidentally."[49] Requiring the defense to establish the existence of torture, in my opinion, will severely restrict the availability of exclusion as a remedy for constitutional violations. To satisfy

48 See Chapter 5.

49 See 6.2.1.

this prong of the test, a defendant has the burden of establishing the existence of torture. It creates a totally arbitrary impediment to law enforcement without protecting the interest of the defendant. This barrier seems nearly insurmountable as a practical matter, because a defendant cannot get any physical evidence on the subject in almost all situations. The state should prove its own case without assistance from the defendant.

8.3.3 The Search and Seizure Exclusionary Rule

The search and seizure exclusionary rule is an essential ingredient of the right to be free from illegal searches and seizures; the rule guarantees that a person shall be secure against illegal searches and seizures. The mechanism to control search and seizure activities consists of three parts. The first part involves the mandate that police must meet certain requirements of a warrant before conducting a search. It is designed to ensure that a neutral judge will review a warrant prior to its issuance, which protects suspects from investigatory overreaching. Without it, I cannot imagine how to assure that a government is acting under lawful authority and performing necessary criminal investigations that require invasions of privacy and the seizure of property. However, as I have already discussed,[50] the protections afforded by a neutral third person are missing as Chinese judges cannot review a search warrant prior to its issuance. The second part consists of the evaluation of the nature of the sanction that will be delivered when faced with law enforcement officers' flagrant disregard for the commands of a warrant. The third part involves the right to be free from illegal searches and seizures.

I contend that the lack of a search and seizure exclusionary rule is caused by a flawed criminal justice policy which seeks to enforce complex search and seizure situations with merely 10 simplistic articles of the Code of Criminal Procedure. The Code of Criminal Procedure should be amended to require that law enforcement officials have probable cause to believe that a crime has been or is being committed in order to conduct a search in criminal investigations. The police should establish a nexus between (1) the criminal activity under investigation; (2) the items to be seized; and (3) the place to be searched. When judges come into possession of physical evidence against defendants that they believe on reasonable grounds was obtained through illegal or unfair methods, they should exclude such evidence.

Chinese courts refuse to exercise their discretion to exclude evidence obtained or derived through illegal means. From 1949 until now, courts have not excluded evidence from criminal trials even if it has been obtained by police during an illegal search. Chinese courts merely concern themselves with whether or not the physical evidence is probative: if the evidence is probative to determine the guilt of the accused, the evidence is admissible, regardless of how it was obtained.[51] There is no action by the courts to ensure adequate protection by a suitable route

50 See 6.3.1.

51 See 6.3.

for an individual's freedom from all restraint or interference by others, unless by clear and unquestionable authority of law. Therefore, with regard to the search and seizure exclusionary rule, in order to protect the right to be free from illegal searches and seizures, China should adopt a strict exclusionary rule—in other words, a new Code of Criminal Procedure should utilize the "mandatory exclusion with exception" approach to control police wrongdoing. I propose minimizing judicial discretion and hope that the admissible illegally obtained physical evidence becomes a rarity rather than the common practice.

8.4 Conclusion

There are countless possible variations of police wrongdoing which offer inexhaustible material for the criminal procedure and evidence scholar. No matter how many times we shake the tree, more fruit remains on the branch for further consideration. Further, if there is any fixed star in our constitutional and criminal procedure constellation, it is that torture is illegal and torture-introduced evidence is inadmissible. We simply do not legally torture defendants and use the evidence obtained by torture. It seems to me, therefore, that condoning illegal activity conducted in the name of the state is hard to justify under any circumstances. There are no exceptions to the confession exclusionary rule under the corpus of human rights law. There can be no torture warrants, and no balancing.[52]

There is no such thing as lawful torture in China. Police torture in China, however, is the prevalent evil, not the isolated anecdote. It is not a few bad apples—it is the apple tree. And allegations of police misconduct continue to fill the air. Police torture deals a traumatic blow at the Chinese criminal justice system. On the whole, China grants the police too much power and has too little judicial supervision over police investigations. It creates imbalance in the existing Chinese criminal justice system. It is such an imbalance and the lack of separation of powers in the criminal justice system that poses a significant and growing threat for the protection of defendants' rights. In the past, the basic assumption in China is that all relevant evidence should be available to judges. The time is ripe for a change in this context. Rights, for example the right to be free from torture, and the right to be free from illegal searches and seizures, would mean nothing without adequate remedies to ensure these rights. The exclusion of evidence obtained contrary to the right to be free from torture, and the right to be free from illegal searches and seizures should be considered as an essential corollary of the right, if such right is to be of any value. To protect freedom from torture and advance the administration of the criminal justice system, it is strongly recommended that China establishes the exclusionary rule in practice immediately.

The law of evidence is not solely designed to assist the truth-finding process of a criminal trial. The exclusionary rule will not change the substantive law of

52 See 3.3.

search and seizure at all. Opponents claim that the rule causes criminals to go free. In the Back-from-the-dead Wife Case (*She Xianglin* Case)[53] and the *Du Peiwu* Case,[54] the criminals went free, but it is Article 118 of Code of Criminal Procedure and police torture that has set them free, not the exclusionary rule per se.

By contrast, in the United States, the exclusionary rule does a good job at deterring police misbehavior, motivating police departments to take the constitution seriously, and ensuring the Fourth Amendment is enforced by the courts. The exclusionary rule stands as a significant bulwark against governmental invasion of liberty. It is essential that China should admonish the use of torture-introduced evidence. Additionally, the courts are not willing conduits for governmental lawlessness. One undoubted benefit of the confession exclusionary rule is that it creates a strong disincentive for coercive tactics.

The time has come for China to try to establish the exclusionary rule in practice so that Article 50 of the Code of Criminal Procedure can be more easily followed by the police and the courts and, at the same time, provide the public with consistent and predictable protection against torture, and illegal searches and seizures. Unlawfully obtained confessions must be excluded in all cases where the defendant has had no legal recourse to a measure that would have prevented the execution of investigatory acts which unlawfully infringe upon his fundamental rights. The prohibition of police torture requires states not merely to refrain from condoning police torture but also to discourage the practice of police torture and not to connive at it. I suggest exclusion of evidence by the exclusionary rule will be the only effective sanction in China. If the confessions obtained by torture can be used, no matter how lawless the investigation, the right to be free from torture might as well be struck from the constitution and criminal procedure.

A comparative view once again offers the prospect for a preferable solution. The approach of the United States is instructive. The search and seizure exclusionary rule commands that evidence obtained in violation of constitutional guarantees be excluded at a criminal trial. By the same token, courts should not soil their hands by admitting in unconstitutionally or illegally obtained evidence. A court is not be a party to the use of illegally obtained confessions or illegally seized evidence. The judiciary should avoid the taint of partnership in police wrongdoing. If law enforcement officials do not adhere to the rule of law and uphold it themselves it will become increasingly difficult for them to persuade individuals in the society to obey the law.

Experiences of police misconduct in China clearly correlate with low confidence in the police and the courts. In order to bolster public trust in the Chinese judicial system, courts should accomplish this by ensuring fairness. Public confidence will keep diminishing in China when apparently innocent individuals are convicted for crimes they did not commit through the evidence by torture. Hence, the key to the Chinese exclusionary rule should focus on the crucial roles the court should play.

53 See 5.2.3.
54 See 6.1.1.

The judiciary should serve as the beacon light of justice and should not forget that its obligation is to prevent tyranny.[55] Every court has an inherent duty and responsibility to ensure that the proceedings have been fair. The judge is the only person who can protect the right to be free from torture, and the right to be free from illegal searches and seizures. Judges must understand their role if they are to fulfill their responsibility with integrity and courage.

In general, when Chinese law enforcement officers violate a person's right to be free from torture, they do so in attempting to obtain confessions for use in criminal proceedings. The application of the exclusionary rule can preclude law enforcement officials from profiting from its own illegality. To give effect to the constitution's prohibition against torture, it is necessary for the judiciary to remove the incentive for violating it. The exclusionary rule allows a court to deliver a public reprimand to the offender along with a public warning to other potential violators that the very goals that they are pursuing by illegal methods will be frustrated if they do not comply with the constitution's or law's commands. I assert that police officers who know both illegally tortured confessions and illegally seized evidence cannot be used can avoid illegal wrongdoing because they will have nothing to gain from them; when the police themselves break the law they and other agencies of government will not use the benefits which flow from the violation. More specifically, once the police know that they would not profit from their lawless behavior, torture will no longer be a useful option. Application of the exclusionary rule to China would serve a deterrence function and compel compliance with the right to be free from torture by removing the incentive for law enforcement agents to disregard it. On the contrary, Chinese police doubts are very likely to be stronger and stronger now than they would be if the exclusionary rule in the judicial interpretations had never been imposed.

It would be intolerable if the guarantee against torture and illegal searches could be violated without practical consequence. The exclusion of evidence will be an effective way of deterring police misconduct and illegal searches in China. The exclusionary rule is needed to make the right to be free from torture, and the right to be free from illegal searches and seizures something real; a guarantee of the right mentioned above that does not carry with it the exclusionary rule by its violation is a chimera. Choosing not to establish the Chinese exclusionary rule in practice will do nothing to solve the problem of miscarriages of justice; on the contrary, it may increase the number of wrong convictions; it certainly will not reduce crime levels in China. As I have already made clear I regard the exclusionary rule as a valuable part of the criminal justice system. To be clear, I do not advocate expanding defendants' rights at the cost of the public safety in China. On the contrary, I do contend that the social contract philosophy underlying the exclusionary rule imposes a strong obligation on the state to protect public order

55 James Wilson, "Altered States: A Comparison of Separation of Powers in the United States and in the United Kingdom" (1990) 18 *Hastings Constitution Law Quarterly* 125, 179.

and the exclusionary rule is as much about the rights of the people as it is about any individual.

I liken the exclusionary rule to wild clover, not poison ivy. Once rooted, the exclusionary rule may spread, ultimately changing the hue of the Chinese criminal justice landscape. It should be emphasized that there is no denying that controlling crime is important. However, crime control and constitutional rights are not dichotomous. This is not a question of sacrificing constitutional rights for safety. The exclusionary rule that I have favored will not damage the criminal justice system and I believe an effective anti-crime campaign can be conducted without torture. It is *our right* to enjoy both. And it is *our duty* to demand both.

Bibliography

Amar, A.R. (1996), "The Fourth Amendment, Boston, and the Writs of Assistance" 30 *Suffolk University Law Review* 65.

—— (1997), *The Constitution and Criminal Procedure: First Principle* (Yale University Press, New Haven).

Andrews, J.A. and Hirst, Michael (2001), *Andrews and Hirst on Criminal Evidence* (4th edn, Jordan, Bristol).

Arenella, Peter (1983), "Rethinking the Functions of Criminal Procedure: The Warren and Burger Courts 'Competing Ideologies'" 72 *Georgia Law Journal* 211.

Ashworth, Andrew (1977), "Excluding Evidence as Protecting Rights" *Criminal Law Review* 725.

—— (2002), *Human Rights, Serious Crime and Criminal Procedure* (Sweet and Maxwell, London).

—— (2002), "Re-Drawing the Boundaries of Entrapment" 2002 *Criminal Law Review* 161.

Ashworth, Andrew and Redmayne, Mike (2005), *The Criminal Process* (Oxford University Press, Oxford).

Atkins, Burton (1989), "Judicial Selection in Context: The American and English Experience" 77 *Kentucky Law Journal* 577.

Baldwin, John (1990), "Police Interviews on Tape" 11 *New Law Journal* 662.

Barak, Abaron (2006), *The Judge in a Democracy* (Princeton University Press, Princeton).

Beloof, Douglas (1999), "The Third Model of Criminal Process: The Victim Participation Model" 1999 *Utah Law Review* 289.

Bentham, Jeremy (1827), *Rationale of Judicial Evidence: Specially Applied to English Practice* (Hunt & Clarke, London).

Berger, Mark (1984), "Rethinking Self-Incrimination in Great Britain" 61 *Denver Law Journal* 519.

Bi Xiaoqing (1998), "中國犯罪嫌疑人和被告人的權利保護與反酷刑制度" [Protection of the Rights of Suspects and Defendants, and Prohibition of Torture in China] in Liu Hainian, Li Lin and Morten Kjaerum (eds), 人權與司法 [*Human Rights and Administration of Justice*] (China Legal System Press, Beijing).

Blackstone, William (1769), *Commentaries on the Laws of England* (Clarendon Press, Oxford).

Boyes, Roger (2004), "Police Chief Sanctioned "Torture to Save a Life"" *The Times*, Nov. 19, at 38.

Bredemeler, Kenneth, (1999), "In Virginia, Freedom from Fear for Crime Victims, Relief for Families" *Washington Post*, July 7, at A14.

Calabresi, Guido (2003), "The Exclusionary Rule" 26 *Harvard Journal of Law and Public Policy* 114.

Cameron, James and Lustiger, Richard (1984), "The Exclusionary Rule: A Cost Benefit Analysis" 101 *Federal Rules Decisions* 109.

Canon, B.C. (1974), "Is the Exclusionary Rule in Failing Health?: Some New Data and a Plea Against a Precipitous Conclusion" 62 *Kentucky Law Journal* 709.

Cape, Ed and others (eds) (2007), *Suspects in Europe: Procedural Rights at the Investigative Stage of the Criminal Process in the European Union* (Intersentia Antwerpen, Oxford).

Cassese, Antonio (1996), *Inhuman States: Imprisonment, Detention and Torture in Europe Today* (Polity Press, Oxford).

Chambliss, William and Seidman, Robert (1971), *Law, Order and Power* (Addison-Wesley Publishing, Reading).

Chang Jian (2003), "評執法指標" [Enforcement Index] 5 *Political Science and Law*, 130–32.

Chao Mingwei (2008), "由杜培武案解讀司法程序層面的公正審判權" [Interpreting the Right to a Fair Trial in the Judicial Procedure from the Case of *Du Peiwu*] 12 *Legal System and Society* 147.

Chen Ruihua (2000), "超期羈押的法律分析" [Legal Analysis of Illegal Detention] *People's Procuratorial Semimonthly* 8.

—— (2008), "向誰辯護，向誰傾聽？以律師會見權問題為切入的分析" [Defend to Whom? Listen to Whom? The Analysis of the Right to Access Counsel] in Lang Sheng (ed.), 刑事辯護與非法證據排除 [*Defence System and the Exclusionary Rule*] (Beijing University Press, Beijing) 75.

Chen Xingliang (2006), "中國刑事司法改革的考察：以劉涌和佘祥林案為標本" [The Examination of Chinese Criminal Justice Reform: Taking the Example of *Liu Yun* and *Yu Xianglin*] 6 *Zhejiang Social Sciences* 60.

Cleaver, Hannah (2003), "Kidnapper Gets Life for Murder of Banker's Son in £700,000 Plot" *Daily Telegraph*, July 29, at 11.

Codagnone, Amy (2009), "Good-Faith Exception to Exclusionary Rule Extends to Illegal Searches Based on Police Recordkeeping Errors—*Herring v. United States*, 129 S. Ct. 695 (2009)" 43 *Suffolk University Law Review* 265.

Conner, Allison (2000), "True Confessions? Chinese Confessions Then and Now" in G. Turner, J.V. Feinerman, and R.K. Guy (eds), *The Limits of the Rule of Law in China* (Washington University Press, Seattle and London).

Cooke, J.E. (ed.) (1961), *The Federalist* (Wesleyan University Press, Middletown).

Cotton, J. and Povey, D. (2000), "*Police Complaints and Discipline: England and Wales, April 1999 to March 2000* (Home Office Statistical Bulletin, Issue 14/00, London, Home Office Research and Statistics Directorate).

Cox, Barry (1975), *Civil Liberties in Britain* (Penguin Books, Middlesex).

Cui Min (2001), "關於沉默權問題的理性思考" [The Rationale Knowledge about "the Right to Silence"] 89 *Journal of Chinese People's University of Public Security* 55.

—— (2003), "再論遏制刑訊逼供" [Rethinking the Elimination of Torture] 76 *Journal of Zhejiang Police College* 26.

Damaška, M.R. (1986), *The Faces of Justice and State Authority: A Comparative Approach to the Legal Process* (Yale University Press, New Haven).

—— (1997), *Evidence Law Adrift* (Yale University Press, New Haven).

Davies, Thomas (1983), "A Hard Look at What We Know (and Still Need to Learn) about the 'Costs' of the Exclusionary Rule: The NIJ Study and Other Studies of 'Lost' Arrests" 8 *American Bar Foundation Research Journal* 611.

Dawson, J.B. (1982), "The Exclusion of Unlawfully Obtained Evidence: A Comparative Study" 31 *International and Comparative Law Quarterly* 536.

Dennis, I.H. (2008), *The Law of Evidence* (3rd edn, Sweet & Maxwell, London).

Dershowitz, Alan (2002), *Why Terrorism Works: Understanding the Threat Responding to the Challenge* (Yale University Press, New Haven).

Devlin, Patrick (1958), *The Criminal Prosecution in England* (Yale University Press, New Haven).

Diamant, Neil, Lubman, Stanley and O'Brien, Kevin (2005), "Law and Society in the People's Republic of China" in Neil Diamant, Stanley Lubman and Kevin O'Brien (eds), *Engaging the Law in China* (Stanford University Press, Stanford).

Dicey, A.V. (1964), *Introduction to the Study of the Law of the Constitution* (10th edn, Oxford University Press, Oxford).

Dixon, David (1997), *Law in Policing: Legal Regulation and Police Practices* (Clarendon Press, Oxford).

Dodd, Vikram (2007), "Guilty, but Blair Refuses to Go" *The Guardian*, Nov. 2, at 1.

Dripps, Donald (2001), "The Case for Contingent Exclusionary Rule" 38 *American Criminal Law Review* 1.

Drizin, S.A. and Colgan, B.A. (2001), "Let the Cameras Roll: Mandatory Videotaping of Interrogations is the Solution to Illinois' Problem of False Confessions" 32 *Loyola University Chicago Law Journal* 424.

Drizin, Steven and Leo, Richard (2004), "The Problem of False Confessions in Post-DNA World" 82 *North Carolina Law Review* 891.

Du Jingji (1998), "A Superficial Discussion of the Tortured Confession and Policies to Deal with It" in Wang Huaixu (ed.), *Research and Practice of Investigation and Interrogation* (China People's Public Security University Press, Beijing).

Duff, Antony (1986), *Trials and Punishment* (Cambridge University Press, Cambridge).

Duff, Peter (2004), "Admissibility of Improperly Obtained Physical Evidence in the Scottish Criminal Trial: the Search for Principle" 8 *Edinburgh Law Review* 152.

Eddleston, J.J. (2000), *Blind Justice: Miscarriages of Justice in Twentieth-Century Britain?* (ABC-CLIO, Oxford).

Fan Chongi and Xa Hong (2007), "聯合國刑事司法準則與中國刑事訴訟法的再修改" [United Nations Criminal Justice Regulations and Revision of Chinese Code of Criminal Procedure] 11 *People's Procuratorial Semimonthly* 24.

Fan Peigen (2002), "我國不宜移植美式非法證據排除規則" [The American Exclusionary Rule Should Not Be Transplanted in China] 2 *Journal of Henan Public Security Academy* 36.

Fang Baoguo (2007), "現實已經發生—論我國地方性刑事證據規則" [The Fact is There—On Rules of Criminal Evidence in China] 25 *Tribune of Political Science and Law (Journal of China University of Political Science and Law)* 41.

Feldman, David (1990), "Regulating Treatment of Suspects in Police Stations: Judicial Interpretation of Detention Provisions in the Police and Criminal Evidence Act 1984" *Criminal Law Review* 453.

Fennelly, J.E. (1991), "Inevitable Discovery, the Exclusionary Rule and Military Due Process" 131 *Military Law Review* 129.

Freedman, Monroe (1967), "The Professional Responsibility of the Prosecuting Attorney" 55 *Georgetown Law Journal* 1037–8.

Fu, H.L. (1998), "Criminal Defense in China: The Possible Impact of the 1996 Criminal Procedure Law Reform" 153 *The China Quarterly* 31.

Galligan, D.J. (1988), "More Scepticism about Scepticism" 8 *Oxford Journal of Legal Studies* 255.

Garland, David (2005), "Panel Excess and Surplus Meaning: Public Torture Lynchings in Twentieth-Century American" 39 *Law and Society Review* 793.

Goldstein, Abraham (1974), "Reflections on Two Models: Inquisitorial Themes in American Criminal Procedure" 26 *Stanford Law Review* 1009.

Greely, Henry and others (2006), "Family Ties: The Use of DNA Offender Databases to Catch Offenders' Kin" 34 *The Journal of Law, Medicine and Ethics* 248.

Griffin, Lissa (2001), "The Correction of Wrongful Convictions: A Comparative Perspective" 16 *American University International Law Review* 1241.

Griswold, Erwin (1955), *The Fifth Amendment Today: Three Speeches* (Harvard University Press, Massachusetts).

Gross, Oren (2003), "Are Torture Warrants Warranted? Pragmatic Absolutism and Official Disobedience" 88 *Minnesota Law Review* 1481.

Gu Minkang (2006), "憲法權利的深層保護—從垃圾袋的處理說起" [Further Protections of Constitutional Rights—Cases of Handling Garbage Bags] 7 *Law* 87.

Guan Jinhua (ed.) (2003), 基本人權保護與法律實踐 [*The Protection of Basic Human Rights and Legal Practice*] (Xiamen University Press, Xiamen).

Hall, J.W., Jr. (1991), *Search and Seizure* (2nd edn, Michie, Charlottesville).

Han Yang (2007), 被訴人的憲法權利 [Constitutional Rights of the Accused] (Chinese People's Public Security University Press, Beijing).

He Weifang (1995), "透過司法實現社會正義：對中國法官現狀的一個透視" [The Realization of Social Justice through Judicature: A Look at the Current Situation of Chinese Judges], in Xia Yong (ed.), 走向權利的時代：中國公民權利發展研究 [Toward an Era of Rights: Research on the Civil Rights Development in China] (China University of Political Science and Law Press, Beijing).

Helmholz, R. (1990), "Origins of the Privilege against Self-Incrimination: The Role of the European Ius Commune" 65 *New York University Law Review* 963.

Ho, H.L. (2008), *A Philosophy of Evidence Law—Justice in the Search of Evidence Law* (Oxford University Press, Oxford).

Holdsworth, William (1945), vol. 5 of *A History of English Law* (3rd edn, Methuen, London).

Hooper John (2003), "Kidnap Case Presents Germans with Ugly Dilemma over Torture" *The Guardian*, Feb. 27, at 18.

Hsieh Kuo-hsing (2004), "美國證據排除法則之思辨" [Rethinking the Exclusionary Rule of Evidence in the United States] 49 *Criminal Law Review* 81.

Hu Ming (2005), "刑訊逼供的證明責任之思考" [The Thinking of the Burden of Proof for Torture] 116 *Journal of Chinese People's Public Security University* 60.

Huang Qiang and Wang Lily (2005), "非法證據排除規則中國化過程中的矛盾分析" [Analyzing the Contradiction of the Exclusionary Rule with Chinese Characteristics] 10 *Chongqing Social Science* 87.

Ian Jun and Yang Xiaoping (2005), "試論公安執法指標對警察權的影響" [The Impact of Enforcement Index towards Police Power] 2 *Journal of Adult Education of Gansu Political Science and Law Institute* 100.

Inman, Marquita (1981), "The Admissibility of Confessions" *Criminal Law Review* 469.

Jessberger, F. (2005), "Bad Torture—Good Torture? What International Criminal Lawyers May Learn from the Recent Trial of Police Officers in Germany," 3 *Journal of International Criminal Justice* 1066.

Ji Xiangde (2006), "民憤的正讀—杜培武佘祥林等錯案的司法性反思" [An Authentic Interpretation of the People's Wrath—Reflection on Unjust Cases of Du Peiwu and She Xianglin, etc.] 28 *Modern Law Science* 155.

Jin Xueren (2002), "公檢法機關之間互相配合——一個沉重而陳舊的刑事訴訟法原則" [Public Security Organs, Procuratorial Organs and People's Courts Act in Concert—A Heavy and Obsolete Principle in Code of Criminal Procedure] 1 *Journal of Huaqiao University (Political and Social Sciences)* 83.

Kamisar, Yale (1983), "Does (Did) (Should) the Exclusionary Rule Rest on a 'Principled Basis' Rather Than an 'Empirical Proposition'? " 16 *Creighton Law Review* 565.

—— (2002), "The Writings of John Barker Waite and Thomas Davies on the Search and Seizure Exclusionary Rule" 100 *Michigan Law Review* 1828.

Kang Huaiu (2005), "讓我看到法律—刑辯律師的真實處境及其他" [Let Me See the Law—The Real Reality of Defense Attorneys] *The Lawyer and Law* 2.

Kaplan, John (1974), "The Limits of the Exclusionary Rule" 26 *Stanford Law Review* 1027.

Kassin, S.M. and Neumann, Katherine (1997), "Coerced Confessions and the Jury: An Experimental Test of the 'Harmless Error' Rule" 21 *Law and Human Behavior* 27.

Katz, Michael (1966),"The Supreme Court and the States: An Inquiry into *Mapp v. Ohio* in North Carolina: The Model, the Study, and the Implication" 45 *North Carolina Law Review* 119.

Kaufman, I.R. (1980), "The Essence of Judicial Independence" 80 *Columbia Law Review* 671.

Langbein, J.H. (2003), *The Origins of Adversary Criminal Trial* (Oxford University Press, Oxford).

Landynski, J.W. 1966, *Search and Seizure and the Supreme Court: A Study in Constitutional Interpretation* (Baltimore, Johns Hopkins University Press) 20.

Leng Shao-Chuan (1977), "The Role of Law in the People's Republic of China as Reflecting Mao Tse-Tung's Influence" 68 *The Journal of Criminal Law and Criminology* 356.

Leo, Richard and Ofshe, Richard (1998), "The Consequences of False Confessions: Deprivations of Liberty and Miscarriages of Justice in the Age of Psychological Interrogation" 88 *Journal of Law and Criminology* 481.

Levy, Leonard (1968), *Origins of the Fifth Amendment: The Right against Self-Incrimination* (Oxford University Press, New York).

—— (1999), *Origins of the Bill of Rights* (Yale University Press, New Haven).

Li Maoguan (1989), "Why Laws Go Unenforced?" *Beijing Review* 18.

Li Wei (1997), "Judicial Interpretation in China" 5 *Willamette Journal of International Law and Dispute Resolution* 93.

Li Yunzhao (2002), "刑訊逼供屢禁不止的原因及對策研究" [The Reasons and Solutions of Endless Torture] 8 *Journal of Beijing University* 156.

Lippman, Matthew (1994), "The Development and Drafting of the United Nations against Torture and Other Cruel, Inhuman or Degrading Treatment or Punishment" 17 *The Boston College International and Comparative Law Review* 276.

Liu Yousheng (2008), "司法官的素質與職業培訓研究" [The Study of Competence and Career Training of Judges] 12 *People's Procuratorial Monthly* 27.

Loewenthal, M.A. (1980), "Evaluating the Exclusionary Rule in Search and Seizure" 49 *University of Missouri-Kansas City Law Review* 29.

Lu, Hong and Miethe, Terance (2007), *China's Death Penalty: History, Law and Contemporary Practices* (Routledge, London and New York).

Lubman, S.B. (2002), *Bird in a Cage: Legal Reform in China after Mao* (Stanford University Press, California).

McWhirter, Robert (2007), "Molasses and the Sticky Origins of the Fourth Amendment" 43 *Arizona Attorney* 18.
Manchester, A.H. (1980), *A Modern Legal History of England and Wales 1750–1950* (Butterworths, London).
Mann, Thomas (1933), *Joseph in Egypt* (Alfred A. Knopf, New York), translated in D.P. Currie (1994), *The Constitution of the Federal Republic of Germany* (Chicago University Press, Chicago).
Markowitz, Paula and Summerfield, Walter, Jr. (1952), "Philadelphia Police Practice and the Law of Arrest" 100 *University of Philadelphia Law Review* 1182.
Mirfield, Peter (1985), *Confessions* (Sweet and Maxwell, London) 47.
Mollica, R.F. "The Psychosocial Impact of War Trauma and Torture on Southeast Asian Refugees" (1987) 144 *The American Journal of Psychiatry* 1571
Montesquieu, B.D. (1975), *The Spirit of the Laws* (Hafner Publishing, New York).
Muhlhahn, Klaus (2009), *Criminal Justice in China: A History* (Harvard University Press, Cambridge).
Murphy, Michael (1966), "Judicial Review of Police Methods in Law Enforcement" 44 *Texas Law Review* 941.
Murphy, Peter (2008), *Murphy on Evidence* (10th edn, Oxford University Press, Oxford).
National Advisory Commission (1968), "Report of the National Advisory Commission on Civil Disorders" (New York).
O'Connor, Michael and Rumann, Celia (2003), "Into the Fire: How to Avoid Getting Burned by the Same Mistakes Made Fighting Terrorism in Northern Ireland" 24 *Cardozo Law Review* 1682.
Oldham, James (1994), "Truth-Telling in the Eighteenth-Century English Courtroom" 12 *Law and History Review* 97.
Orfield, Myron, Jr. (1987), "The Exclusionary Rule and Deterrence: An Empirical Study of Chicago Narcotics Officers" 54 *University of Chicago Law Review* 1016.
—— (1992), "Deterrence, Perjury, and the Heater Factor: An Exclusionary Rule in the Chicago Criminal Courts" 63 *University of Colorado Law Review* 75.
Orland, Leonard (2002), "A Russian Legal Revolution: The 2002 Criminal Procedure Code" 18 *Connecticut Journal of International Law* 150.
Packer, Herbert (1968), *The Limits of the Criminal Sanction* (Stanford University Press, Stanford).
—— (1988), "Two Models of the Criminal Process" in George F. Cole (ed.), *Criminal Justice: Law and Politics* (5th edn, Pacific Grove Brooks/Cole, California).
Pakter, Walter (1985), "Exclusionary Rules in France, Germany, and Italy" 9 *Hastings International and Comparative Law Review* 4.
Parise, Agustin (2010), "Legal Transplants and Codification: Exploring the North American Sources of the Civil Code of Argentina (1871)" 21 *Jindal Global Law Review* 40.

Perrin, L.T. and others (1998), "If It's Broken, Fix It: Moving beyond the Exclusionary Rule" 83 *Iowa Law Review* 678.

Pollock, Joycelyn (2008), Ethical Dilemmas and Decisions in Criminal Justice (6th edn, Cengage Learning, Australia).

Posner, Richard (1981), "Rethinking the Fourth Amendment" *The Supreme Court Review* 49.

Powe, L.A., Jr. (2000), *The Warren Court and American Politics* (Belknap Press of Harvard University Press, Cambridge).

Raitt, Fiona (2001), *Evidence* (3rd edn, W. Green/Sweet and Maxwell, Edinburgh).

Ran, Yanfei (2009), "When Chinese Criminal Defense Lawyers Become the Criminals" 32 *Fordham International Law Journal* 1014–15.

Rawls, John (1996), *Political Liberalism* (Columbia University Press, New York).

Reddy, Peter (2005), *Torture: What You Need to Know* (Ginninderra Press, Charnwood).

Roberts, Paul (2011), "Does Article 6 of the European Convention on Human Rights Require Reasoned Verdicts in Criminal Trials?" *Human Rights Law Review* 213, 214.

Roberts, Paul and Zuckerman, Adrian (2004) *Criminal Evidence* (Oxford University Press, Oxford).

Ross, Margaret and Chalmers, James (2006), *Walker and Walker: The Law of Evidence in Scotland* (Tottel, Edinburgh).

Roth, Kenneth (2005), "A History of Torture" in Kenneth Roth, Minky Worden and Amy Bernstein (eds) *Torture: Does It Make Us Safer? Is It Ever OK?—A Human Rights Perspective* (Human Rights Watch, New York).

Sanders, Andrew and Young, Richard (2007), *Criminal Justice* (3rd edn, Oxford University Press, Oxford).

—— (2007), "From Suspect to Trial" in M. Maguire, R. Morgan and R. Reiner (eds), *The Oxford Handbook of Criminology* (4th edn, Oxford University Press, Oxford).

Scalia, Antonin (1989), "The Rule of Law as a Law of Rules" 56 *University of Chicago Law Review* 1175.

Scarman. Lord (1981), The Brixton Disorders April 10–12, 1981, *Report of an Inquiry* (Cmnd. 8427).

Scheiber, Harry (1992), "Constitutional Structure and the Protection of Rights" in A.E. Howard (ed.), *The United States Constitution: Roots, Rights, and Responsibilities* (Smithsonian Institution Press, Washington and London).

Schwartz, M.A. (2001), "Should Juries be Informed that Municipality Will Indemnify Officer's § 1983 Liability for Constitutional Wrongdoing" 86 *Iowa Law Review* 1209.

Schwarzschild, Maimon (1994), "Class, National Character, and the Bar Reforms in Britain: Will There Always Be an England?" 9 *Conn Journal of International Law* 185.

Scott, Walter (1999), *Guy Mannering* (Edinburgh University Press, Edinburgh).

Shanks, B.F. (1983), "Comparative Analysis of the Exclusionary Rule and Its Alternatives" 57 *Tulane Law Review* 651.

Sharpe, Sybil (1996), "Covert Policing: A Comparative View" 25 *Anglo-American Law Review* 165.

Silberman, Charles (1978), *Criminal Violence, Criminal Justice* (Random House, New York).

Silove, Derrick, "The Psychosocial Effects of Torture, Mass Human Rights Violations, and Refugee Trauma: Toward an Integrated Conceptual Framework" (1999) 187 *Journal of Nervous and Mental Disease* 206.

Skolnick, J.H. (1975), *Justice without Trial: Law Enforcement in Democratic Society* (2nd edn, John Wiley and Sons, New York).

—— (2004), "American Interrogation: From Torture to Trickery" in Sanford Levinson (ed.), *Torture: A Collection* (Oxford University Press, Oxford).

Smith, M.H. (1978), *The Writs of Assistance Case* (University of California Press, Berkeley).

Specter, Arlen (1962), "*Mapp v. Ohio*: Pandora's Problems for the Prosecutor" 111 *University of Pennsylvania Law Review* 4.

Stewart, Potter (1983), "The Road to *Mapp v. Ohio* and Beyond: The Origins, Development and Future of the Exclusionary Rule in Search-and-Seizure Cases" 83 *Columbia Law Review* 1369.

Sun Yequan (2003), "做一個刑辯律師究竟有多難—律師參與刑事訴訟活動有關問題的思考" [How Difficult to be a Defense Attorney—Thinking of the Related Questions about Participating Criminal Procedure Activities] *Chinese Lawyer* 69.

Tamm, Quinn (1959), reported in 8 *Civil Liberties in New York*, No. 2, p. 4, col. 5 (Nov.).

Tanner, Murray (2005), "Campaign-Style Policing in China and Its Critics" in Borge Bakken (ed.), *Crime, Punishment and Policing in China* (Rowman and Littlefield Publishers, Lanham).

Tapper, Colin (2007), *Cross and Tapper on Evidence* (11th edn, Oxford University Press, Oxford).

Tiffany, L., Mclntyre, D., and Rotenberg, D. (1967), *Detection of Crime: Stopping and Questioning, Search and Seizure, Encouragement and Entrapment* (Little, Brown, Boston).

Traynor, Roger (1962), "*Mapp v. Ohio* at Large in the Fifty States" 1962 *Duke Law Journal* 319.

Trevaskes, Susan (2007), *Courts and Criminal Justice in Contemporary China* (Lexington Books, Lanham).

Turack, D.C. (1999), "The New Chinese Criminal Justice System" 7 *Cardozo Journal of International and Comparative Law* 49.

Twining, William (1985), *Theories of Evidence: Bentham and Wigmore* (Weidenfeld & Nicolson, London).

Twining, W.L. and Twining, P.E. (1973), "Bentham on Torture" 24 *The Northern Ireland Legal Quarterly* 305.

Wang Bin (2008), 刑事搜查制度研究 [The Research of Search] (Chinese People's Public Security University Press, Beijing).

Wang Gangping (ed.) (1997), *The Crime of Tortured Confession* (People's Procuratorate Press, Beijing).

Wang Haiyan and Hu Changlong (2002), 刑事證據基本問題研究 [The Study of Basic Questions of Criminal Evidence] (Law Press, Beijing).

Wang Jiancheng (2003), "漠視程序的慘痛代價—從杜培武案件引發的思考" [The Price of Ignoring Procedure—Thinking Triggered from Yu Xinglin Case] in Cheng Guangzhong and Jiang Wei (eds), 訴訟法論叢第8卷 [The Procedure Law VIII] (Legal Press, Beijing) 275.

Wang Min (2001), "淺析民警刑訊逼供的心理狀態及治理對策" [Analyzing the Psychological Situations and Governance of Police Torturers] 83 *Policing Studies* 21.

Wang Zhao and Zhou Jing (2003), "杜培武案的證據學思考" [The Case of *Du Peiwu* as Viewed from the Science of Evidence] 19 *Shantou University Journal (Humanities and Social Sciences Bimonthly)* 54.

Wang Zhjian and Yang Yamin (2009), "我國非法證據排除規則的模式選擇" [The Choosing of the Model for Chinese Exclusionary Rule] *Law Science* 145.

Wigmore, J.H. (1922), "Using Evidence Obtained by Illegal Search and Seizure" 8 *The American Bar Association Journal* 479.

Wilson, James (1990), "Altered States: A Comparison of Separation of Powers in the United States and in the United Kingdom" 18 *Hastings Constitution Law Quarterly* 125.

Woo, M.Y.K. (2000), "Law and Discretion in Contemporary Chinese Courts" in Karen Turner and others (eds), *The Limits of the Rule of Law in China* (Washington University Press, Seattle).

Worden, Andrew (2009), "'A Fair Game?' of Law and Politics in China, and the 'Sensitive' Case of Democracy Activist Yang Jianli" 40 *Georgetown Journal of International Law* 458.

Wu Danhong (2006), "非法證據排除規則的實證研究—以法院處理刑訊逼供辯護為例" [A Positive Study of Exclusion of Illegally Obtained Evidence—Cases Concerning Using Torture to Coerce a Confession] 28 *Modern Law Science* 144.

Xue Hongtao (2008), "國際人權公約在中國的實施" [The Practice of International Human Rights Conventions in China] *Human Rights* 22.

Yang Yuan (2009), "淺談我國沉默權應當緩行" [The Right to Silence in China Should Not be Established Currently] *Legal System and Society* 32.

Ye Xiaoxin (ed.) (1989), 中國法制史 [The Chinese Legal History] (Beijing University Press, Beijing).

Zander, Michael (1999), *Cases and Materials on the English Legal System* (8th edn, Butterworths, London).

—— (2007), *Cases and Materials on the English Legal System* (10th edn, Cambridge University Press, Cambridge).

Zhang Jun, Jiang Wei and Tian Wenchang (eds) (2001), 刑事訴訟: 控辯審三人談 [Criminal Procedure: Talks between the Procuratorate, Lawyer and Judge] (Law Press, Beijing).

Zhang Songmei (2001), "中國尚不具備確立沉默權的社會條件" [China Does Not Have the Social Condition to Establish the Right to Silence] *Law Science* 27.

—— (2001) "沉默權生長的社會條件" [The Social Condition for the Right to Silence] *Public Administration and Law* 45.

Zheng, Shiping (1997), *Party v. State in Post-1949 China* (Cambridge University Press, Cambridge).

Zhou Fuming (2007), "我國確立非法證據排除規則的必要性和可行性" [The Necessity and Feasibility of Establishing the Exclusionary Rule in China] 1 *Law Science* 142.

Zion, S.E. (1965), "Detectives Get a Course in Law: They Return to Classroom to Study Court Decisions" *New York Times*, Apr. 28, at 50.

Zuckerman, Ashworth (1991), "Miscarriages of Justice and Judicial Responsibility" *Criminal Law Review* 498.

Index

For Product Safety Concerns and Information please contact our EU representative GPSR@taylorandfrancis.com Taylor & Francis Verlag GmbH, Kaufingerstraße 24, 80331 München, Germany

Batch number: 10725973

Printed by Printforce, the Netherlands